C++ Primer for C Programmers

J. Ranade Workstation Series

LOCKHART • *OSF DCE: Guide to Developing Distributed Applications,* 0-07-911481-4

WIGGINS • *The Internet for Everyone: A Guide for Users and Providers,* 0-07-067019-8

CHAKRAVARTY • *Power RISC System / 6000: Concepts, Facilities, and Architecture,* 0-07-011047-6

SANCHEZ, CANTON • *High-Resolution Video Graphics,* 0-07-911646-9

DEROEST • *AIX for RS / 6000: System and Administration Guide,* 0-07-036439-7

LAMB • *MicroFocus Workbench and Toolset Developer's Guide,* 0-07-036123-3

JOHNSTON • *OS / 2 Connectivity and Networking: A Guide to Communications Manager / 2,* 0-07-032696-7

SANCHEZ, CANTON • *PC Programmer's Handbook, 2 / e,* 0-07-054948-6

WALKER, SCHWALLER • *CPI-C Programming in C: An Application Developer's Guide to APPC,* 0-07-911733-3

SANCHEZ, CANTON • *Graphics Programming Solutions,* 0-07-911464-4

CHAKRAVARTY, CANNON • *PowerPC: Concepts, Architecture, and Design,* 0-07-011192-8

LEININGER • *UNIX Developer's Toolkit,* 0-07-911646-9

HENRY, GRAHAM • *Solaris 2.X System Administrator's Guide,* 0-07-029368-6

PETERSON • *DCE Guide to Developing Portable Applications,* 0-07-911800-3

LEININGER • *Solaris Developer's Toolkit,* 0-07-911851-6

C^{++} Primer for C Programmers

Jay Ranade

Saba Zamir

Second Edition

McGraw-Hill, Inc.

New York San Francisco Washington, D.C. Auckland Bogotá
Caracas Lisbon London Madrid Mexico City Milan
Montreal New Delhi San Juan Singapore
Sydney Tokyo Toronto

Library of Congress Cataloging-in-Publication Data

Ranade, Jay.
C++ primer for C programmers / Jay Ranade, Saba Zamir.—2nd ed.
p. cm.
Includes index.
ISBN 0-07-051487-9
1. C++ (Computer program language) I. Zamir, Saba, date.
II. Title.
QA76.73.C153R36 1994
005.13'3—dc20 94-27453
CIP

1 2 3 4 5 6 7 8 9 0 DOH/DOH 9 0 9 8 7 6 5 4

ISBN 0-07-051487-9

The sponsoring editor for this book was Jerry Papke, the editing supervisor was Stephen M. Smith, and the production supervisor was Suzanne W. Babeuf.

Printed and bound by R. R. Donnelley & Sons Company.

This book is dedicated to the memory of my grandfather,
Pundit S.R.D. Ranade (1895–1957)

Jay

To the light in her eyes, and the life in her soul,
Who loves to be loved, who we love to hold,
Beautiful child—vibrant and wild—this one's just for you.

To Sheena Zamir

Saba

Contents

Preface

Any new discipline in the art of programming or system development involves many thinkers and contributors who jostle with various ideas and concepts. These ideas then reach the domain of developers and implementors, who see usefulness or plain absurdity from a practical point of view. As the discipline evolves and matures, some of the ideas drop out while others become more firm and acceptable. The First Edition of this book was written while ideas regarding C^{++} were still in the evolutionary stage. It was therefore necessary to revise this book to produce a Second Edition that retains only those styles and elements that have been accepted and have withstood the test of time.

The changes in the first half of this edition are so subtle that they may not be noticeable even to someone who has read the First Edition. But the changes in the second half are significant. Since the publication of the First Edition a little over two years ago, we have been inundated with reader mail. There have been good suggestions from many of these readers, which were incorporated in this edition. Several technical corrections were made as well, also based on reader comments. We apologize for not being able to thank every reader who responded to the First Edition, but if it was not for them, there would be no Second Edition.

A common sentiment among the readers who wrote to us was that this is the "easiest book to understand." Nothing could have pleased us more. They also complained that the source code diskette did not add any value to the book. So we took it out.

If this edition is as successful as the first one, we will update the book again. So we would still like to solicit your comments and suggestions. Please sent them to the followiong address:

J. Ranade Series
P.O. Box 338
Grand Central Station
New York, NY 10163
U.S.A.

We wish you effortless reading!

Jay Ranade
Saba Zamir

Acknowledgments

Thanks are owed to all the people who took the time to read the First Edition, and then wrote to us and offered useful suggestions that culminated in the Second Edition. We are indebted to Kathy Schueller for her thorough review of this book. We also acknowledge Jerry Papke, our senior editor, for his support; and Stephen Smith, editing supervisor, for an excellent job of producing the Second Edition.

Saba Zamir would like to thank her mother (Ammi) and father (Abjani) for helping to simplify her life. Saba would also like to thank her husband, David, for helping out whenever he could. Saba is especially indebted to her son, Richad, for being so cute and entirely adorable!

Jay Ranade
Saba Zamir

C++ Primer for C Programmers

Part

1

Introduction/Comparison to C

Chapter

1

An Introduction to C++

1.1 Introduction

If you are a C programmer, then you must have a basic understanding of data types, storage classes, operators, control structures, functions, pointers, structures, and all of those other features that make C the versatile and powerful language that it is. You are now in a position to go one step further. You are now ready for C++.

C++ is a successor of C. It was invented by Bjarne Stroustrup of AT&T Bell Laboratories in the mid 1980s. It builds upon the facilities provided by C and provides new features that are significant improvements on C. C++ is gaining immense popularity as a software development platform tool.

1.2 An Analogy

We will present a simple analogy that will help you understand one of the key concepts in C++ that make it a more powerful and flexible language than C. This key concept is defined as the *class mechanism.* This analogy will be expanded to introduce the concept of a *derived class.* The discussion will continue with an explanation of *virtual functions.* We will conclude with a synopsis that will help you understand the concept of *object-oriented programming.* It is this powerful new programming tool that makes C++ the language of the future.

1.3 CLASSES

Assume that you are a busy manager in a large company and you have not one but two secretaries: Mary and John. If these employees could be represented by numbers (after all, each employee is assigned an employee number), then we could represent them in C in the form of a *structure*. Recall how a structure is defined in C. It is a compound data type which gathers together, in a fixed pattern, different types of information that comprise a given entity. In our example, we can name this given entity `secretary`. This would be the structure name. The members of this structure would be `mary` and `john`. This is how the declaration would look:

```
struct secretary
   {
   int mary;
   int john;
   };
```

Mary and John perform three functions: they type, file and answer phones. Their function prototypes can be represented in C as follows:

```
void type(int);
void file(int);
void answer_phones(int);
```

For the sake of simplicity, we will assume that the functions above return no value, that is, they are of type `void`, and are passed one argument of type `int`.

A typical C program that contains the above structure declaration and function prototypes could look something like this:

```
/* function prototypes follow */
void type(int);
void file(int);
void answer_phones(int);

/* structure declarations follow */
struct secretary
   {
   int mary;
   int john;
   };

main()
{
   .
   .
   type(..);
```

```
    .
    file(..);
    .
    answer_phones(..);
    .
}

void type(..)
{
    .
}

void file(..)
{
    .
}

void answer_phones(..)
{
    .
}
```

In our program, mary and john are grouped together in a structure called secretary. Some functions that perform various tasks are also declared and defined.

Now suppose there are other functions in the program, in addition to the ones just listed:

```
void design_systems(int);
    .
    .
```

Secretaries do not design systems; that is not a part of their job description. We would like to somehow separate those functions which will be performed by members of secretary from other functions. Restating, we will group together the functions that can be performed by the members of the structure secretary with its members mary and john.

C++ allows us to do so, by declaring the relevant functions *within the structure declaration itself.* Doing so will take these structures out of the domain of other structures and/or functions that may exist in the program. Here's the redefined declaration:

```
struct secretary
    {
    int mary;
    int john;

    void type(int);
    void file(int);
    void answer_phones(int);
    };
```

Functions declared within a structure are called *member functions*. Thus, functions `type()`, `file()`, and `answer_phones()` are member functions for the class whose name is `secretary`.

In C, structure variables that are of the type specified in the tag-name are defined as follows:

```
struct secretary a;
```

The above statement defines `a` as a structure of type `secretary`. In C++, structure variables are defined as follows:

```
secretary a;
```

The above statement defines `a` as a structure of type `secretary`. Notice the absence of the keyword `struct` from the declaration.

In C, structure members can be referenced using the `.` operator:

```
a.mary = 5000;
```

The structure member `mary` of structure `a` is set to 5000.

In C++, members are referenced the same way:

```
a.mary = 5000;
```

Member functions are also referenced using the `.` operator:

```
a.type(5000);
```

The above statment invokes the function `type()`, which was declared as a member function of the structure of type `secretary`, and passes it an argument of type `int`. This conforms to the function prototype declaration.

We are now going to touch on a subject that is similar to what C programmers recognize as *scope*. Scope references the visibility of a variable within a program. C++ enhances this concept by giving the application programmer the capability to *restrict the visibility or access of a variable and/or functions to specific parts of the program through the use of classes*.

Now let's go back to our original example:

```
struct secretary
   {
   int mary;
   int john;

   void type(int);
   void file(int);
```

```
void answer_phones(int);
};
```

The nature of this declaration is such that the structure members mary and john can be accessed by any function in the program. One of these members could even be passed as an argument to the function design_systems()!

You, on the other hand, are quite particular about the functions that Mary and John may perform. You don't want them to design_systems. (They probably don't want to design systems either!) All you want them to do is file, type, and answer_phones.

C++ allows you to restrict the access of the members of a structure to specific functions only. Restrictions such as these can be specified by declaring a *class* instead of a structure and incorporating the key words private and public in the class declaration. Doing so would result in restricting the use of applicable variables/member functions to specific parts of the program. Here is how it is done:

```
class secretary
   {
   private:
   int mary;
   int john;

   public:
   void type(int);
   void file(int);
   void answer_phones(int);
   };
```

The keyword private is followed by a colon, and then mary and john are declared. The keyword public is also followed by a colon, and then the function prototypes are declared. The keyword private specifies that members declared as such can be accessed only by the functions that are declared in their class. In C++, this is known as data hiding; i.e. the data for the members declared as private are hidden from all functions but those that are declared in their class. The keyword public specifies that members are accessible from anywhere within program scope. Functions that are public can work with any variable in the program, unless that variable has been declared as a private member of some other class.

Thus, the functions type(), file(), and answer_phones() can only access the private members that belong to their class: mary and john. Restating, only mary and john can be passed as arguments to these functions. The function design_systems() cannot access mary or john, since it is not a member function of the class secretary. The following statement will generate an error:

```
design_systems(mary);  /* won't work */
```

In C++, the default specification for class members is private. The following declaration is equivalent to the one you just saw (it states that the variables mary and john are private), while the member functions type(), file(), and answer_phones() are public:

```
class secretary
   {
   int mary;
   int john;

   public:
   void type(int);
   void file(int);
   void answer_phones(int);
   };
```

Classes with different tag-names can have member functions of the same name. Hence, it is necessary to specify the class to which a member function belongs when it is defined. This is done by prefixing the function name with the class name and the scope resolution operator: :: For example, the function type() would be defined as follows:

```
void secretary::type(int mary)
{
   .
   <code for function type()>
   .
}
```

The definition above states that the function type() is a member function of the class secretary, it returns no value, and it expects to be passed an argument of type int.

It is interesting to note here is that class members other than mary and john can be passed to this function as well, as long as they have not been declared as private members of some other class. This is because the function is declared in the public area of the class declaration. However, mary and john cannot be passed as arguments to any function other than type(), file(), and answer_phones().

Functions can be defined within a program after they have been declared. C++ allows function definitions within the declaration as well:

```
class secretary
   {
   int mary;
   int john;

   public:
```

```
void type(int)  {..<code for type()..}
void file(int)  {..<code for file()..}
void answer_phones(int)
 {..<code for answer_phones()..}
};
```

Notice the absence of the semicolon after each definition. Member functions larger than one or two lines are best defined outside of the class body.

Let's stop for a moment and think about what we have learned so far. What we just described are the concepts of *classes* and *information hiding* in C++. Classes offer a method for grouping together variables and the functions that can be performed on these variables. They also provide a mechanism for restricting access to specific data. Restrictions such as these have many benefits. Mary or John is to blame if a secretary did not type or file correctly. However, someone else is responsible if the system is not designed properly! You are able to localize problems, and thereby fix them quickly and efficiently.

We are now in a position to take the next step forward. We will now describe the concept of *derived classes*. Let's go back to where we left off in our analogy.

1.4 DERIVED CLASSES

The company is growing. Work is piling up on your desk. Mary and John are capable secretaries, but the workload is just too much. It seems that you need to hire another secretary. You put an ad in the paper.

As you skim through the pile of resumes on your desk, you find one that catches your eye. This young lady's name is Priscilla, and she is a bright young lady indeed! Not only does she know how to file, type, and answer phones, she also knows how to add numbers! (She probably knows a few other things too, but that's the subject of another book.) This young lady performs all of the functions that we grouped under the class type `secretary`, plus one more: `add_numbers`. Priscilla gets the job; her title: *accounting secretary*.

Let's take a look at the original declaration of the class `secretary`:

```
class secretary
   {
   int mary;
   int john;

   public:
   void type(int);
   void file(int);
   void answer_phones(int);
```

```
};
```

C++ allows us to derive the class accounting_secretary from secretary. Thus, the derived class *inherits* members of the class that it is derived from. Here's the declaration:

```
class accounting_secretary:public secretary
   {
   int priscilla;

   public:
   void add_numbers(int);
   };
```

The class accounting_secretary is called the *derived* class and secretary is called the *base* class. Notice that the name of the derived class is preceded by the keyword class, and is followed by a single colon. The colon is followed by the keyword public, and the name of the base class. The keyword public precedes the name of the base class and indicates that the public members of secretary are also to be the public members of accounting_secretary. Thus, accounting_secretary inherits the public members of secretary, which are type(), file(), and answer_phones(). At the same time, accounting_secretary has a member function that is unique to it: add_numbers().

The interesting thing to note here is that members of the derived class do not have access to the private members of their base class. Private members mary or john cannot be passed as arguments to the function add_numbers(), because they are private members of the base class.

Incidentally, C++ does provide a *friend* mechanism to gain access to private members of a base class, but a discussion of this topic will be reserved for later chapters.

The foremost benefit to be derived from *inheritance* is that code for the functions that the derived class inherits from the base class does not have to be rewritten, and therefore, it does not have to be retested. This allows for the reuse of existing code to create a new type. One class is used as a building block for another.

Let's take a breather and review what we have learned so far:

- We learned how to declare classes and the reasons for doing so.

- We learned how to derive one class from another and the benefits in doing so.

Now we are ready to take the next step forward, which brings us one step closer to understanding the powerful tool called *object-oriented programming*. This is understanding what C++ calls *virtual functions*.

1.5 VIRTUAL FUNCTIONS

Take yet another look at the declarations for secretary and accounting_secretary:

```
class secretary
   {
   int mary;
   int john;

   public:
   void type(int);
   void file(int);
   void answer_phones(int);
   };

class accounting_secretary:public secretary
   {
   int priscilla;

   public:
   void add_numbers(int);
   };
```

As mentioned previously, Priscilla knows how to type, file, answer_phones, and add_numbers. However, the way Priscilla files documents is *different* from the way Mary and John file. We will modify our declaration for accounting_secretary accordingly:

```
class accounting_secretary:public secretary
   {
   int priscilla;

   public:
   void add_numbers(int);
   void file(int);
   };
```

Within the program, each file() function can be defined as follows:

```
void secretary::file(int mary)
{
   .
   <code for file() that belongs to class secretary>
   .
}

void accounting_secretary::file(int priscilla)
{
   .
```

```
    <code for file() that belongs to
      class accounting_secretary>

}
```

Sometimes, we want to execute the `file()` function defined for the base class. At other times, we want to execute the `file()` function defined for the derived class. Now, the question is, how can we invoke the correct function without having to state explicitly which one it is? The answer is *through the use of a pointer, which is made to point to the class whose function is to be executed.* Take a look at the fragment of code below, and you will understand exactly how this works:

```
// Declare class secretary:
class secretary
   {
   int mary;
   int anna;

   // Notice use of keyword virtual in file()
   public:
   void type(int);
   virtual void file(int);
   void answer_phones(int);
   };

// Declare derived class
class accounting_secretary:public secretary
   {
   int priscilla;

   // Notice no use of keyword virtual in file()
   public:
   void add_numbers(int);
   void file(int);
   };

// Define functions with common names:
void secretary::file(int mary)
{
   ..<Code for file() in secretary>..
}

void accounting_secretary::file(int priscilla)
{
   ..<Code for file() in accounting_secretary>..
}

// Code for main():
main()
{
// a is class of type secretary
// b is class of type accounting_secretary
```

```
// arg1 and arg2 are arguments sent to functions
// ptr is a pointer to class of type secretary
secretary a;
accounting_secretary b;
int arg1, arg2;
secretary *ptr;

arg1 = 5000;

// ptr is set to address of base class
// secretary::file() is executed
ptr = &a;
ptr->file(arg1);

arg2 = 6000;

// ptr is set to address of derived class
// accounting_secretary::file() is executed
ptr = &b;
ptr->file(arg2);
}
```

Let's step through this program and see what happens. We start off by declaring the base and derived classes. In the declarations, notice:

- The use of //. In C, we can insert comments anywhere in our code using the notation: /* `comment` */. In C++, one line comments can be inserted using the double slash: // `comment`. The traditional style (/*...*/) can also be used.

- The use of the keyword `virtual`. This keyword indicates that the function `file()` can have different versions for different derived classes. However, the programmer does not have to worry about which function to invoke; the compiler takes care of these details at run time. Thus, the selection of the appropriate function that is to be executed is *dynamic* (determined at run time), as opposed to *static* (determined at compile time).

The true value of the last point may not be apparent to you at this early stage of the book. For now, it is enough that you simply be aware of this capability. Details will follow later on in the book. We continue with the discussion of the program.

Next, we see the definition of the functions declared. The function that has different versions must be declared as virtual in the base class. It can (but need not) be redefined for each derived class. It is necessary to define the function for the class in which it is first declared. In other words, the following function definition must exist:

```
void secretary::file(..)
{

}
```

Next, we see the main() function, which drives all of the other functions, just as in C. Within main(), variables a and b of the class types secretary and accounting_secretary and a pointer to a class of type secretary are declared. This is a pointer to the base class. ptr is set to point to a using the address of (&) operator. The statement

```
ptr->file(arg1);
```

executes the function that belongs to the class that ptr is pointing to. Therefore, the statement

```
ptr->file(arg1);
```

results in secretary::file(int) being executed. The statement

```
ptr->file(arg2);
```

results in accounting_secreatary::file(int) being executed.

1.6 Object-Oriented Programming

We have now covered the three main concepts that are the building blocks for object-oriented programming:

- The *class* mechanism, which allows *encapsulation* of different data types and operations that can be performed by them. This mechanism allows data hiding and management of access privileges.
- Derivation of classes, or *inheritance*, which allows the reuse of existing code with minor variations to create a new type.
- *Dynamic selection* by the compiler, instead of the programmer, of the appropriate function that is to be executed based on the object that is being pointed to.

An *object* is created via the class mechanism. A second object can be derived from the first. A third can be created from a combination of the two, and so on. Access privileges of one object to another can be *restricted*, as required. Exactly which object is executed at any particular time is the compiler's problem, not the programmer's.

Object-oriented programs are easier to change, maintain, and reuse than structured programs, at the cost of perhaps being a little more difficult to design. C++ is an object-oriented programming language, and incorporates the three features just described, plus a host of other features that make it a better C.

We will briefly touch on the basic similarities and differences between the two languages in the next chapter. This will help you feel comfortable with the basics and confident that you will be able to assimilate the knowledge that you will gain in subsequent chapters. The remainder of the book will present brief references to C, and detailed explanations of features specific to C++. Parallel examples in both languages will help you truly appreciate the power that C++ has to offer over C.

Chapter

2

Similarities and Differences between C and C++

2.1 INTRODUCTION

In this chapter we will describe the features of C++ that are derived from C. For those of you who are experienced C programmers, you will notice little or no difference between C syntax rules and those of C++. The basic constructs are the same, since, after all, C++ is a direct descendant of C. In C++ terminology, if C is a class, then C++ is derived from it! However, we recommend that you do read this chapter, since it will help you feel comfortable and confident as you proceed to the next chapter. Instances of how C++ improves on classical C concepts will also be described.

This chapter is meant to be brief introduction to the language only, and the topics touched on here will be covered in detail in the remainder of the book. For now, we just want to get you started.

2.2 SOURCE CODE NAMING CONVENTIONS

Different operating systems have varying rules for the names of C and C++ programs. You should consult your system manual for rules that are applicable to your system. Generally speaking, C programs are postfixed with a "`.c`" and C++ programs are postfixed with a "`.C`". For example, your first C program may have been called "`test_1.c`". Along the same line, your first C++ program can be called "`test_1.C`".

2.3 Which Compiler?

All programs in this book have been compiled and run using the Turbo C++ compiler Version 3.1, in a Microsoft Windows environment on an IBM Personal Computer.

Please note that the programs used in this book are portable. As a matter of fact, one of the strengths of C++ is that it is a highly portable language. These programs will compile and execute using any C++ compiler, which may or may not be installed in a Windows environment.

This compiler understands C programs if they are postfixed with a `.c`, and C++ programs if they are postfixed with a `.cpp`. We will use this same convention throughout the book. If you are working with some other operating system or compiler, simply refer to the relevant documentation for applicable instructions. More likely than not, the programs will compile and execute exactly as they would on our system. The code and output should remain the same. Although the wording of the error messages may vary if you are using a different compiler, the context of the messages should remain the same.

2.4 Creation and Execution of a Program

One of the basic assumptions of this book is that you are somewhat familiar with C and know how to compile and run programs written in that language. If this assumption is true, then you must know that before a program can be run, it has to be typed using your favorite (or nonfavorite) editor and stored in a file. Once the file has been created, it is compiled, linked, and run, as required by the particular implementation that is being used. Some implementations allow the above steps to be performed by typing commands at the operating system commmand line prompt. Other systems allow the whole process to be implemented via menus and dialog boxes. Our system is completely menu driven, and allows the user to edit, compile, and run programs using dialog boxes within an integrated environment. For all others, simply "compile" and "run" as instructed by your system documentation.

2.5 Borland's C++ 3.1 Compiler

We will step through the edit, compile, and run process within the Integrated Development Environment that is provided by Borland's Turbo C++ Version 3.1 compiler. You may select options by positioning and clicking the left mouse button. Or you may simply move the arrow keys to highlight the relevant option and press return. We will adopt the latter method. Options may also be selected via their corresponding hot keys, or by typing the letter designating that command.

We begin our discussion by briefly overviewing the *I*ntegrated *D*evelopment *E*nvironment (IDE) which is Borland's Programmers Platform.

2.5.1 Borland's Program Manager Group

Before you can use a compiler, you obviously have to install it on your PC. You will need to execute the `INSTALL` program that is provided with this compiler to properly load all applicable files onto your machine. This program assumes that you already have Microsoft Windows installed, and that Program Manager will start up when you start up Windows. After successful installation, on exit and reentry into the Windows environment, Borland C++ will automatically create a new Program Manager group, which will contain the group of icons that are related to this platform. There are a total of 20 icons here, which are grouped together under the heading Borland C++ 3.1. Please refer to Figure 2.1 for a picture of this group.

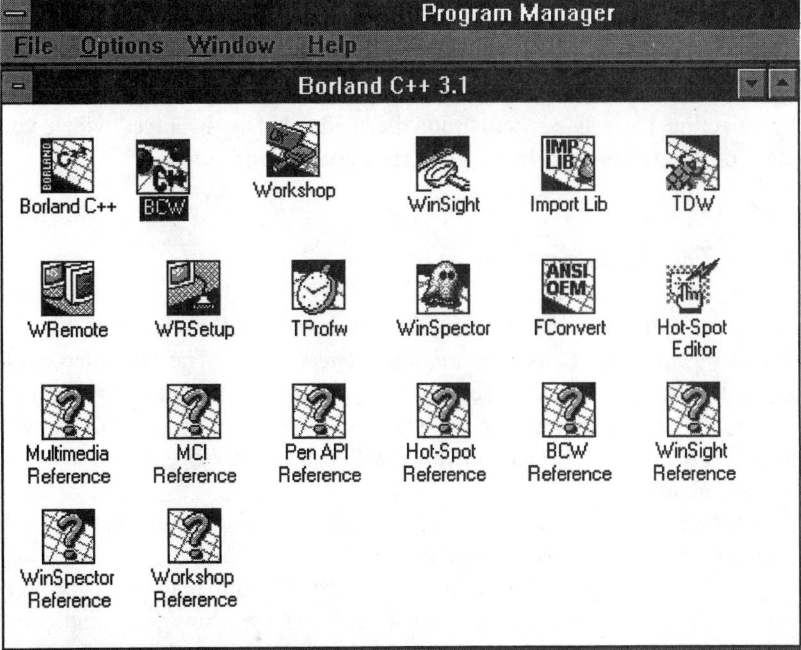

Figure 2.1 Borland C++ 3.1 Icon Group

We will be exploring the menu options available in the Borland C++ for Windows compiler only (second icon from the left). We encourage you to explore the functionality available for the remaining icons; please refer to your C++ documentation for further details.

Position your cursor in the window displayed in Figure 2.1 and double click the left mouse button on the window that says BCW (second icon from the left in the top row). Double click on this now, and you will be placed in the IDE platform. This environment contains windows, menus, dialog boxes, a speed bar, scroll bars, and an edit and status line.

2.5.2 The IDE Platform

At the top of the IDE screen are the menu options. These will be discussed in detail shortly. Below the menu options is the *Speed Bar*. The speed bar contains a group of icons that provide a shortcut method for implementing frequently used tasks. Position the mouse arrow in any of these icons and a brief description of the functiuonality of that icon will appear in the status field. Please refer to Figure 2.2 for the message that will display (*Display Context Sensitive Help*) when the mouse is positioned on the *?* (Help) icon (the first one on the left).

The arrow keys at the bottom of the screen allow you to scroll the window from left to right. The arrow keys on the right of the screen allow you to scroll the window from top to bottom.

The screen itself can be *maximized* (cover the entire area of the terminal that you are working on) or *minimized* (changed back to an icon) by selecting the related item from the menu that is displayed when you click on the left button in the top left corner of the screen.

2.5.3 The Edit Screen

As you take another look at the edit screen, you will notice that the title line at the top says *C:\borlandc\bin\noname00.cpp*. The compiler automatically opens up an edit session for you and names the C++ file that it expects you to create as *noname00.cpp*. You can accept this default name, or change it by clicking on the File menu option, which we will explain shortly.

So much for the basics! Let's step through the menu bars that are displayed for each menu option.

Position the mouse arrow under *File* (first menu option on the left) and click on it (or position the cursor on it via the arrow keys and press return). The File menu bar will be displayed. Refer to Figure 2.3 for a picture of this menu bar.

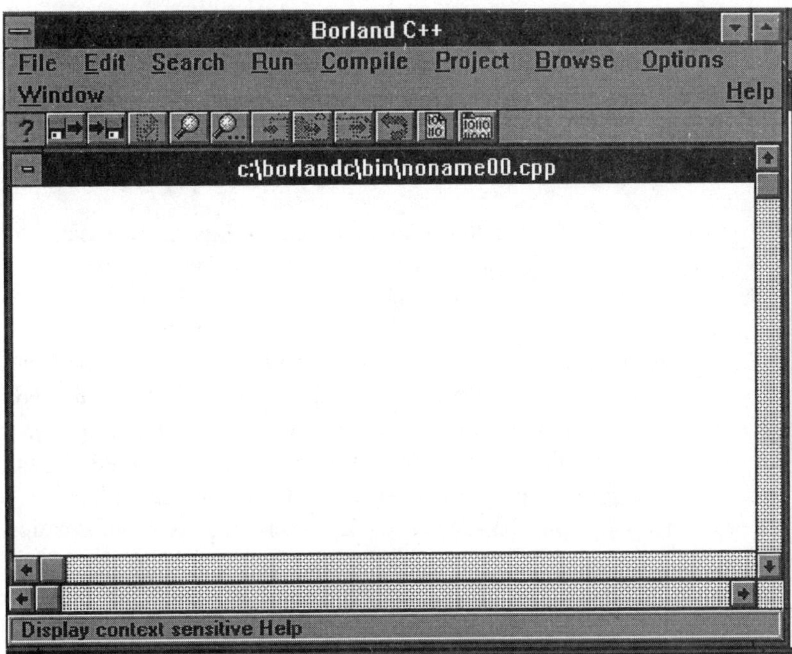

Figure 2.2 IDE Environment of Borland C++ 3.1 Compiler

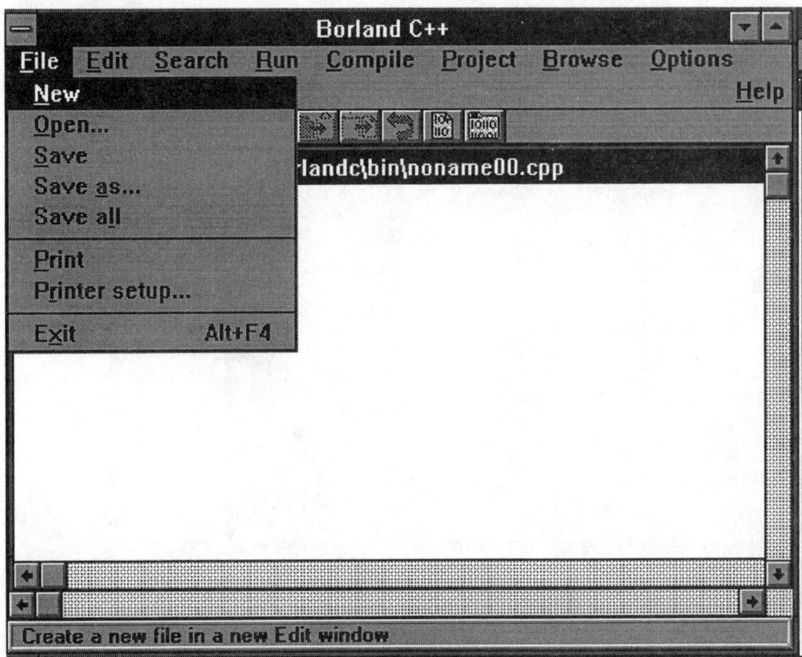

Figure 2.3 File Menu Bar in IDE

You can select any option in the menu bar in one of three ways:

- Drag the mouse to highlight the chosen option, and then click on it.

- Type the letter that is underlined for that menu option, if one is underlined. For example, typing *N* will result in your selecting the *New* menu option in the File menu bar.

- Press the hot key(s) for that option, if one(s) exists. For example, pressing the alt key in parallel with function key number 4 will result in the *Exit* option in the File menu bar.

Each menu command that is followed by ellipses (...) implies that a *dialog box* will be activated if this command is chosen. The dialog box will overlay the current window. For example, if you select the *Open* command from the File menu bar, the *Open a File* dialog box will display. Please refer to Figure 2.4 for a picture of this dialog box.

For each dialog box that is opened up, you could type information applicable to that dialog box and then click on *OK* to have the system accept what you just typed. Or, you may click on *Cancel* to have the system discard anything that may have been entered. Click on *Help* for help information related to that window.

Please refer to Figures 2.5 through 2.13 for pictures of the menu bars that are displayed for each of the menu options available.

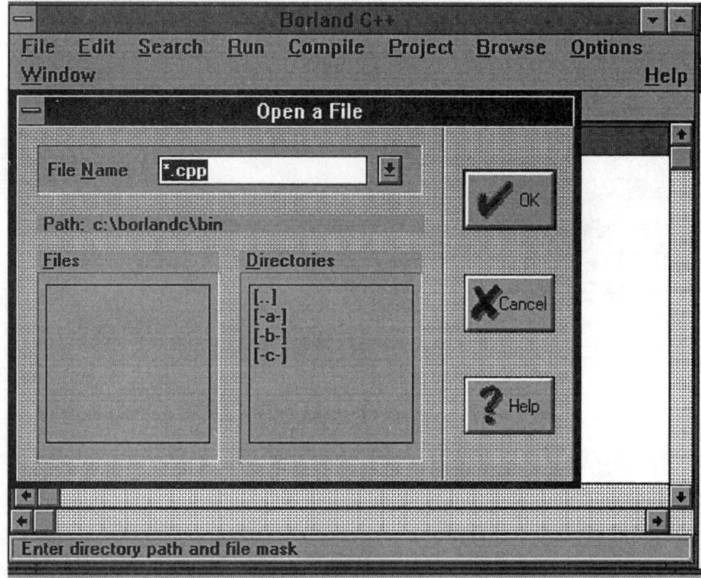

Figure 2.4 Open a File Dialog Box

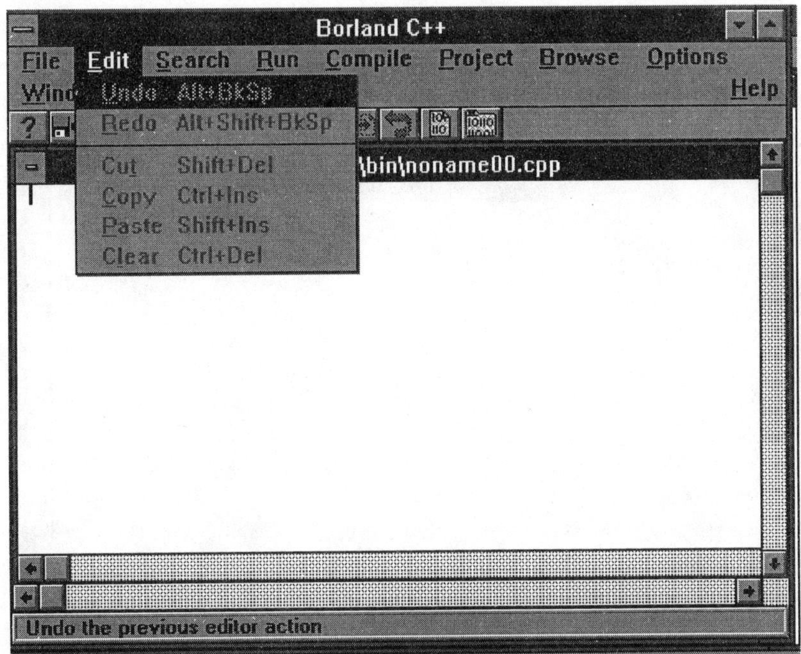

Figure 2.5 Edit Menu Bar in IDE

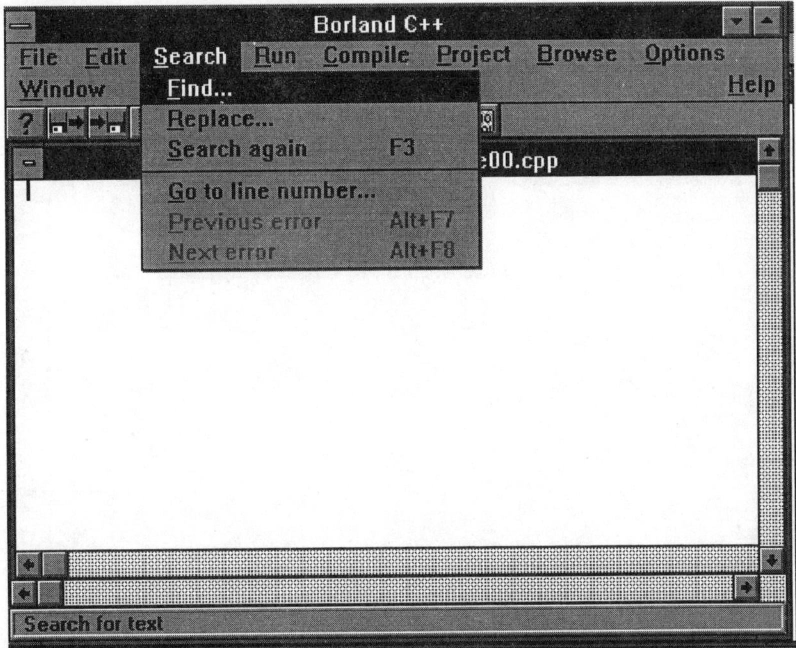

Figure 2.6 Search Menu Bar in IDE

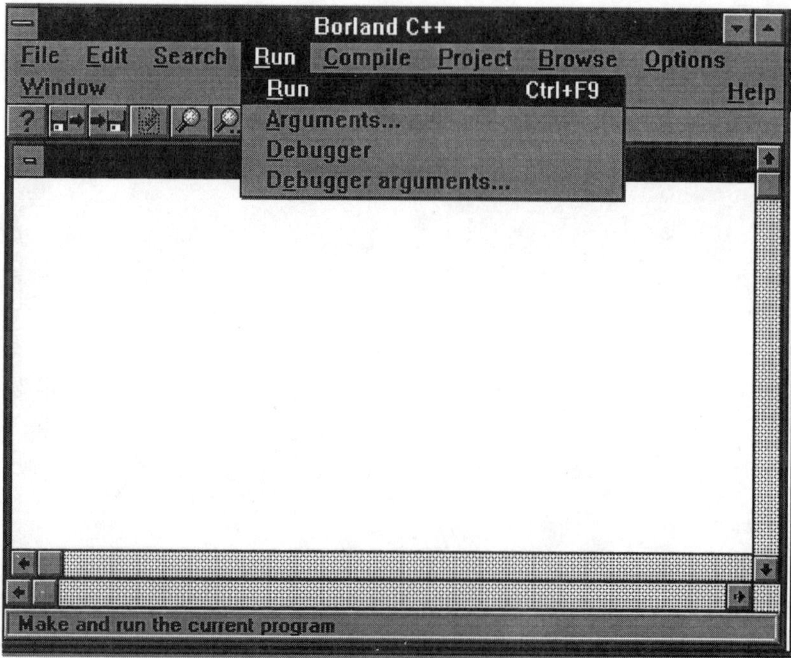

Figure 2.7 Run Menu Bar in IDE

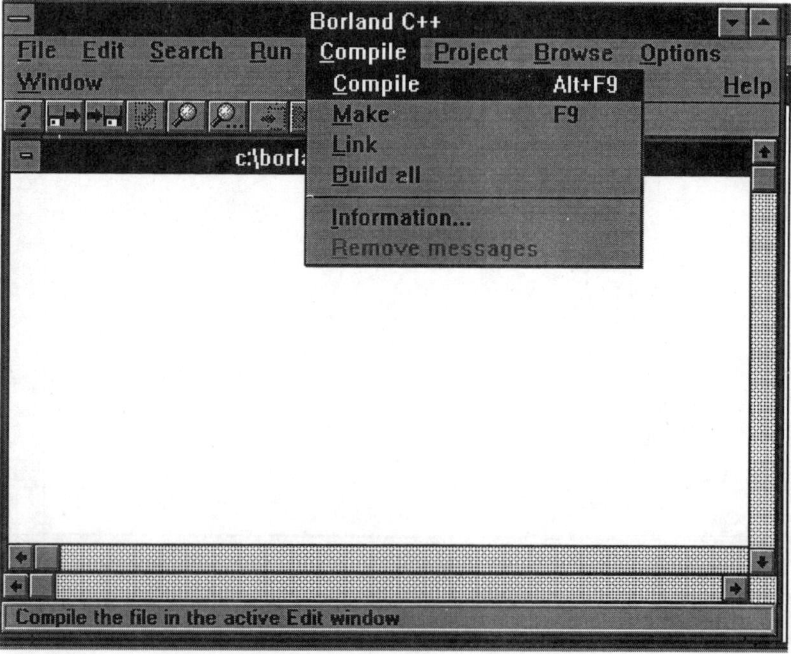

Figure 2.8 Compile Menu Bar in IDE

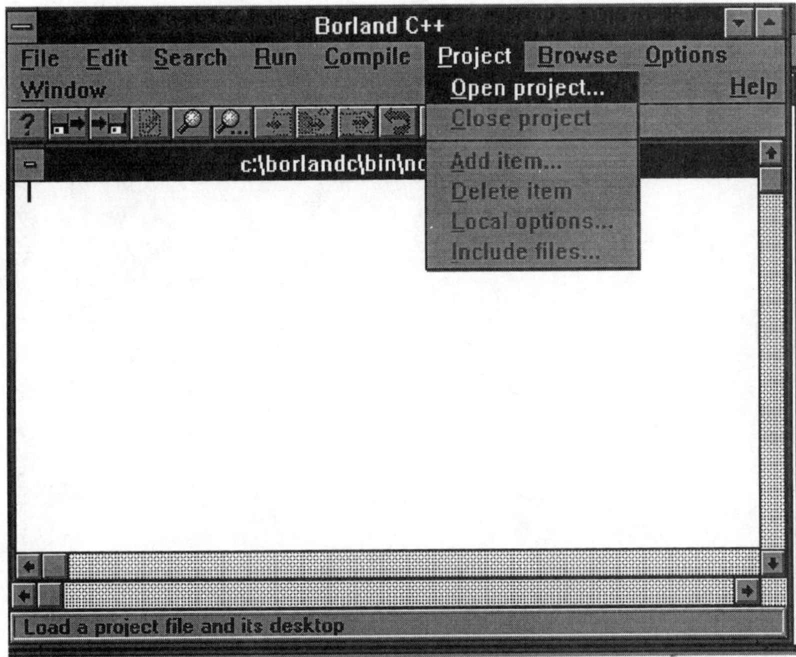

Figure 2.9 Project Menu Bar in IDE

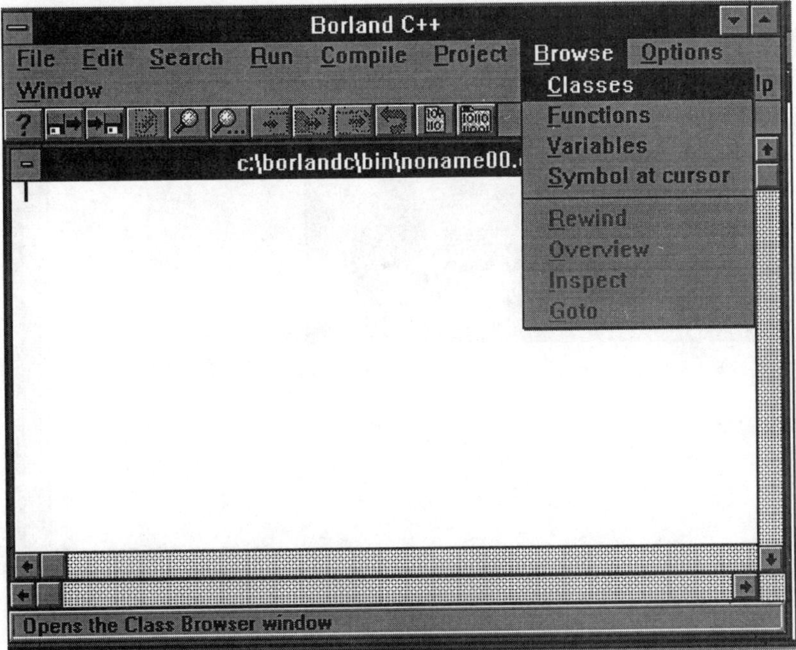

Figure 2.10 Browse Menu Option in IDE

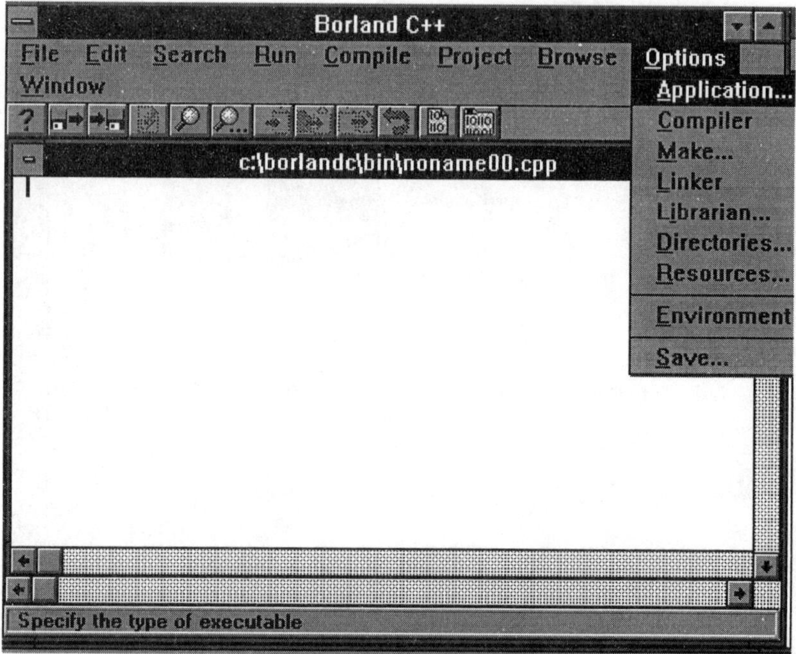

Figure 2.11 Options Menu Bar in IDE

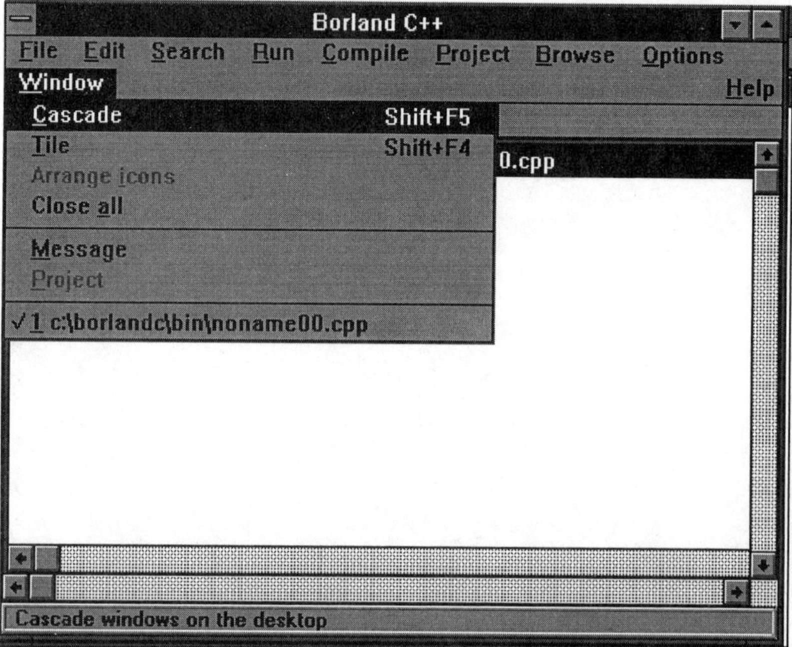

Figure 2.12 Window Menu Bar in IDE

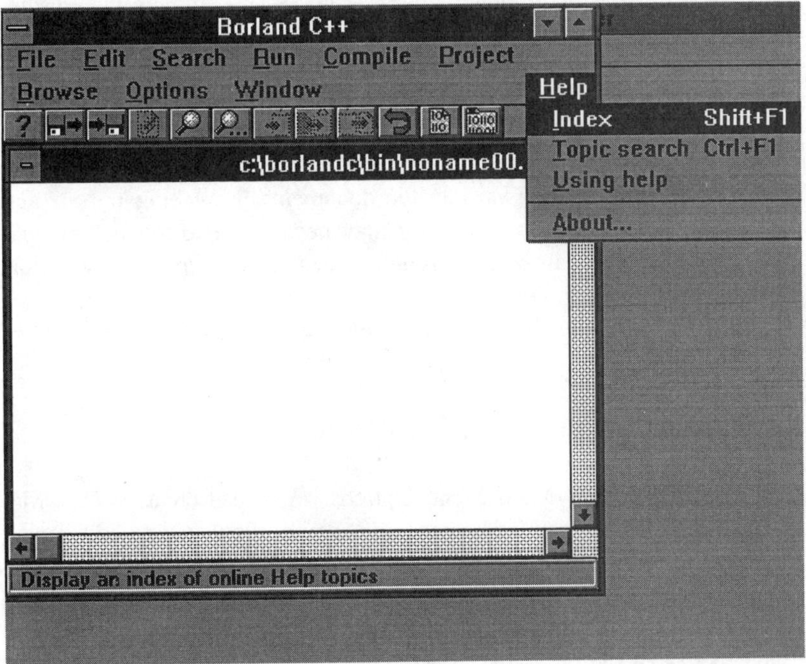

Figure 2.13 Help Menu Bar in IDE

It is beyond the scope of this primer to explain the functionality available in each menu bar, so we refer you to the appropriate system manual for further details. We will, however, describe how you can obtain on-line help for practically any feature.

2.5.4 On-Line Help

Selecting the *Help* menu option will display four commands in its menu bar. If you select *Using Help*, then information similar to what we are about to describe will be displayed. If you select *About...*, then copyright information relating to the product will be displayed. *Topic Search* will allow you to search for help information specific to any topic that you may enter. Let's choose *Index* (shift + F1) and see what happens.

Clicking on *Index* places you in the Borland/Turbo C++ Help window. Please refer to Figure 2.14 for a picture of this screen.

Below the window title is displayed a list of topics. If you position your cursor on any of these topics, the arrow pointer will change into the shape of a hand with a pointed index finger. This implies that further information can be viewed for this topic simply by double clicking on the item that the hand is positioned on. Please refer to Figure 2.15 for the window that was displayed when we double clicked on Dialog Boxes in this window.

You can exit out of any subsequent Help windows by clicking on *Back*. You can scroll forward in the document by clicking on >> and backwards by clicking on <<. You may never have to touch a manual again, because you can scroll through almost the entire documentation available simply by browsing through it on-line.

We now briefly explain how to edit/compile and run a typical C++ program.

2.5.5 Edit/Compile and Run Process

Choose *File* from the Main Menu Options. You can create a new file, or edit a preexisting one. Choosing *Open* will allow you to edit a pre-existing file. The dialog box in Figure 2.4 will be displayed.

We will create a new file. Simply click on *New* in the *File* menu, and type in the C++ (or C) program. The Edit menu option provides features designed to edit the program. For the most part, if you make a mistake, simply move the arrow keys to the place where the file has to be edited, use the *Backspace* or *Delete* keys to delete characters, and retype. As you type, it is good practice to save the file frequently.

To save a file, select the *Save as...* command in the *File* menu bar. Clicking on this command will result in the Save File as dialog box displaying. Please refer to Figure 2.16 for a picture of this window.

Click on the directory where you wish to save the file. Then, either select the file name from the list that displays under *Files* by clicking on it, or type a new name in File Name. Clicking on *OK* will result in the file being saved.

You may accept the default name (`noname001.cpp`), or type in the name of your choice, as we just indicated. Make sure that C programs are postfixed with a `.c`, and C++ programs with a `.cpp`.

Once the file has been saved, compile it by selecting the *Compile* Option from the Main Menu. If there are errors, the compiler will inform you as such. Simply reedit the file, save, and recompile.

Once your program compiles with no errors, select *Run* from the main Menu. Incidentally, if you select *Run* directly after saving a file, this option will compile and execute your program at the same time. The output of a successful run will be displayed on a new screen that will overlay any prior screens.

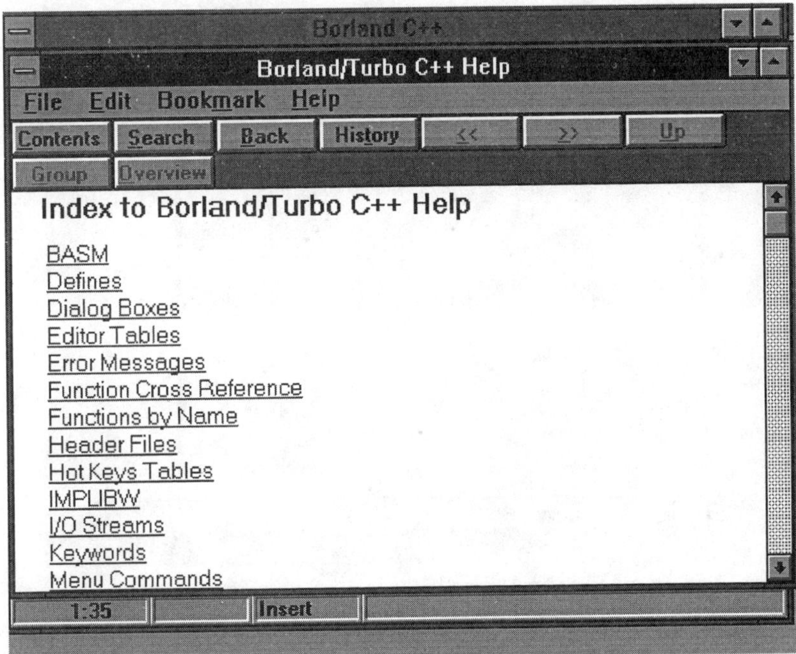

Figure 2.14 Index Sub-Option in the Help Menu Bar

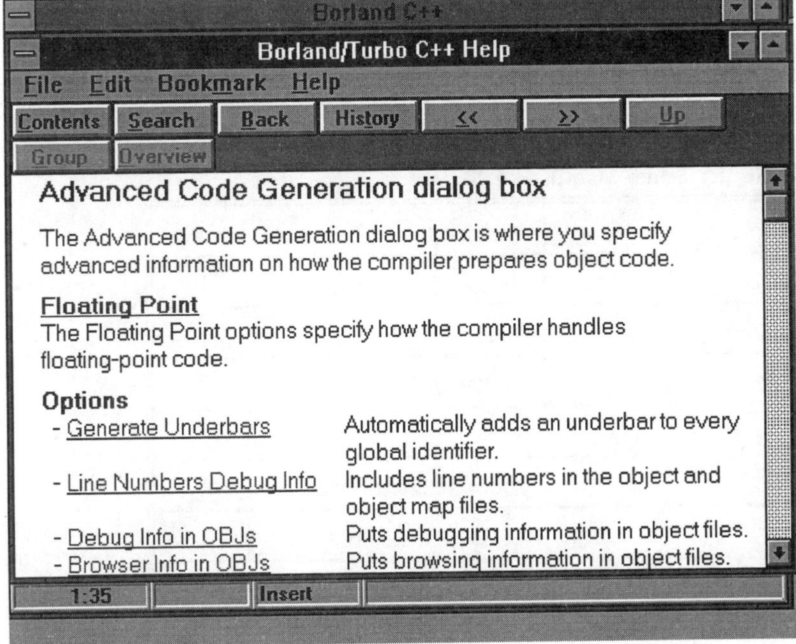

Figure 2.15 Dialog Boxes Help Information

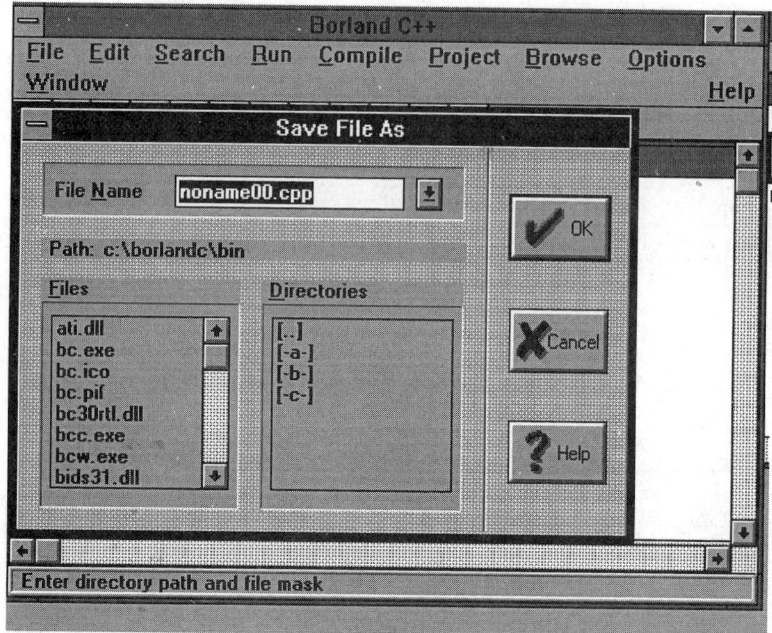

Figure 2.16 Save File As Dialog Box

Table 2.1 lists some commonly used hot keys that allow you to speed up your work.

The menu bar, dialog boxes, windowing schemes, hot keys, and so on, may vary depending on your compiler, but the basic procedure of selecting options and executing them will not be that much different from what you have just read.

Table 2.1 Some Useful Hot Keys

Hot Key	Result
F1	Help
F2	Save
F3	File/Open
F4	Run
F5	Zoom active window
F6	Go to next window
F10	Go to menu bar

2.6 Compile Process for Non-Menu-Driven Systems

Most C++ compilers typically use the command CC to compile the program. Let's compile a program that we will call source.cpp:

```
CC source.cpp
```

We can run this program simply by typing its name without its prefix:

```
source
```

In a UNIX environment, the name of the executable file will be `a.out`. Hence, you will type the following at the operating system prompt:

```
$ a.out
```

2.7 Similarities between C++ and C

Now that we've got the generalities out of the way, let's get on with what this chapter is all about. First, the features of C++ that are similar to C will be discussed.

2.7.1 Fundamental Data Types

C++ contains the same fundamental data types as C:

```
char  short  int  long  float  double
```

The adjective `const` can be applied to any of the above data types to indicate that the value of a variable of this type cannot be changed, once it has been initialized:

```
const int age = 35;
```

You know how it is, some people just don't age beyond 35!
In C++, a constant must be initialized when it is declared.

2.7.2 Operators

C++ contains the same arithmetic operators as C:

Operator	Meaning	Operator	Meaning
+	Plus	-	Minus
*	Multiply	/	Divide

The comparison operators are carried over from C to C++:

Operator	Meaning	Operator	Meaning
==	Equal to	!=	Not equal to
>	Greater than	<	Less than
<=	Less than or equal to	>=	Greater than or equal to

The bitwise operators are also the same:

Operator	Meaning	Operator	Meaning
~	Complement	&	And
^	Exclusive or	!	Inclusive or
<<	Logical left shift	>>	Logical right shift

C++ adds quite a few operators of its own. You have already encountered three of these in Chapter 1:

Operator	Meaning	Operator	Meaning
::	Scope resolution	<<	Put to
>>	Get from		

You will notice that the *put to* and *get from* operators are the same as the logical left shift and logical right shift operators. This is an example of *operator overloading* in C++. What this means is that an operator can be "overloaded" to mean different things at different times. We will touch upon this topic later in this chapter.

The operators *new* and *delete* will be introduced later in the chapter.

2.7.3 Expressions

C++ forms expressions by combining one or more operators, just as C does. Following are valid expressions in C and C++:

```
a = a + b;
if (a < b)
   a = b;

if (a == b)
   a = "temp";
```

2.7.4 Control Structures

C++ supports the same control structures as C. We can summarize these in pseudocode:

- ```
  if (this statement is true)
  {
  do this;
  and this;
  }
  else
  {
  do this;
  and this:
  }
  ```

- ```
  while (this condition is true)
  {
  do this;
  and this;
  }
  ```

- ```
  do
  {
  this;
  and this;
  }
  while (this condition is true);
  ```

- ```
  for (initialize counter; perform conditional test;
                           reevaluate counter)
  {
  ```

```
do this;
and this;
}
```

■ `switch (on integer expression)`

```
{
case constant1:
   do this;
case constant2:
   do this;
default:
   do this;
}
```

2.8 Differences between C++ and C

Now we will briefly describe those features of C++ that are not found in C. You were introduced to several of these features in Chapter 1.

2.8.1 Output

When you first started to learn C, one of the first complete programs that you wrote probably looked something like this:

```
main()
{
   printf ("This is C!!!\n");
}
```

Assuming that this nice little program was called test2_1.c, and using an IBM or IBM compatible computer, it was compiled, linked, and executed as follows:

```
cl test2_1.c
$ test2_1
This is C!!!
```

The equivalent of this program in C++ (we'll call it test2_2.cpp) is as follows:

```
// test2_2.cpp

#include <iostream.h>
main()
{
   cout << "This is C++!!!\n";
}
```

Compiling and running the code give the following output:

```
This is C++!!!
```

The include file <iostream.h> contains the standard input and output facilities for C++. The name of this header file can vary with different compilers. The operator << (put to) writes the argument that follows it to the argument that precedes it. cout is defined as the standard output stream in <iostream.h>. Thus, the phrase

```
This is C++!!!
```

is output to the terminal.

2.8.2 Input

C provides many functions that allow input of data, for example, getchar(), getc(), and gets(). C++ allows input of data through the input stream cin. Here's a program that demonstrates its use:

```
// test2_3.cpp

#include <iostream.h>
main()
{
   int num;
   cout << "Please enter number: ";
   cin >> num;
   cout << "\nThe number you entered was " << num  << "\n";
}
```

Compiling and running this program give this output:

```
Please enter number: 7
The number you entered was 7
```

All variables that will be used in the program must be declared, just as in C. The variable num is declared of type int. We are prompted to enter a value via the statement

```
cout << "Please enter number: ";
```

Notice that the newline character \n is missing. This allows us to enter the number on the same line.

The number entered is read from the standard input stream cin, using the >> (get from) operator and output, as usual, via cout.

Notice the use of three output operators to cout in the final statement. The output is, in effect, being concatenated together.

2.8.3 Functions

Functions can be invoked from anywhere in the program, which is a practice similar to that of C. The function prototype, which specifies the return value and type of arguments, must be declared before main().

C++ adds the concept of *function overloading*. This allows functions that perform similar tasks but work with different data types of objects to have the same name. Take a look at this program:

```
// test2_4.cpp

void print(int);
void print(float);

#include <iostream.h>

main()
{
   // num is int
   // num2 is float
   int num = 5;
   print(num);

   float num2 = 5.5;
   print(num2);
}

void print(int num)
{
   cout << " Num is: " << num << "\n";

}

void print(float num2)
{
   cout << " Num is: " << num2 << "\n";
}
```

The output for this program is as follows:

```
 Num is: 5
 Num is: 5.5
```

Notice that two functions with the same name are defined. One function takes an integer as an argument, and the other accepts a float. The compiler matches the argument type in the program to the function prototypes, and chooses the right function to call, based upon the data types involved. In the first instance, it invokes the `print()` function that operates on an integer argument, and in the second instance, it invokes the `print()` function that operates on a float.

C++ has the capability of overloading *operators* as well. For example, the operator plus (+) can be overloaded to mean multiply (*). In the `<iostream.h>` file, the logical left shift operator << has been overloaded to mean *put to*, and the logical right shift operator >> has been overloaded to mean *get from*.

2.8.4 Pointer Declaration and Indirection

In C++, pointers are declared and referenced similar to the method used by C:

```
int *ptr;       // ptr is pointer to int
ptr = &var;     // ptr contains the address of the variable var
*ptr = 50;      // set var to 50, through indirection
```

C++ adds the concept of a constant pointer:

```
char *const ptr2;    //ptr2 is a constant pointer to char
```

The declaration above declares `ptr2` as a constant pointer to a `char` data type. The programmer cannot modify the address to which `ptr2` is initialized:

```
ptr2 = &var2; // ptr2 contains address of var2
ptr2 = &var3; // won't work!!  ERROR
```

C++ also adds the concept of a pointer to a constant:

```
char const *ptr3; //ptr3 is a pointer to a constant

ptr3 = &var3;   // ptr3 contains address of var3
ptr3 = &var4;   // ptr3 now contains address of var4 - that's ok
var5 = 50;       // var5 initialized to 50;
*ptr3 = 60;     // trying to set var5 to 60 - won't work!!  ERROR
```

The last statement will generate an error because `ptr3` is declared as a pointer to a constant. It can point to any variable of the correct data type, but the contents of what it is pointing to cannot be changed through indirection, since they remain constant.

2.8.5 Structures and Unions

C++ allows the declaration of structures similar to that in C. However, it adds the capability of declaring member functions within structures as well. The analogy presented in Chapter 1 described this feature in detail.

2.8.6 Classes and Derived Classes

Classes and derived classes have also been discussed in Chapter 1.

2.8.7 References

C++ allows the use of a *reference*, which is simply another name of the variable that is being initialized. Following is a reference declaration:

```
int richard = 666;

// notice use of &, it follows variable
// type and precedes variable name
int& rich = richard;
```

The declaration above will result in `rich` being an alternative name for `richard`.

If we add 2 to `rich`:

```
rich += 2; // richard equals 668
```

we have, in effect, added 2 to `richard`. A reference must be initialized at the time that it is declared.

2.8.8 Constructors, Destructors, new, and delete

A *constructor* is a member function in a declared class that dynamically initializes a variable of its class. It is distinguished from other member functions in that it has the same name as its class.

A *destructor* deallocates memory for a class member. A destructor also has the same name as its class, except that it is preceded by a tilde (~). Constructors and destructors are discussed in detail in later chapters.

2.9 REVIEW

In this chapter, we briefly reviewed some of the concepts introduced in Chapter 1, which described features such as data encapsulation, inheritance, and dynamic run-time binding of functions. These combined features make C++ more structured, expandable, and easier to maintain than non-object-oriented languages. We also described non-menu- and menu-driven compilation processes for C++ programs. By now you should have a feel for the basic building blocks of C++.

Chapter

3

C++ Standards for Tokens and Control Structures

3.1 INTRODUCTION

In this chapter we will describe some of the basic building blocks of a C++ program, i.e., the *tokens* that make up a program. Tokens are grouped together to form different types of control structures. Control structures that utilize tokens to implement program logic will be described next.

3.2 TOKENS

A program comprises *word-like units* and *whitespace*. The whitespace separates the word-like units. The word-like units are known as *tokens*. The combination of tokens and white-space make up a program, and allow the compiler to parse or break it up before it proceeds to the next step of the compilation process.

A program is made up of one or more of the following components:

keywords
identifiers
constants
string-literals
operators

Whitespace can be blanks, tabs, new line characters, and comments. As we discuss each type, you will find that they are inherently similar to what you have encountered in C.

3.2.1 Keywords

The following words cannot be used as identifiers, since they are reserved for C and C++:

```
auto        default    float    register   switch
break       do         for      return     typedef
case        double     goto     short      union
char        else       if       sizeof     unsigned
const       enum       int      static     void
continue    extern     long     struct     while
```

The following keywords have been added by C++:

```
class     inline     overload     public
delete    new        private      this
friend    operator   protected    virtual
```

Some compilers support the additional keywords:

```
asm       template
catch     volatile
```

Now that you know the words that you cannot use as identifiers in your programs, let's discuss the rules for the names that you can create.

3.2.2 Identifiers

Identifiers are the names that you choose to give to variables, constants, functions, classes, and the like. The first character must be a letter or an underscore. The remainder of the name may contain digits. Letters may be upper- or lowercase. The allowable length of the identifier name varies with different implementations. Our system allows up to 32 characters of significance, but yours may not. Please refer to the documentation for your compiler for rules specific to your implementation. You cannot use reserved words or keywords to name identifiers.

3.2.2.1 Case Sensitivity

As in C, C++ identifiers are case sensitive. A variable declared as follows:

```
int variable;
```

is not the same as this one:

```
int Variable;
```

or this one:

```
int VARIABLE;
```

Here's a small program that illustrates what we have discussed so far:

```
// test3_1.cpp
// iostream.h is necessary for cout
#include <iostream.h>
main()
{
   int   float;   // ERROR - invalid use of keyword as name
   int   sum;     // valid identifier name
   int  Sum;      // valid identifier name
   float = 2;
   Sum = 0;
   sum = 5;
   Sum = sum + float;
   cout << "Sum is  " << Sum << "\n";
}
```

Compiling this program gives several error messages. ***Please note that we will list only those messages that are directly related to the error in the program, and will be conforming to this convention throughout the remainder of the book.*** Often, other errors are simply offshoots of the real problem, or do not make sense in the context of the actual problem. Here's the message displayed for this program:

```
Error:  Too many types in declaration
```

This is because `float` is a keyword, and it cannot be used as the name of an identifier. This problem can be fixed by changing `float` to a name that is not a keyword or a reserved word, such as `var1`. Here's the rewrite of `test3_1.cpp`:

```
// test3_1.cpp
// iostream.h is necessary for use of cout
#include <iostream.h>
main()
{
   int var1;      // valid identifier name
   int sum;       // valid identifier name
   int Sum;       // valid identifier name

   var1  = 2;
   Sum   = 0;
   sum   = 5;
   Sum = sum + var1;
```

```
   cout << "Sum is " << Sum << "\n"
}
```

Compiling and executing the above code result in the correct output:

```
Sum is 7
```

3.2.3 Data Types

Data types can be constant or variable. C++ contains the same data types as C:

integer
character
floating point

3.2.3.1 Integer Data

An integer is a number that does not have a fractional part. Integer constants can be short or long and signed or unsigned. Integer constants can be represented as decimal values, octal (by prefixing the number with a `0`) or hexadecimal (number is prefixed with a `0x` or `0X`). Integer constants can be short, which is the default, or long, suffixed with an `l` or an `L`. They can also be signed, which is the default, or unsigned, suffixed with a `u` or a `U`. The unsigned and long prefixes can be used together to represent an unsigned, long constant. The following declarations are valid:

```
int  i = 10;    // short integer, decimal
int  j = 10l;   // long integer constant
int  k = 10ul;  // unsigned long integer constant
```

3.2.3.2 Character Data

A character is enclosed in single quotes:

```
char  yes = 'y';  // character constant yes initialized to y
```

Character constants can comprise more than one character enclosed within the single quotes. These are the escape sequences, or combinations of characters that have special significance for the compiler. Table 3.1 lists the escape sequences that are recognized by our compiler.

Table 3.1 Escape Sequences

Escape sequence	Action taken by the compiler
\a	Rings bell
\b	Backspace
\f	Formfeed
\n	New line character (linefeed)
\r	Carriage return
\t	Tab (horizontol)
\v	Tab (vertical)
\\	Backslash
\'	Single quote
\"	Double quote
\?	Question mark
\nnn	Octal bit pattern, where nnn is an octal number
\xnn	Hexadecimal bit pattern, where xnn is a hexadecimal number

These escape sequences should be familiar to you, since the ANSI C standard provides the same sequences.

3.2.3.3 Floating Point

Floating point data comprise an integer part, a decimal fraction, and optional suffixes. This type of data is declared as follows:

```
float half = 0.5;
```

Floating point data can also contain an exponential value and is declared as follows:

```
float big_number = 465.012e3
```

A floating point constant is suffixed with an `f` or an `F`:

```
float constant_half = 0.5f;
```

A double data type is similar to a float, except that twice as much storage space is reserved for variables and constants of this type. Constants such as these can also be suffixed with an `l` or an `L` to indicate that they are long.

3.2.3.4 Const Data Types

The qualifier `const` can precede the declaration of any data type to indicate that the value of the variable cannot be changed. Thus `const` can be used as an alternative way to specify a constant. The following is a `const` declaration:

```
const ten 10; // ten will always equal the value 10
```

3.2.3.5 Storage Requirements

The compiler assigns storage to different data types based on their declaration. Table 3.2 summarizes storage requirements and permissable values for the data types discussed. Remember that these storage specifications are for our computer, which uses 16 bits to store a word. If you are working on an IBM or IBM compatible PC, then the storage specifications will probably be the same.

3.2.3.6 String Literals

A string literal is a collection of characters enclosed within double quotes. A string literal is terminated by the null character, `\0`, just as in C. Following is an example:

```
char string[16] = "This is a string";  // string literal
```

Escape sequences can be freely interspersed between string literals. Take a look at this short program:

```
// test3_2.cpp
// iostream.h is required for cout

#include <iostream.h>
main()
{
   char string[36] = "This is line 1 \n and this is line 2";
   cout << string;
}
```

Compiling and running this program result in the following output:

```
This is line 1
 and this is line 2
```

Table 3.2 Data Types and Storage Requirements

Data type	Declaration in C++	Storage	Permissable values
Integers	int	16 bits	-32,768 to +32,768
Integers, short	short int	16 bits	-32,768 to +32,768
Integers, long	long int	32 bits	-2,147,483,648 to +2,147,483,647
Integers, unsigned	unsigned int	16 bits	0 to 65,535
Integer constants, long	Add suffix l or L	32 bits	-2,147,483,648 to +2,147,483,647
Integer constants, unsigned	Add suffix u or U	16 bits	0 to 65,535
Character	char	8 bits	ASCII code
Float	float	32 bits	3.4×10^{-38} to $3.4 \times 10^{+38}$
Double	double	64 bits	1.7×10^{-308} to $1.7 \times 10^{+308}$
Double, long	Add suffix l or L	80 bits	3.4×10^{-4932} to $1.1 \times 10^{+4932}$

Notice the space before the `and` on the second line of output. We inserted a space after the new line character `\n` so that you could differentiate it from the remainder of the string. There would be no space on the second line of output if it had been initialized as follows:

```
char string[36] = "This is line 1 \nand this is line 2";
```

3.2.4 Operators

Operators are symbols that indicate the computation to be performed on two or more variables or constants within an expression.

In C++, we find the same operators as in C, plus a few of its own. Take a look at the following program, which illustrates the use of those that are used more frequently:

```
// test3_3.cpp
// iostream.h is necessary for cout

#include <iostream.h>
main()
{
   int i, j;                        // comma operator
   int i = j = 0;                   // assignment operator
   int  k[5] = {1, 2, 3, 4, 5};  // array subscript
                        // assignment
                        // comma
   struct person
      {
      int age;
      char sex;
      } ;

// structure anna of type person is declared
// ptr is pointer to structure of type person
   person anna;
   person *ptr;

// less than or equal and increment opertors are used
   for (j=0; j <= 5; j++)
   {
      // array subscript and assignment operators are used
      k[j] = 0;
   }

   // dot operator is used
   anna.age = 25;
   anna.sex = 'F';

   cout "Age is " << anna.age << "\n";
   cout << "Sex is " << anna.sex << "\n";

   // address of operator is used
   ptr = &anna;

   // set pointer to address of structure anna
   // arrow operator is used
   ptr -> age = 30;

   cout << "Using Indirection now \n";
   cout << "Age is " << ptr->age << "\n";
```

```
    cout << "Sex is " << ptr->sex << "\n";

    // add 25 to original value of anna.age
    anna.age += 25;

    cout << "Age is " << anna.age << "\n");
}
```

Compiling and running this program result in the following output:

```
Age is 25
Sex is F
Using Indirection now
Age is 30
Sex is F
Age is 55
```

In this program several of the most frequently used operators are used to perform different functions. You should be familiar with all of them. Now look at the complete list of operators that have been carried forward from C to C++ in Table 3.4.

An expression such as this:

```
a = a + b;
```

can be written as follows:

```
a += b;
```

Table 3.3 lists the set of operators that can be derived.

Table 3.3 Derived Operators in C++

Expression	Meaning
*=	Expression 1 = expression 1 * expression 2
/=	Expression 1 = expression 1 / expression 2
%=	Expression 1 = expression 1 % expression 2
-=	Expression 1 = expression 1 - expression 2
<<=	Expression 1 = expression 1 << expression 2
>>=	Expression 1 = expression 1 >> expression 2
&=	Expression 1 = expression 1 & expression 2
^=	Expression 1 = expression 1 ^ expression 2
|=	Expression 1 = expression 1 | expression 2

Table 3.4 Operators in C++

<table>
<tr><th>Operator</th><th>Function</th></tr>
<tr><td>()</td><td>Function call</td></tr>
<tr><td>[]</td><td>Array subscript</td></tr>
<tr><td>.</td><td>Dot; accesses member of structure or union</td></tr>
<tr><td>-></td><td>Arrow; points to member of structure or union</td></tr>
<tr><td>!</td><td>Logical NOT condition</td></tr>
<tr><td>~</td><td>One's complement</td></tr>
<tr><td>-</td><td>Unary minus</td></tr>
<tr><td>++</td><td>Increments</td></tr>
<tr><td>--</td><td>Decrements</td></tr>
<tr><td>&</td><td>Gets the address of</td></tr>
<tr><td>*</td><td>Performs indirection</td></tr>
<tr><td>(type)</td><td>Type casts</td></tr>
<tr><td>sizeof</td><td>Gets size of variable or constant specified</td></tr>
<tr><td>*</td><td>Multiplies</td></tr>
<tr><td>/</td><td>Divides</td></tr>
<tr><td>%</td><td>Modulus; gets the remainder</td></tr>
<tr><td>+</td><td>Adds</td></tr>
<tr><td>-</td><td>Subtracts</td></tr>
<tr><td><<</td><td>Performs left shift at the bit level</td></tr>
<tr><td>>></td><td>Performs right shift at the bit level</td></tr>
<tr><td><</td><td>Evaluates less than condition</td></tr>
<tr><td>></td><td>Evaluates greater than condition</td></tr>
<tr><td><=</td><td>Evaluates less than or equal to condition</td></tr>
<tr><td>>=</td><td>Evaluates greater than or equal to condition</td></tr>
<tr><td>==</td><td>Evaluates equal to condition</td></tr>
<tr><td>!=</td><td>Evaluates not equal to condition</td></tr>
<tr><td>&</td><td>Performs bitwise AND</td></tr>
<tr><td>^</td><td>Performs bitwise XOR</td></tr>
<tr><td>|</td><td>Performs bitwise OR</td></tr>
<tr><td>&&</td><td>Performs logical AND</td></tr>
<tr><td>||</td><td>Performs logical OR</td></tr>
<tr><td>?:</td><td>Conditional; evaluates two expressions</td></tr>
<tr><td>=</td><td>Assigns value</td></tr>
<tr><td>,</td><td>Separates variables, constants, and expressions inside functions, control structures, etc.</td></tr>
</table>

Table 3.5 lists the operators that are used by the preprocessor and Table 3.6 lists the operators added by C++.

Table 3.5 Operators Used by Preprocessor

Operator	Meaning
#	Define a variable or constant, or include a file
##	Concatenate two strings together

Table 3.6 Operators Added in C++

Operator	Meaning
::	Resolved scope
.* ->*	Dereferences pointer to a class member
new	Initializes, assigns storage dynamically
delete	Deallocates storage assigned by new

Table 3.7 displays the associativity and precedence of C++ operators. Precedence refers to the order in which operators are evaluated. Associativity refers to the order in which operators that have the same precedence are evaluated.

The order of the operators, from top to bottom, indicates the precedence. The associativity is indicated in the right hand column.

The operators introduced by C++ will be discussed in detail as they are encountered in subsequent chapters. For now, we want you to feel comfortable that the majority of operators in C++ are the same as in C.

3.2.4.1 Operator Overloading

Now that you know what operators you can work with in C++, let's briefly touch upon an interesting feature that is not available in C: operator overloading. (This feature will be discussed in detail in later chapters.) Overloading allows you to redefine the meaning of operators.

You have seen instances of operator overloading in the use of `cout` and `cin`. `cout` uses the left shift operator << to output a stream of data, while `cin` uses the right shift operator >> to accept input.

Table 3.7 Associativity and Precedence of C++ Operators

<table>
<tr><th>Operators</th><th>Associativity</th></tr>
<tr><td>() [] -> :: .</td><td>Left to right</td></tr>
<tr><td>! ~ - ++ -- & *</td><td>Right to left</td></tr>
<tr><td>sizeof new delete .* ->* / %</td><td>Left to right</td></tr>
<tr><td>+ -</td><td>Left to right</td></tr>
<tr><td><< >></td><td>Left to right</td></tr>
<tr><td>< <= > >=</td><td>Left to right</td></tr>
<tr><td>== !=</td><td>Left to right</td></tr>
<tr><td>&</td><td>Left to right</td></tr>
<tr><td>^</td><td>Left to right</td></tr>
<tr><td>|</td><td>Left to right</td></tr>
<tr><td>&&</td><td>Left to right</td></tr>
<tr><td>||</td><td>Left to right</td></tr>
<tr><td>? conditional operator</td><td>Right to left</td></tr>
<tr><td>= += /= %= += -=</td><td>Right to left</td></tr>
<tr><td>&= ^= |= ,</td><td>Left to right</td></tr>
</table>

What is important to note at this point is that almost all of the operators described can be overloaded. (The few exceptions will be discussed in later chapters.) However, their precedence and associativity cannot be changed.

3.3 Control Structures

C++ has the same control structures as C. These control structures utilize different combinations of tokens to perform the logic or devise the flow of control within a program. These structures are as follows:

The if and if-else statements
The while statement
The do-while statement
The for statement
The switch-case construct

Each type will be briefly described via pseudocode. Their use will be illustrated in small C++ programs.

3.3.1 The if Statement

The syntax of the *if* statement is as follows:

```
if (expression is true)
   {
   do this;
   and this;
   }
```

The *else* statement can be appended to the *if*:

```
if (expression is true)
   {
   do this;
   and this;
   }
else
   {
   do this;
   and this;
   }
```

The following program illustrates their use:

```
// test3_5.cpp
// iostream.h is necessary for cout

#include <iostream.h>
main()
{
   int income;
   char meal_1[] = "Go out - Eat steak";
   char meal_2[]  = "Stay home - Eat spaghetti";

   income = 55;

   if (income > 50)
      {
      cout << meal_1 << "\n";
      }
   else
      {
      cout << meal_2 << "\n";
      }
}
```

Compiling and executing the program result in the following output:

```
Go out - Eat steak
```

3.3.2 The while Statement

The syntax of the *while()* statement is as follows:

```
while (expression is true)
   {
   do this;
   and this;
   }
```

The following program illustrates its use:

```
// test3_6.cpp
// iostream.h is necessary for cout

#include <iostream.h>

main()
{
   int income;
   char meal_1[] = "Go out - Eat steak";
   char meal_2[] = "Stay home - Eat spaghetti";

   income = 150;

   while (income > 50)
      {
      cout << meal_1 << "\n";
      income -= 45;
      }
   cout << "Out of money! \n" << meal_2 << "\n";
   cout << "I don't think I can stand another steak anyway!! \n"

}
```

Compiling and running the above program give us the following output:

```
Go out - Eat steak
Go out - Eat steak
Go out - Eat steak
Out of money!
Stay home - Eat spaghetti
I don't think I can stand another steak anyway!!
```

3.3.3 The do-while Statement

The syntax of the *do-while* statment is as follows:

```
do
   {
```

```
   this;
   and this;
   }
   while (expression is true);
```

The following program illustrates its use:

```
// test3_6.cpp
// iostream.h is necessary for count

#include <iostream.h>
main()
{
   int income, i;
   char have_fun_type[2][10] =
      {{" See play"},
       {" See movie"}};
   char out_of_choices[] = "Stay home - watch TV";

   i = 0;
   income = 115;
   do
      {
      cout << "Income is " << income
         << have_fun_type[i] << "\n";
      i++;
      income -= 45;
      }
      while (income > 50);
      // end do-while() construct
   cout << "Income is " << income << " "
        << out_of_choices << "\n";
}
```

Compiling and running this program result in the following output:

```
Income is 115 See play
Income is 70 See movie
Income is 25 Stay home - watch TV
```

3.3.4 The for Statement

The syntax of a *for* statement is as follows:

```
for (initialize variable;
        perform conditional test;
           reevaluate variable)
   {
   do this;
   and this;
   }
```

The following program illustrates its use:

```
// test3_7.cpp
// iostream.h is necessary for cout

#include <iostream.h>
main()
{
   int income;
   char compulsion[] = "Spend money";

   for (income = 200; income > 20; income -= 45)
      {
      cout << "Income is " << income << " "
         << compulsion << "\n";
      }

   cout << "Income is " << income << "."
      << " Can't spend anymore. Have to wait till pay-day. \n";
}
```

Compiling and running the above program give the following output:

```
Income is 200 Spend money
Income is 155 Spend money
Income is 110 Spend money
Income is 65 Spend money
Income is 20. Can't spend anymore. Have to wait till pay-day.
```

3.3.5 The switch-case Construct

The syntax of a *switch-case* construct is as follows:

```
switch(on integer expression)
   {
   case 1:
      {
      do this;
      and this;
      }
   case 2:
      {
      do this;
      and this;
      }
   default:
      {
      do this;
      and this;
      }
   }
```

The following program illustrates its use:

```
// test3_8.cpp
// iostream.h is necessary for cout

#include <iostream.h>
main()
{
  int income;
  income = 200;

  while (income > 0)
  {           // start while()
     switch(income)
     {        // begin switch case construct

        case 25:
        {
        cout << "Income is " << income << "."
           << "Spend only on lunch. \n";
        income -= 10;
        break;
        }
        case 100:
        {
        cout << "Income is " << income << "."
           << "Spend with less abandon \n";
        income -= 75;
        break;
        }
        case 200:
        {
        cout << "Income is " <<  income << "."
           << "Spend with abandon \n";
        income -= 100;
        break;
        }
        default:
        {
        cout << "Income is << " << income << "\n"
           << "Stay home";
        }
     }  // end switch
  }  // end while()
}  // end main()
```

Compiling and running test3_8.cpp give the following output:

```
Income is 200 Spend with abandon
Income is 100 Spend with less abandon
Incomeis 25 Spend only on lunch
Income is 15 Stay home
Income is 15 Stay home
```

We were obliged to hit the *control break* key to stop program execution. (Please note that you may have to press a different combination of keys to stop program execution. If the control break key does not work, try pressing *control-alt-delete*. Refer to your system manual for further assistance.) This was done because once income falls below 25, it is neither incremented nor decremented, and hence the default condition is executed forever, or at least until the break key is hit.

3.4 REVIEW

In this chapter, the fundamental building blocks required to write a C++ program were described. In particular, we did the following:

- Reviewed the keywords that have been carried forward from C to C++.

- Found a few new ones that have been added to C++.

- Described `int`, `char`, `float`, `double`, and string data types. The rules for these data types are the same as in C.

- Reviewed the operators that have been carried forward from C to C++.

- Discovered a few new ones that have been added to C++.

- Finally, we put it all together through control structures. We realized that all C control structures have also been carried forward from C to C++.

So far, so good! C++ does not seem to be deviating too much from the C language that you already know! That's the whole point of Part 1 of this book. You need to feel comfortable with the basics of C++, before we get into the real stuff! Your transition will be that much easier if the introduction builds a strong foundation.

Chapter

4

Storage Classes and Scope in C++

4.1 Introduction

In the last chapter we learned the different data types that exist in C++. In this chapter, the storage classes of these types will be discussed. A *storage class* implies the location in which the variable will be stored and its duration or lifetime through the execution of the program that contains it. An *object* is a location in memory in which fixed or variable values can be stored. Tied closely to storage class is *scope*. Scope is that part of a program in which the variable is active; that is, it can be accessed.

A variable's storage class can be implied *explicitly*, by stating it as such, or *implicitly*. It defaults to the storage class implied by its context. The following storage classes have been carried forward from C to C++:

```
automatic
static
external
register
```

You should already be familiar with each type, since they are used in C programs. Their use will be illustrated in C++ programs.

4.2 Automatic Declarations

The keyword `auto` is used to declare automatic variables. Variables that are declared without specifiers default to `auto`. Take a look at this code:

```
auto int a;    // automatic variable
char  b;       // automatic variable by default
```

In C++, the scope of an automatic variable is only for the block, or any blocks within that block, in which it appears. The scope of an automatic variable in C is the same. Take a look at the following example;

```
// test4_1.cpp

#include <iostream.h>
main()
{
   // i and j are auto variables by default
   int i;
   int j;

   cout << " i in outer block is " << i << "\n";
   cout << " j in outer block is " << j << "\n";
   cout << " k in outer block is " << k << "\n";

   { //    inner block
      int k;      // auto variable by default
      cout << " i in inner block is " << i << "\n";
      cout << " j in inner block is " << j << "\n";
      cout << " k in inner block is " << k << "\n";
   }

   //    outer block again
   cout << " i back in outer block is " << i << "\n";
   cout << " j back in outer block is " << j << "\n";
   cout << " k back in outer block is " << k << "\n";

} // end main()
```

Compiling this program results in the following error messages:

```
Error:  Undefined symbol 'k' in function main()
Error:  Undefined symbol 'k' in function main()
```

This is because the variable k is auto by default. It is declared inside the inner block, and it exists, or can be accessed, only within this block. The compiler does not know the value of k in the outer block, and hence generates error messages. The error can be fixed simply be declaring k in the outer block and deleting its declaration in the inner block. After doing so, recompiling and executing the program give the following output:

```
i in outer block is 8886
j in outer block is 18
k in outer block is 0
```

```
i in inner block is 8886
j in inner block is 18
k in inner block is 0
i back in outer block is 8886
j back in outer block is 18
k back in outer block is 0
```

So where did the values 8886, 18, and 0 magically appear in the variables `i`, `j`, and `k`? Well, recall from your knowledge of C that if automatic variables are not initialized within their scope, they contain random or garbage values. The same rule holds true in C++. If the original declarations of `i`, `j`, and `k` are modified as follows:

```
    .
    .
int i = 1;
int j = 2;
int k = 3;
    .
    .
```

then the output changes to this:

```
i in outer block is  1
j in outer block is  2
k in outer block is  3
i in inner block is  1
j in inner block is  2
k in inner block is  3
i back in outer block is 1
j back in outer block is 2
k back in outer block is 3
```

4.3 STATIC DECLARATIONS

Static variables are declared as such by preceding their declaration with the key word *static*. Like automatic variables, these variables are also local to the function, block or subsumed blocks in which they exist. However, there is one important difference. Their values persist, or *stick*, even when the variables go out of scope. When the program comes back to the same function, processing proceeds with the last values that were stored in them. Also, static variables in the absence of initializers are automatically initialized to 0 or null. Take a look at the following program:

```
// test4_2.cpp

#include <iostream.h>
```

```
// function prototype follows
void sum(void);

main()
{
   // j is a static declaration
   static int j;

   sum();
   cout << "Inside main(), j is  " << j << "\n";
   sum();
   cout << "Inside main(), j is  " << j << "\n";
}

void sum(void)
{
   static int j

   j = j+1;
   cout << "Inside sum() j is %d " << j <<  "\n";
}
```

Compiling and running the program result in the following output:

```
Inside sum() j is 1
Inside main(), j is 0
Inside sum() j is 2
Inside main(), j is 0
```

j is declared as a static variable inside the functions main() and sum(). Inside sum(), 1 is added to j, and thus j is set to 1. Then, processing goes back to main(), and, we see that the value of j is 0. This is because the variable j in main() is out of scope in the function sum(). In the absence of explicit initializers, statics are set to 0. Hence the value 0 is output for the value of j in main(). Next, control is returned to sum(), and here the old value of 1 that was placed in j persists, (because it is static), and now j is set to 2. Inside main(), the value of j is still 0.

In C++, static members of classes have special rules associated with them. These will be discussed in detail when we discuss classes.

4.4 External Declarations

External variables differ from static and automatic variables in that their scope is *global* instead of local. External variables in C++ behave similarly to their C counterparts. They can exist outside or inside functions, and are available to all functions that are within the same file (this is known as file scope). The values of external variables persist, just as those of static types do. In the absence of explicit initializers, externals are also set to 0 or null. Take a look at the following program:

```
// test4_3.cpp
#include <iostream.h>

// i is a global extern declaration
int   i;

// function prototypes follow
void function_1(void);
void function_2(void);

main()
{
   cout << " i inside main() is " << i << "\n";
   function_1();
}

void function_1(void)
{
   i = i + 1;
   cout << " i inside function_1() is " << i << "\n";
   function_2();
}

void function_2(void)
{
   i = i + 1;
   cout << " i inside function_2() is " << i << "\n";
}
```

Compiling and running this program result in the following output:

```
i inside main() is 0
i inside function_1() is 1
i inside function_2() is 2
```

i outputs as 0 in main(), since it was not explicitly initialized. Inside function_1(), it outputs as 1. There is no need for a declaration of i inside function_1(), since it has been declared globally outside of main(). Inside function_2(), it outputs as 2, since the value set in function_1() persists.

As in C, externals can be declared as extern inside the function in which they are used. The compiler would accept the following change to the original program without any change in output.

```
   .
   .
void function_1(void)
{
```

```
   extern int i;
   .
   .
}

void function_2()
{
   extern int i;
   .
   .
}
```

The rule that must be followed is that the extern declaration should be outside and above the function that references it, and within the same source code file. The compiler will generate an error for the following program:

```
// test4_4.cpp
#include <iostream.h>

// i is an external declaration
int i;

main()
{
   i = 5;
   cout << " i is " << i << "\n";
   cout << " j is " << j << "\n";
}

// j is declared after being referenced
int j;

Error:   Undefined symbol 'j' in function main()
```

This problem can be fixed by simply moving the declaration of j next to i. Another fix would be to leave the code the way it was in the original program, and add an extern declaration for both i and j inside main():

```
.
.
int i;
   .
   .
main()
{
   extern int i;
   extern int j;
   .
   .
}
```

```
int j;
```

Compiling and running this program would produce the following output:

```
i is 5
j is 0
```

And now, a word of advice. C++ capitalizes on the concept of privacy of data, and you will learn how in subsequent chapters. We recommend that you use external variables only when absolutely necesary since privacy of data is lost, they take up storage space throughout the duration of the program because they are global in scope, and in a program of any fair length it may be hard to keep track of what value is stored in them in different functions at different times.

4.5 Register Declarations

Register variables behave like automatic variables in that they are local in their scope. However, when a variable declaration is preceded with the keyword *register*, it means that a request has been made to the compiler to store that variable in a register, if one is available. This can significantly reduce the size of a program and improve its performance, since operations on registers are faster than those performed for variables stored in memory.

The following are valid register declarations:

```
register int  a;    // register declaration
register char b;    // register declaration
```

The keywords `auto` and `register` cannot appear in an external declaration.

4.6 Duration of Variables

The duration of a variable is the period of time that a variable is assigned memory.

As indicated previously, static and external storage class variables are assigned memory for the complete duration of the program. Auto and register variables are assigned memory while they are within their enclosing block or function.

In C, you can dynamically assign storage to variables at the time that a program is executed via calls to `calloc()` and `malloc()`. In C++, you can dynamically allocate storage to variables via the operators new and delete. These will be discussed next.

4.6.1 The Operators new and delete

The operator new is used to dynamically allocate storage to different data types from the *free store* or *heap*. The free store is a pool of unallocated memory that is provided to the program when it is run. The variable continues to be allocated space until memory is deallocated via the operator delete.

On successful allocation, the operator new returns a pointer to that location in memory. A null pointer is returned on unsuccessful allocation. The operator delete uses the same pointer to deallocate memory for that type when it is no longer required. A word of caution here: if for some reason the value of the pointer returned by new is changed, then delete will duly delete the amount of memory allocated by new, but at the new location being pointed to. The results could be quite disturbing. Make sure the value of the pointer does not change through the duration of the program.

The use of the delete operator is not mandatory, since memory will obviously be automatically deallocated on termination of the program. Take a look at the following program, which illustrates the use of these operators:

```
// test4_5.cpp

#include <iostream.h>

main()
{
   // ptr1 is a pointer to int data type
   // ptr2 is a pointer to a double data type
   int *ptr1;
   double *ptr2;

   // memory is allocated for 1 object of type int
   // memory is allocated for 1 object of type double
   ptr1 = new int;
   ptr2 = new double;

   // 5 is stored in area allocated by new, and pointed
   // by ptr1.
   // 6.45 is stored in area allocated by new, and
   // pointed to by ptr2.
   *ptr1 = 5;
   *ptr2 = 6.45;

   cout << "ptr1 is " << ptr1 << "\n";
```

```
    cout << "ptr2 is " << ptr2 << "\n";
    cout << "*ptr1 is " << *ptr1 << "\n";
    cout << "*ptr2 is " << *ptr2 << "\n";

    // memory allocated by new and pointed to
    // by ptr1 is deallocated.
    delete ptr1;

    cout << "ptr1 is " << ptr1 << "\n";
    cout << "ptr2 is " << ptr2 << "\n";
    cout << "*ptr1 is " << *ptr1 << "\n";
    cout << "*ptr2 is " << *ptr2 << "\n";
}
```

Compiling and running this program result in the following output:

```
ptr1 is 0x8f4d11ac
ptr2 is 0x8f4d11b4
*ptr1 is 5
*ptr2 is 6.45
ptr1 is 0x8f4d11ac
ptr2 is 0x8f4d11b4
*ptr1 is 4520
*ptr2 is 6.45
```

ptr1 and ptr2 indicate the locations in memory assigned by the operator new, for two objects of types int and double, respectively. These pointers are displayed as hexadecimal values. A null pointer or 0 would have been returned if there was not enough memory to store objects of that type.

ptr1 shows us the contents of the memory location to which it points. As expected, this is the value 5. Likewise, the value 6.45 is stored in the area to which ptr2 points, and is printed via cout.

Next, the operator delete is used to delete the memory allocated by new and pointed to by ptr1. ptr1 and ptr2 still contain the same values. This is what we expected, since ptr1 and ptr2 have not been reset to point to anything else. However, the contents of what was stored in the area to which ptr1 pointed are lost; the value 4520 (or garbage) is stored in it instead. This is because the operator delete has already deallocated that memory and returned it to the free store. *ptr2 still contains the value 6.45, since we have not used delete to deallocate memory to which ptr2 pointed.

The operators new and delete can be used to allocate memory to arrays, classes, and other data types. These operators will be discussed in greater detail when constructors and destructors are described later in the book. For now, we just want you to understand the concept of dynamic duration as it exists in C++.

4.7 REVIEW

In this chapter, we discussed storage classes and discovered that C++ carries the same types as C, plus a couple more. Table 4.1 illustrates the major concepts discussed:

Table 4.1 Storage Classes in C++

Storage class	Scope	Memory allocation	Initialization by compiler
auto	Local to block, subsumed block,or function in which it is declared. Values do not persist.	While in scope	None
static	Local to block, subsumed block, or function in which it is declared. Values persist.	Duration of program	0
extern	Globally available to all functions within the same file, if declared outside and above them. Values persist.	Duration of program	0
register	Local to block, subsumed block, or function in which it is declared. Values do not persist.	While in scope	None
new, delete	Depends on type of object created.	Until delete is called, or program terminates	None

Chapter

5

Functions in C++

5.1 INTRODUCTION

In this chapter we will discuss how functions are put together in C++ programs. A *function* is a self-contained block of code, the inner workings of which are invisible to the remainder of the program.

All C programs comprise one function called `main()`. In addition to this, they may have one or more functions that interact with each other to produce the output. One function can call another and it can even call itself. Arguments can be sent to functions. The argument itself is not sent; instead, a copy of that argument is sent. (Exceptions to this are arrays and external variables.) Inside the called function, the original copies of arguments can be manipulated through pointers only (unless these arguments happen to be arrays or externals). Hence, if the value of an argument is to be changed inside another function, then a pointer to that argument has to be sent as well.

Values can be returned from the called function. The return and argument data types for returned values must be declared in the function prototype area. The return type, function name, and number and type of arguments must correspond with the actual use of the function.

In C++, the rules are the same. C++ adds quite a few nice features of its own.

5.2 MAIN()

As noted previously, all C and C++ programs have a central entry point to the program called `main()`. In C, you are not required to state the return value of main(). In C++, even though you are not required to specifiy the return type, main() is defined to match one of the following prototypes:

```
int main();                           // prototype 1
int main(int argc, char *argv[]);     // prototype 2
```

These prototypes should be familiar to you. argc is the count of arguments that are being sent to main(). argv is a pointer to each one of those arguments.

The first prototype implies that a status is being returned to the operating system upon successful or unsuccesful execution of the program. Since C++ declares main() to return a value, it is good programming practice to actually do so, on program termination, indicating successful or unsuccessful execution of your program. A return value of 0 indicates successful execution. Take a look at the following program:

```
// test5_1.cpp
#include <iostream.h>

int main(void)
{
   cout << "This program returns a 0 \n";
   return (0)
}
```

Compiling and running this program result in the following output:

```
This program returns a 0
```

Recall that void indicates the absence of a type. If this keyword precedes the function name, it means that the function returns no value. If it is within the function parameter list, it indicates that the function takes no arguments. In C++, a function declared as follows:

```
int function_1(void);
```

is equivalent to the following:

```
int function_1();
```

The compiler will ensure that no arguments are passed to function_1().

Now let's get back to our original program and modify it to return a string.

```
// test5_2.cpp
#include <iostream.h>

int main(void)
{
   cout << "This program returns abc \n";
   return("abc");
}
```

Compiling and running this program result in the following output:

```
Error:  Expression type does not match the return type in
        function main()
```

This is because C++ expects `main()` to return a value of integer type only.

Let's review what we have just learned:

- C++ forces `main()` to return an integer value to the operating system.
- It is good programming practice to return an integer value upon successful execution of a program.
- Errors will be generated by the compiler if a value other than an integer type is returned.

5.3 Function Prototyping

ANSI C standards encourage function prototyping. That is, the return value, function name, and number and type of arguments can be specified in the function prototype, right before `main()`. The function itself must correspond to the specifications set down in the prototype area, or errors will be generated.

What you might find interesting is that C borrowed the function prototype concept from C++. While ANSI C allows function prototyping, C++ requires it. Take a look at the following program:

```
// test5_3.cpp

#include <iostream.h>
void function_1(i)
{
   cout << "i is " << i << " \n";
}

int main(void)
{
```

```
   int i = 1;
   function_1(i);
}
```

While C may have let you get away with the code above (replacing `cout` with `printf()` and `#including <stdio.h>` instead of `<iostream.h>`), the C++ compiler will generate the following error messages:

```
Error:  Function 'function_1' should have a prototype
```

The problem can be fixed by adding the function prototype of `function_1()` to the program, like this:

```
// test5_4.cpp

#include <iostream.h>
void function_1(int i);

int main(void)
{
   int i = 1;
   function_1(i);
}

void function_1(int i)
{
   cout << "i is " << i << " \n";
}
```

Compiling and running this program result in the following output:

```
i is 1
```

Now let's modify the program again to illustrate what happens if the return value, number of arguments, or argument types do not correspond with the actual function definition:

```
// test5_5.cpp

#include <iostream.h>
void function_1(int i);

int main(void)
{
   int i, j;
   i = j = 1;

   // function_1() is sent illegal number of arguments
   function_1(i, j);
}
```

```
void function_1(int i)
{
   cout << "i is " << i << " \n";
}
```

Compiling this program will result in the following error message:

```
Error:   Extra parameter to call in function_1(int)
```

This error is generated because the function call itself, that is:

```
function_1(i, j);
```

does not correspond with the function prototype:

```
void function_1(int i);
```

Some C compilers might have let you get away with the above code. However, the problem would have surfaced when the program was run. The C++ compiler would catch the discrepancy at compilation time, thereby prompting the programmer to fix the problem before the program is run. Just as in C, it is not necessary to specify the argument name in the function prototype. However, you are still required to specify the argument name in the function definition. (A function definition contains the body of the function.) The compiler will accept the following modification to the program:

```
// test5_6.cpp

#include <iostream.h>

// notice missing parameter name in prototype
void function_1(int);

int main(void)
{
   int i = 1;
   function_1(i);
}

void function_1(int i)
{
   cout << "i is " << i << " \n";
}
```

Compiling and executing this program result in this output:

```
i is 1
```

But this won't work:

```
// test5_7.cpp

#include <iostream.h>

void function_1(int);

int main(void)
{
   int i = 1;
   function_1(i);
}

// notice missing parameter name
void function_1(int)
{
   cout << "i is " << i << " \n";
}
```

The compiler generates the following message:

```
Error:  Undefined symbol i
```

If you modify the definition of function_1() as follows:

```
   .
   .
void function_1(int i)
{
   cout << "i is " << i << " \n";
}
```

then the program will compile correctly. The output of the program will be:

```
i is 1
```

i is displayed as the value that was stored in it in the function main(), before the call to function_1().

Another variant that is acceptable to the compiler is as follows:

```
// test5_8.cpp

#include <iostream.h>

// notice use of variable x in prototype
void function_1(int x);
```

```
int main(void)
{
   int i = 1;

   function_1(i);
}

// notice use of variable x in definition
void function_1(int x)
{
   cout << "i is " << x << " \n";
}
```

In test5_7.cpp, the name of the actual argument (which is passed from the calling function to the called function) is i. The name of the formal argument (which is declared within the parentheses at the time that the function is defined) is x. Compiling and running this program result in the same output:

```
i is 1
```

Note, however, that the value of x is output to cout. We would have received the *undefined symbol* error message again if the value of i had been output. x is used as a mask name for any argument that is passed to this function. x is the only variable name that function_1() understands.

This strong type checking, regardless of the style used, ensures that illegal values are not passed to functions. Thus,

- C++ programs require function prototyping.

- The function prototype must agree with its corresponding function call and definition.

5.4 Function Definition

A function definition is the actual body of the function itself. It comprises the following components:

- Return type of the function, i.e., the data type that will be returned

- Name

- Argument list

- Code

Each component will be discussed, and illustrated via small C++ programs.

5.4.1 Return Type

As stated previously, the return type of the function in the function definition must correspond with its prototype in the program. If a return type is not specified explicitly in the function prototype, then a default return type of `int` is assumed by the compiler. In this case, it is necessary that you insert a `return` statement in the called function and return an `int`, or an error message will be generated. Take a look at the following program:

```
// test5_9.cpp

#include <iostream.h>
function_1(int i);

int main(void)
{
   int i = 1;
   function_1(i);
}

function_1(int i)
{
   cout << "i is " << i << " \n";
   return(0);
}
```

Compiling and running this program give the expected output:

```
i is 1
```

Let's see what happens if a character instead of an integer is returned:

```
function_1(int i)
{
   .
   .
   return('c');
}
```

Surprisingly, the program compiles and executes as before. This is because *the compiler performs type conversions when it can.* The character is converted to `int`, and therefore there are no problems. Let's try to return a string next:

```
function_1(int i)
{
    .
    .
    return("abc");
}
```

This version of the program generates an error, because the compiler is unable to convert data type of string to integer. This problem was encountered when compiling `test5_2.cpp` as well. We recommend that you always indicate the return type in the function prototype and leave nothing to chance.

A summary of features of return types follows:

- The return type in a function definition must agree with its corresponding prototype.
- If it does not, then the compiler will perform some type conversions and try to find a correspondence. If it fails in its efforts, then it will generate error messages.
- A default type of `int` is assumed for those functions in which the return type is not specified.

5.4.2 Function Names and Function Overloading

In C, you were required to assign a different function name to each function in your program. In C++, two or more distinct functions can have the same name. This is called function overloading. You encountered this feature in Chapter 1. This is a powerful new capability that will be discussed at length in this chapter.

Take a look at this C program:

```
// test5_10.c

void sum_integer(int i);
void sum_float(float j);

main()
{
    // variables are initialized
    int i = 5;
    float j = 5.5;

    sum_integer(i);
    sum_float(j);
}
```

```
void sum_integer(int i)
{
   i += 5;
   printf (" i is %d \n", i);
}

void sum_float(float j)
{
   j += 5;
   printf (" j is %f \n", j);
}
```

Compiling and running this program give the following output:

```
i is 10
j is 10.500000
```

Notice here that `sum_integer()` and `sum_float()` do exactly the same thing. They add a value of 5 to the argument passed to them, and then display that value via the `printf()` statement.

Now take a look at an equivalent C++ program:

```
// test5_11.cpp

#include <iostream.h>

// notice two functions of same name
void sum(int i);
void sum(float j);

main(void)
{
   int i = 5;
   float j = 5.5;

   sum(i);     // call sum() to add integer
   sum(j);     // call sum() to add float
}

void sum(int i)
{
   i += 5;
   cout << "i is " << i << " \n";
}

void sum(float j)
{
   j += 5;
   cout << "j is " << j << " \n";
}
```

Compiling and running the program above result in the following output:

```
i is 10
j is 10.5
```

What you see here is a very simple case of function overloading. The function name `sum()` is *overloaded*. What this means is that the same function is given multiple implementations. The execution of the correct implementation is performed by the compiler, not the programmer. The compiler matches up the type of the arguments in the function call with the types in the function definition, and executes the one that matches the type of the argument in the function call. That's all there is to it.

Now let's modify the program and see what happens if different data types are sent to the two functions:

```
// test5_12.cpp

#include <iostream.h>
void sum(int i);
void sum(float j);

main(void)
{
   char i = 'c';
   float j = 3.14323;

   // send ASCII c to sum()
   // send floating point to sum()
   sum(i);
   sum(j);
}

void sum(int i)
{
   cout << "Inside sum(int) \n";
}

void sum(float j)
{
   cout << "Inside sum(float) \n";
}
```

This program compiles properly. The output is as follows:

```
Inside sum(int)
Inside sum(float)
```

Now how did the C++ compiler figure out which function to invoke each time? The process is really very simple. First, it compares the definition of overloaded functions with the definition parameters in the function call. If there is a match, then that function is implemented. If there is no match, then C++ performs type conversions and implements the function that allows the easiest type conversion.

In our example, `sum(int)` was called the first time around because the ASCII character 'c' was converted to integer, and thereby matched the function definition of `sum(int)`.

The second time around, the value 3.14323 matched the data type of float, and `sum(float)` was called.

Now let's modify this program and see what happens if an integer is sent to a function that expects a character:

```
// test5_13.cpp

#include <iostream.h>

// sum(char) expects char as argument
// sum(float) expects float as argument
void sum(char);
void sum(float);

main(void)
{
   int i = 65;
   float j = 6.5;

   // send integer to sum()
   // send float to sum()
   sum(i);
   sum(j);
}

void sum(char i)
{
   cout << "Inside sum(char) \n";
}

void sum(float j)
{
   cout << "Inside sum(float) \n";
}
```

Compiling this program results in the following error message:

```
Error:   Ambiguity between 'sum(char)' and 'sum(float)'
```

This message was generated because the compiler expected to find a character sent to `sum(char i)` instead of an `int`, and it was unable to perform the necessary type conversions the other way round. Function overloading will be discussed again in later chapters. For now, we just want you to understand the concept behind it, how it works in its simplest application, and what advantages it offers over rules for function names as they exist in C. A summary follows:

- In C++, more than one function can have the same name.
- The data types of the arguments in the function calls must match the data types in the function prototypes and definitions.
- If they don't, the compiler will perform type conversions. It will generate error messages if it is unable to match data types.

5.4.3 Argument List

As stated previously, the number and types of arguments in a function definition must match the corresponding function prototype. If there is not exact correspondence, then the C++ compiler will attempt to convert the types of the actual arguments so that they can match the formal arguments in the called functions. The `const` and `volatile` modifiers can precede the types of the formal arguments to indicate specific instructions to the compiler. We discuss these modifiers next.

5.4.3.1 The const Modifier

You can precede an argument type with the modifier `const` to indicate that this argument cannot be changed. The argument to which it applies cannot be assigned a value or changed in any way.

The following program illustrates its use:

```
// test5_14.cpp

#include <iostream.h>

// const argument is sent as argument to function_1()
void function_1(const int i);

main(void)
{
   int i = 1;

   // i is passed as actual argument
   function_1(i);
}

// const modifier precedes argument name
```

```
void function_1(const int i)
{
   cout << " i is " << i << " \n";
}
```

Compiling and running this program give the following output:

```
i is 1
```

So far, so good. Now let's modify the program and change the value of i.

```
// test5_15.cpp

#include <iostream.h>
void function_1(const int i);

main(void)
{
   int i = 1;
   function_1(i);
}

void function_1(const int i)
{
   // const argument is incremented
   i++;
   cout << "i is " << i << " \n";
}
```

Compiling this program results in an error:

```
Error:  Cannot modify a const object
```

This is because an attempt is being made to change the value of the argument i, which was specified as type const.

5.4.3.2 The volatile Modifier

The volatile modifier is the flip side of const. This keyword can be used to precede formal arguments to indicate that they are liable to be changed during the course of the normal execution of the program. Declaring arguments as such also prevents the compiler from storing them in registers. Let's modify test5_13.cpp to use the keyword volatile instead of const:

```
// test5_16.cpp

#include <iostream.h>

// notice use of volatile keyword
void function_1(volatile int i);

main(void)
{
   int i = 1;
   function_1(i);
}

// notice use of keyword volatile
void function_1(volatile int i)
{
   i++;
   cout << "i is " << i << " \n";
}
```

This program gives the following output:

```
i is 2
```

5.4.3.3 Default Initializers

In C++, you can have arguments default to values that you specify at the time that the function is declared in the function prototype. Take a look at the following program:

```
// test5_17.cpp

#include <iostream.h>

// notice initialization of argument
void function_1(int i, int j = 2);

main(void)
{
   int i = 1;
   int j;

   function_1(i, j);
}
void function_1(int i, int j)
{
   cout << "i is " << i << "\n";
   cout << "j is " << j << "\n";
}
```

Compiling and running this program give the following output:

```
i is 1
j is 8689
```

The argument j is initialized to garbage because initialization in the prototype only does not have the required effect.

Now let's modify the program to see what happens if the parameter j is initialized inside main().

```
// test5_18.cpp

#include <iostream.h>
void function_1(int i, int j = 2);

main(void)
{
   int i = 1;

   // j is initialized inside main()
   // j is sent as argument to function_1()
   int j = 5;
   function_1(i, j);
}

void function_1(int i, int j)
{
   cout << "i is " << i << " \n";
   cout << "j is " << j << " \n";
}
```

The output for this program is:

```
i is 1
j is 5
```

The value of j is output as 5 instead of 2. The default value of 2 assigned in the function prototype area is overridden by the value that is explicitly assigned to j within main().

Now let's modify the program again to see what happens if j is initialized at the time that the function is called.

```
// test5_19.cpp

#include <iostream.h>
void function_1(int i, int j = 2);

main(void)
{
   int i = 1;
   int j;

   // j is initialized at time of function call
```

```
   function_1(i, j = 8);
}
void function_1(int i, int j)
{
   cout << "i is " << i << " \n";
   cout << "j is " << j << " \n";
}
```

Compiling this version results in the output:

```
i i 1
j is 8
```

Okay. Now let's see what happens if a value is assigned to an argument at the time that the function is defined.

```
// test5_20.cpp

#include <iostream.h>

// j is assigned in prototype
void function_1(int i, int j = 2);

main(void)
{
   int i=1;

   function_1(i);
}

// j is reinitialized in function definition
void function_1(int i, int j = 8)
{
   cout << "i is " << i << " \n";
   cout << "j is " << j << " \n";
}
```

Compiling this program gives an error:

```
Error:  Default argument value redeclared for parameter 'j'
```

Okay. Now let's try something else. Let's try to initialize more than one argument:

```
// test5_21.cpp

#include <iostream.h>

// notice initialization of multiple arguments
void function_1(int i = 1, int j, int k = 2);

main(void)
```

```
{
   int i, k;
   int j = 2;

   function_1(i, j, k);
}

void function_1(int i, int j, int k)
{
   cout << "i is " << i << " \n";
   cout << "j is " << j << " \n";
   cout << "k is " << k << " \n";
}
```

Compiling this program results in the following error:

```
Error:   Default value missing following parameter 'i'
```

This is because C++ has another rule about default arguments. This rule states that only the last arguments in a parameter list can be initialized, the variable `i` is not one of the last. Okay. Let's modify `test5_18.cpp` to initialize the variables `j` and `k` only, and see what happens:

```
// test5_22.cpp

#include <iostream.h>

// only j and k are initialized
void function_1(int i, int j = 2, int k = 3);

main(void)
{
   int i = 1;
   int j, k;

   function_1(i);
}
void function_1(int i, int j; int k)
{
   cout << "i is " << i << " \n";
   cout << "j is " << j << " \n";
   cout << "k is " << k << " \n";
}
```

This program compiles properly. Here's the output:

```
i is 1
j is 2
k is 3
```

The output is as we expected.

Now we can summarize the rules that apply to default arguments in parameter lists.

- Arguments assigned values in the function prototype only do not result in the expected assignments.
- Arguments can be initialized within function calls.
- Arguments cannot be reinitialized in a function if they have been previously initialized elsewhere in the program.
- Only the last arguments in the list can be assigned values.

5.4.3.4 Ellipses

In C++ you can enter ellipses in the formal paramater declaration of a function to indicate that the function will be called with different sets of arguments on different occasions. Type checking is not performed for these arguments. You have encounterd this feature in C as well, perhaps without even knowing about it. The function `printf()` is nothing but a function that takes a variable number of arguments. If you do not specify the correct argument data types in the format specification, then the results can be erratic, since there is no type checking.

Implementation of a variable number of arguments is a little bit complicated. The header file `stdarg.h` has to be included, and macros defined in this header file are used to obtain the necessary output. Since this is only a primer, we will leave a detailed explanation of the implementation of these functions to your reference manual. For now, we just want you to be aware of this capability.

5.4.3.5 Reference Arguments

A *reference* is simply another name for a variable. Take a look at the following code:

```
// test5_23.cpp

#include <iostream.h>
main(void)
{
   // devil is assigned a value
   // satan is another name for devil
   int devil = 666;
   int &satan = devil;
```

```
   cout << "devil is " << devil << " \n";
   cout << "satan is " << satan << " \n";
}
```

The program's output is:

```
devil is 666
satan is 666
```

The variable devil, which is of type integer, is initialized to 666. Then, the reference type satan is set equal to devil. A reference is implied when the & sign is used to precede its name. A reference must be initialized at the time that it is declared. Restating a little bit differently, satan is simply another name for devil. devil was initialized to 666. After setting the reference type satan equal to devil, satan also contains the value 666. Notice that the value of satan is output, and not &satan. &satan would give the address of where this reference type is stored in memory.

Let's change the value of the reference, and see what happens:

```
// test5_24.cpp

#include <iostream.h>
main(void)
{
   int devil = 666;
   int &satan = devil;

   cout << "devil is " << devil << " \n";
   cout << "satan is " << satan << " \n";

   // value of satan is changed
   satan = 999;
   cout << "devil is " << devil << " \n";
   cout << "satan is " << satan << " \n";
}
```

The output for this program follows:

```
devil is 666
satan is 666
devil is 999
satan is 999
```

As you can see, changing the value of the reference type satan results in changing the value of the variable to which it was assigned, i.e., devil. This makes sense. After all, satan is just another name for devil!

Now that you understand what a reference is, let's see how it can be used as an argument in functions.

Recall that in C language arguments are passed to functions by value. In other words, the variable itself is not passed to the function, but a copy of that variable. What this meant for you as a programmer was that if you wanted to change the value of that variable in the called function, you had to pass a pointer to it, and then manipulate its contents via that pointer. Here's a simple C program that illustrates this feature.

```
/* test5_25.c */

#include <stdio.h>
void function_1(int *j);

main()
{
   int i;
   int *j;       /* j is pointer to integer */
   i = 1;        /* initialize i */
   j = &i;       /* set j to contain address of i */

   printf ("i is %d \n", i);
   function_1(j);
   printf ("i is %d \n", i);
}

void function_1(int *j)
{
   /* increment contents of what j is pointing to */
   *j += 1;
}
```

Compiling and running this program result in the following output:

```
i is 1
i is 2
```

In C++, you can pass arguments by value and by reference. Take a look at the program below, which is the C++ equivalent of test5_25.c. The only difference is that it uses a reference instead of a pointer to change the contents of i in the called function.

```
// tests5_26.cpp

#include <iostream.h>
int function_1(int j);

main(void)
{
   int i = 66;

   // j is a reference to integer type
   int &j = i;
```

```
   cout << "j is " << j << " i is " << i << " \n";

   // send reference to i
   i = function_1(j);

   cout << "j is " << j << " i is " << i << " \n";
}

int function_1(j)
{
   j = 3;
   return j;
}
```

Compiling and running this program result in the following output:

```
j is 66 i is 66
j is 3 i is 3
```

The argument `j` is passed by reference, not value. Therefore, this argument provides direct access to the object that it was made to reference (i.e., `i`), and its contents are modified without the use of pointers in the called function.

Let's review references:

- References are just other names for the variables to which they are assigned. A reference is prefixed with an & sign on the left side of the assignment operator, and must be initialized at the time that it is defined.

- References provide a convenient way of passing arguments to functions by reference, instead of value, as was the case in C.

5.5 Inline Functions

When a function is called, there is a certain amount of processing overhead that goes along with it. In C++, you can reduce this overhead by preceding a function name at the time that it is defined with the keyword `inline`. The compiler compiles the code for the function when it encounters this keyword. Then, it simply substitutes this code for that function each time it is called within the program. This is called *inline expansion*. Since the function has already been compiled, the usual overhead incurred in a function call is avoided. Take a look at this program:

```
// test5_27.cpp

#include <iostream.h>
int increment(int i);

// notice keyword inline
inline increment(int i)
{
   i++;
   return i;
}

main(void)
{
   int i = 0;
   while (i < 3)
      {
      i = increment(i);
      cout << "i is " << i << " \n";
      }
}
```

The output for this program is:

```
i is 1
i is 2
i is 3
```

Okay. Now let's modify the program to move the definition of the inline function below main().

```
// test5_28.cpp

#include <iostream.h>
int increment(int i);

main(void)
{
   int i = 0;
   while (i <= 3)
      {
      i = increment(i);
      cout << "i is " << i << " \n";
      }
}

// inline function definition follows its function call
inline increment(int i)
{
   i++;
   return i;
}
```

Compiling this program gives an error. This is because inline functions must be defined before they are called.

Therefore, inline functions:

- Reduce function overhead
- Must be defined before they are called

5.6 Recursive Functions

In C++, recursive functions exist as they do in C. In recursion, a function calls itself. Take a look at this program:

```
// test5_29.cpp

#include <iostream.h>
void decrement(int i);

main(void)
{
   int i = 2;
   i = decrement(i);
   cout << "i is " << i << "\n";
}

int decrement(i)
{
   cout << "Inside decrement() \n";
   i--;
   if (i > 0)

      // function calls itself
      decrement(i);
   else
      return(i);
}
```

The output for this program looks like this:

```
Inside decrement()
Inside decrement()
i is 0
```

The function `decrement()` calls itself recursively until the test condition evaluates to *TRUE* (or a zero value). When `i` evaluates to zero, program control returns back to `main()`.

5.7 REVIEW

In this chapter we learned many interesting features about functions in C++:

- `main()` returns a value of type `int` to the operating system.
- Function prototypes are mandatory.
- The return type, function name, and number and type of arguments in the prototype must agree with those in the actual function call and definition.
- The compiler attempts to perform type conversions of arguments and return types whenever it can, to create a correspondence if one does not exist.
- Function names can be *overloaded*, that is, assigned the same name. The decision of which function is executed at any time in the program is left up to the compiler, not the programmer.
- The `const` modifier notifies the compiler that a variable of this type cannot be modified.
- The `volatile` modifier notifies the compiler that a variable of this type can and probably will be modified.
- Default initializers can be assigned to function parameters in their prototypes.
- Functions can be called with variable number and types of parameters, via ellipses.
- C++ contains reference types. These are simply other names for the variables to which they are assigned.
- References provide a convenient way of passing arguments to functions by reference, rather than value.
- C++ allows the definition of inline functions, which helps reduce function call overhead.
- C++ allows recursive functions, that is, functions that can call themselves.

Part

2

The Power of C++

Chapter

6

Fundamental Concepts of the Class Mechanism

6.1 INTRODUCTION

In Chapter 1 we presented an analogy that was designed to help you understand the key concept in C++: the class mechanism. In this chapter, this concept will be discussed at length. Not only will you understand how to declare, define, and use classes, but, more important, you will learn the reason for using a class as opposed to the traditional C structure, and the advantages in doing so. In the next chapter, rules specific to class member declarations and definitions will be discussed.

Most of you should be familiar with traditional C structures. These will be reviewed first. Then, we will describe structures as they exist in C++.

6.2 STRUCTURES IN C AND C++

A structure is a special data type that gathers together, in a fixed pattern, other valid data types. Here's a simple structure declaration:

```
struct family
   {
   char *husband;
   char *wife;
   char *son;
   char *daughter;
   };
struct family Anderson;
```

The structure family comprises four variables which are pointers to character arrays. These variables are called husband, wife, son, and daughter, respectively. Anderson is a structure of type family. The members of Anderson can also be initialized at the time they are declared, and accessed through a pointer:

```
Anderson.husband = "John Anderson";
Anderson.wife = "Mary Anderson";
Anderson.son = "Joey Anderson";
Anderson.daughter = "Marla Anderson";
```

The members of Anderson can be accessed through a pointer, as follows:

```
struct family
   {
   char *husband;
   char *wife;
   char *son;
   char *daughter;
   };
struct family Anderson =
 {{"John Anderson"}, {"Mary Anderson"},
  {"Joey Anderson"}, {"Marla Anderson"}};

/* ptr points to structure of type family */
stuct family *ptr;

main()
{
   /* ptr points to 1st member of Anderson */
   ptr = &Anderson;

   printf ("husband is %s \n", ptr->husband,
      "wife is %s \n",  ptr->wife,
      "son is %s \n",  ptr->son,
      "daughter is %s \n", ptr->daughter);
}
```

Compiling and running this program result in the following output:

```
husband is John Anderson
wife is Mary Anderson
son is Joey Anderson
daughter is Marla Anderson
```

A structure with a tag-name of family is declared, Anderson is defined as a structure of this type, and the members are initialized. Next, ptr is declared as a pointer to structures of that type. Inside main(), ptr is set to point to the location in memory where the structure Anderson is stored. The structure members of Anderson are printed through a printf() statement, using ptr to point to the correct member. Simple enough to understand, right? Okay. Now let's see how structures are handled in C++.

Everything that has been said about structures in C is true for C++ as well. Take a look at the following C++ program:

```
// test6_1.cpp

#include   <iostream.h>

struct family
   {
   char *husband;
   char *wife;
   char *son;
   char *daughter;
   };

// Anderson is declared as a structure of type family
// notice that keyword struct or structure is missing
family Anderson =
   {{"John Anderson"}, {"Mary Anderson"},
    {"Joey Anderson"}, {"Marla Anderson"}};

// ptr points to structur of type family
family *ptr;

main(void)
{
   // ptr points to 1st member of Anderson
   ptr = &Anderson;

   cout <<"husband is  " << ptr->husband <<"\n"
   <<"wife is      " << ptr->wife    <<"\n"
   <<"son is       " << ptr->son     <<"\n"
   <<"daughter is " << ptr->daughter<<"\n";
}
```

Running this program gives the following output:

```
husband is John Anderson
wife is Mary Anderson
son is Joey Anderson
daughter is Marla Anderson
```

Notice that the keyword struct (or structure) is missing when Anderson and ptr are declared. In C++, this keyword is optional. However, it is not optional when the structure template is declared.

If you take another look at main(), you will realize that it can perhaps be logically divided into two parts. The first part initializes ptr to point to the structure Anderson. The second part simply outputs the contents of each member. Since functions are used to divide a program into its logical components, where each function performs a coherent task on its own, let's modify test6_1.cpp and create two functions to do the job:

```
// test6_2.cpp

#include <iostream.h>

struct family
   {
   char *husband;
   char *wife;
   char *son;
   char *daughter;
   };

family Anderson =
   {{"John Anderson"}, {"Mary Anderson"},
    {"Joey Anderson"}, {"Marla Anderson"}};

// ptr points to structure of type family
family *ptr;

// function prototypes follow
family  *initialize(family *ptr);
void output(family *ptr);

main(void)
{
   // set pointer to initialize()
   // send ptr to output()
   ptr = initialize(ptr);
   output(ptr);
}

family *initialize(family *ptr)
{
   ptr = &Anderson;
   return ptr;
}

void output(family *ptr)
{
   cout <<"husband is " << ptr->husband <<"\n"
   <<"wife is " << ptr->wife    <<"\n"
   <<"son is " << ptr->son     <<"\n"
   <<"daughter is " << ptr->daughter<<"\n";
}
```

The output for this program looks like this:

```
husband is John Anderson
wife is Mary Anderson
```

```
son is Joey Anderson
daughter is Marla Anderson
```

Now assume that 1000 lines of code, comprising, say, 15 additional functions, are added to the original program. The calls to these additional functions are made from `main()`. The program would look something like this:

```
// test6_3.cpp

#include    <iostream.h>

struct family
   {
   char *husband;
   char *wife;
   char *son;
   char *daughter;
   };
family Anderson;

family Anderson =
   {{"John Anderson"}, {"Mary Anderson"},
    {"Joey Anderson"}, {"Marla Anderson"}};

// ptr points to structure of type family
family *ptr;

// function prototypes follow
family  *initialize(family *ptr);
void output(family *ptr);

// function prototypes for the 15 additional functions are
// added  here......

main(void)
{
   // ptr receives pointer to Anderson
   ptr = initialize(ptr);

   // Calls to the 15 additional functions are made here
   output(ptr);
}

// The code for function initialize() is stil the same
family *initialize(family *ptr)
{
   ptr = &Anderson;
   return ptr;
}

// Code for 15 additional functions is over here.....
```

```
// The code for function output() is still the same
void output(family *ptr)
{
  cout <<"husband is " << ptr->husband <<"\n"
     <<"wife is " << ptr->wife    <<"\n"
     <<"son is " << ptr->son     <<"\n"
     <<"daughter is " << ptr->daughter<<"\n";
}
```

Suppose this program produces the following output:

```
husband is Mark Davis
wife is Jennifer Davis
son is Michael Davis
daughter is Maria Davis
```

On verification of the output, it appears that somewhere in the course of the program, `ptr` has been erroneously made to point to some other structure of type `family`, (perhaps called `Davis`), and its structure members have been initialized to the member names of the Davis family. What this means for you as a programmer is many hours of headache and wasted time, tracing through the 1000 line program, trying to locate the function in which `ptr` was reset to point to the location in memory of the `Davis` family, instead of `Anderson`. This is where C++ comes to the rescue.

6.3 The Class Mechanism in C++

C++ has a class mechanism that allows you to specify a unique set of objects which comprise that class, and the operations allowed on these objects. Let's modify the original version of the program (`test6_2.cpp`) to use a class instead of a structure, and see how classes work.

```
//   test6_4.cpp

#include <iostream.h>
class family
     {
     // notice use of keyword private
     // member list follows this keyword
     // ptr is declared inside family
     private:
     char *husband;
     char *wife;
     char *son;
     char *daughter;
     family *ptr;
```

```
    // notice use of keyword public
    // member functions follow this keyword
    public:
    void initialize(void);
    void output(family *ptr);
    };

// Anderson is object of type family
family Anderson;

main(void)
{
    // initialize() is qualified by class object name.
    // notice the dot operator.
    Anderson.initialize();
}
// initialize() is qualified by class name
void family::initialize(void)
{
    // initializing member list of object Anderson
    // class members are qualified by class object name
    Anderson.ptr = &Anderson;
    Anderson.ptr->husband = "John Anderson";
    Anderson.ptr->wife = "Mary Anderson";
    Anderson.ptr->son = "Joey Anderson";
    Anderson.ptr->daughter = "Marla Anderson";
    Anderson.output(Anderson.ptr);
}

// output() is qualified by class name
void family::output(family *ptr)
{
    cout <<"husband is " << ptr->husband   <<"\n"
         <<"wife is " << ptr->wife      <<"\n"
         <<"son is " << ptr->son      <<"\n"
         <<"daughter is " << ptr->daughter  <<"\n";
}
```

This program produces the following output:

```
husband is John Anderson
wife is Mary Anderson
son is Joey Anderson
daughter is Marla Anderson
```

Now let's step through this program and understand why a class was used instead of a structure, and why it was declared that way.

The keyword `class` is followed by the class tag-name, called `family`, (just like a structure tag-name in C), and then an opening curly brace (once again, like C structure declarations). What this does is create a unique type, a class type called `family`.

Next, you see the keyword private, followed by colon, and then a list of declarations. The list of declarations that are enclosed within the opening and closing curly braces within a class declaration is known as the *member list*. The keyword private is an access specifier, which indicates access privileges for the declarations that follow it. This keyword specifies that the variables that follow can be used only by the member functions that exist within that class (or its *friends*, but we will postpone discussion of the friend mechanism to a later chapter). But what are member functions? Let's continue to analyze the declaration before we answer that question.

Following the keyword private are the declarations for husband, wife, son, daughter, and then one for family *ptr. husband, wife, son, and daughter are known as class members (just like structure members). ptr is declared to be a pointer to a class of type family. Notice that the keyword class does not precede the class tag-name family, just as struct is not required to precede the declaration of a structure of that type. The compiler understands that family is a class name, because it was specified as such at the beginning of the class declaration.

Next is the keyword public, followed by a colon, and a list of function declarations. These functions are called *member functions*, or *methods*. Since these functions are declared as public, they can be accessed by members of their class as well as nonmembers. They can be passed arguments and accessed from anywhere within program scope.

Inside main(), there is a function call to the class member function initialize(). Notice that this function is prefixed with Anderson, and a dot (.). Recall how structure members are accessed in C. A code fragment from test6_1.c is redisplayed for your convenience:

```
struct family
   {
   char *husband;
   char *wife;
   char *son;
   char *daughter;
   };
struct family Anderson;

Anderson.husband = "John Anderson";
Anderson.wife  = "Mary Anderson";
Anderson.son = "Joey Anderson";
Anderson.daughter = "Marla Anderson";
```

The structure members are prefixed with the name given to structures of that type and the dot operator.

In C++, class (or structure members) are referenced the same way. initialize() is a member function of the class family, Anderson is an object of that type. A function call to initialize() is as follows:

```
Anderson.initialize();
```

Now take a look at the function definition of initialize():

```
void family::initialize(void)
{
    .
    .
```

Notice that the function name is preceded by the class name and scope resolution operator ::. Recall from Part 1 of the book how C++ allows different functions to have the same name. It is possible that there may be other functions in our program that have the name initialize(). However, the compiler understands this to be a member function of the class family simply because it is preceded with the class name! To say it a little bit differently, this function is qualified by a class name. Now you should be able to understand why :: is called the scope resolution operator; it resolves the scope of the function name that it precedes, it allows the compiler to understand whether the function definition that follows belongs to a class or structure, or is simply an independent entity on its own. Let's continue with the code:

```
    Anderson.ptr = &Anderson;
    Anderson.ptr->husband = "John Anderson";
    Anderson.ptr->wife = "Mary Anderson";
    Anderson.ptr->son = "Joey Anderson";
    Anderson.ptr->daughter = "Marla Anderson";
    Anderson.output(Anderson.ptr);
```

The class member ptr is assigned the location in memory of the class object name Anderson. Then, the remaining members are initialized. Finally, the function member output() is called and this call is also qualified by the class object name.

The program ends with a definition of the function output(). This function is also qualified by class name. The return value and type and number of arguments agree with the class declaration.

Summarizing,

- Classes are declared via the keyword class.

- Classes, like structures, have tag-names. The tag-name family is assigned to the class in the sample program.

- A class comprises a list of declarations of variables and/or functions. Our class member list comprises the pointers to character arrays called husband, wife, son, and daughter, respectively. In addition to this, ptr is declared as a pointer to a class of type family. The functions initialize() and output() are the member functions in the class member list.

- The keyword *class* does not have to precede the declaration of variables that are objects or instances of that type. In the sample program, Anderson is an object or an instance of a class of type family.

- Access specifiers, such as private and public, are used to specify access privileges of the member list within the class. In the program, the class members husband, wife, son, daughter, and ptr are private. The member functions initialize() and output() are public. What this means is that any valid argument can be passed to initialize() and output() from anywhere within the program. However, the private class members can be accessed by the functions initialize() and output() only. To reiterate, husband, wife, son, daughter, and ptr can be assigned values or manipulated through the functions initialize() and output() only.

- Member function calls are qualified by the class object name and the dot operator.

- Member function definitions are qualified by the class name and the scope resolution operator.

- The return value type, function name, and number and type of arguments of a member function must agree with its corresponding declaration within the class.

So why bother with classes anyway? Let's go back to the scenario that was presented in test6_3.cpp. In that program, ptr had somehow been erroneously set to point to the location in memory of the Davis family structure. The problem was that you as a programmer had to sift through 1000 lines of code comprising more than 15 functions to figure out where ptr had been reset. However, if 1000 lines of code were added to test6_4.cpp, and something were to go wrong, you could narrow down your search to two functions only: initialize() and output(). This is because the variables that have the incorrect value in them were specified as private members of a class, which means that they could be manipulated by these two functions only.

Thus, *a class mechanism allows you to group together variables and functions that can be performed on these variables as a single and unique type*. It also allows you to *localize problems quickly*, through the access privileges specified within the class declaration.

In addition to this, suppose you were required to modify the program at a later date, and the modifications pertained to the members of the class family only. Given that these members are declared as private, all you have to do is modify the logic within the two functions that are the member functions of this class. Just think of the ease of maintenance of such programs, think of the power that is placed at your fingertips!

Now that you understand the fundamental concept of classes, a few variations will be made to `test6_4.cpp` to see how the compiler responds to these changes. `main()` will be modified to qualify `initialize()` by class name, instead of class object name. All subsequent changes to the original program will be highlighted by imbedding a double asterisk within the comment. Make sure you pay special attention to these changes.

```
//   test6_5.cpp

#include <iostream.h>

class family
   {
   // notice use of keyword private
   // member list follows this keyword
   // ptr is declared inside family
   private:
   char *husband;
   char *wife;
   char *son;
   char *daughter;
   family *ptr;

   // notice use of keyword public
   // member functions follow this keyword
   public:
   void initialize(void);
   void output(family *ptr);
   };

// Anderson is object of type family
family Anderson;

main(void)
{
//   **   initialize()   is   qualified   by   class   name   only
family::initialize();
}

// initialize() is qualified by class name
void family::initialize(void)
{
   // initializing member list of object Anderson
   // class members are qualified by class object name
```

```
   Anderson.ptr = &Anderson;
   Anderson.ptr->husband = "John Anderson";
   Anderson.ptr->wife = "Mary Anderson";
   Anderson.ptr->son = "Joey Anderson";
   Anderson.ptr->daughter = "Marla Anderson";
   Anderson.output(Anderson.ptr);
}

// output() is qualified by class name
void family::output(family *ptr)
{
   cout << "husband is " << ptr->husband << "\n"
   << "wife is " << ptr->wife << "\n"
   << "son is " << ptr->son << "\n"
   << "daughter is " << ptr->daughter << "\n";
}
```

Compiling this program results in the following unfriendly message from the compiler:

```
Error:  Use . or -> to call family::initialize()
```

The declaration

```
family Anderson;
```

could just as well have been a declaration such as this:

```
family Anderson, Davis, Samuel;
```

The compiler needs to know which one of these objects or instances is being operated on. That is why it is necessary to prefix the object name that is being operated in the function call in `main()`. Thus, the statement `family::initialize` is incorrect. You must prefix the call to `initialize()` with the class instance name, which is `anderson`, for this example.

Now let's modify the original version (`test6_4.cpp`) and reference the class members in the function `initialize()` without qualifying them by the class object name. Remember, the changes are highlighted by a double asterisk within the comment.

```
//    test6_6.cpp

#include <iostream.h>

class family
   {
   // notice use of keyword private
   // member list follows private declaration
   private:
```

```
   char *husband;
   char *wife;
   char *son;
   char *daughter;
   family *ptr;

   // notice use of keyword public
   // member functions follow this keyword
   public:
   void initialize(void);
   void output(family *ptr);
   };

// Anderson is object of type family
family Anderson;

main(void)
{
   // initialize() is qualified by class object name.
   Anderson.initialize();
}

// initialize() is qualified by class name
void family::initialize(void)
{
   // initializing member list of object Anderson
   // ** class members are not qualified by class object name
   ptr = &Anderson;
   ptr->husband = "John Anderson";
   ptr->wife = "Mary Anderson";
   ptr->son = "Joey Anderson";
   ptr->daughter = "Marla Anderson";
   output(ptr);
}

// output() is qualified by class name
void family::output(family *ptr)
{
   cout << "husband is " << ptr->husband << "\n"
   << "wife is " << ptr->wife << "\n"
   << "son is " << ptr->son << "\n"
   << "daughter is " << ptr->daughter << "\n";
}
```

When this program is compiled, (much to our amazement) there are no errors. The output is the same as for `test6_6.cpp`. Let's see why.

`ptr` is set to the location in memory of the object `Anderson`. Hence, each time `ptr` is used to initialize members of the class, the object `Anderson` is being operated on. That is why there is no need to qualify `ptr` by object name; the compiler understands.

Let's modify the original version again, and try to initialize `ptr` in `main()`. `ptr` will be sent as an actual argument to `initialize()`, and the class declaration and function definitions will be modified accordingly.

```
//    test6_7.cpp

#include <iostream.h>

class family
   {
   // notice use of keyword private
   // member list follows private declaration
   private:
   char *husband;
   char *wife;
   char *son;
   char *daughter;
   family *ptr;

   // notice use of keyword public
   // ** ptr is sent as an argument to initialize()
   public:
   void initialize(family *ptr);
   void output(family *ptr);
   };

// Anderson is object of type family
family Anderson;

main(void)
{
   // ** accessing private member in main()
   Anderson.ptr = &Anderson;

   // ** send ptr to initialize()
   Anderson.initialize(Anderson.ptr);
}

// ** initialize() receives ptr as argument
void family::initialize(family *ptr)
{
   // initializing member list of object Anderson
   // class members are not qualified by class object name
   ptr->husband = "John Anderson";
   ptr->wife = "Mary Anderson";
   ptr->son = "Joey Anderson";
   ptr->daughter = "Marla Anderson";
   output(ptr);
}

// output() is qualified by class name
void family::output(family *ptr)
{
   cout << "husband is " << ptr->husband << "\n"
   << "wife is " << ptr->wife << "\n"
   <<"son is " << ptr->son << "\n"
```

```
   <<"daughter is " << ptr->daughter<< "\n";
}
```

Compiling this program results in the following message:

```
Error:   family::ptr is not accessible
```

The reason for this message should be obvious, if you take a moment to think of what happened. `ptr` is declared as a private member of the class `family`. It can be manipulated only by its class member functions. It cannot be initialized in `main()`.

Let's try one more variation to the original program before closing this chapter. This time the function prototypes of `initialize()` and `output()` will be declared outside the class declaration.

```
//   test6_8.cpp

#include <iostream.h>
class family
   {
   // notice use of keyword private
   // member list follows private declaration
   private:
   char *husband;
   char *wife;
   char *son;
   char *daughter;
   family *ptr;

   // notice use of keyword public
   // member functions follow
   public:
   void initialize(void);
   void output(family *ptr);
   };

// Anderson is object of type family
family Anderson;

// ** function prototypes of class members functions follow
void initialize(void);
void output(family *ptr);

main(void)
{
   // initialize() is qualified by class object name
   Anderson.initialize();
}

// initialize() is qualified by class name
void family::initialize(void)
{
```

```
    // initializing member list of object Anderson
    // class members are not qualified by class object name
    ptr->husband = "John Anderson";
    ptr->wife = "Mary Anderson";
    ptr->son = "Joey Anderson";
    ptr->daughter = "Marla Anderson";
    output(ptr);
}

// output() is qualified by class name
void family::output(family *ptr)
{
    cout << "husband is " << ptr->husband << "\n"
    << "wife is " << ptr->wife << "\n"
    << "son is " << ptr->son << "\n"
    <<" daughter is " << ptr->daughter << "\n";
}
```

Compiling this program results in the following messages:

```
Error:
Class member 'initialize' declared outside its class
Class member 'output' declared outside its class
```

The compiler matched the return value, function name, and type and number of arguments of each function prototype with the declarations inside the class. Since it found the declarations of its member functions outside the class definition, this error message was issued. Member functions cannot be redeclared anywhere except within their class.

If any of the factors had not matched, the compiler would not have issued this message. For example, the following declarations would have been acceptable:

```
void initialize(int i, int j);
void output(int k, char l);
```

However, declarations such as these would have the compiler believe that these functions do not belong to any class or structure. It would expect to find two sets of definitions each for both `initialize()` and `output()`. The set that belongs to the class would be prefixed by the class name and scope resolution operator, as we have illustrated in previous programs. The set that does not belong to the class would simply be defined as is:

```
   .
   .
void initialize(int i, int j)
{
   .
   .
```

```
}
void output(int k, char l)
{
    .
    .
}
```

6.4 REVIEW

Let's summarize what we have learned in this chapter:

- Classes offer a mechanism for grouping together variables and functions that can be performed on those variables within a single unique type.
- Classes allow quick localization of problems and ease of maintenance of programs.
- The member list within a class comprises variable declarations and, optionally, member functions.
- Public member function calls are prefixed with the class object name.
- Member function definitions are prefixed with the class name and the scope resolution operator.
- Member functions within a class cannot be redeclared outside their classes.

Chapter

7

Scope and Member Access of Classes

7.1 Introduction

Rules specific to classes, class members and member functions will be discussed in this chapter. If you understand the fundamental concepts described in the previous chapter, you should be able to breeze quickly through this one. If you are not comfortable yet, then this chapter should help in achieving that end. Some of the information here may seem redundant, but this will help reinforce the ideas introduced in previous chapters. It is essential that you understand classes completely in order to recognize their full potential and power.

7.2 Class Declarations

Classes are declared as follows:

```
class class_name
   {
   // member list follows
   // member functions are also known as methods
   member_1;
   member_2;
   member_3;
   member_function_1();
   member_function_2();
   };
```

Objects or *instances* of classes are defined as follows:

```
// instance_1 is an instance of class type class_name
class_name instance_1;
```

7.3 Class Name Scope

Class name has to be unique within its scope. You cannot assign the same class name to two different types of classes. Take a look at the following program:

```
//    test7_1.cpp

#include <iostream.h>

class increment
   {
   // public member list follows
   public:
   int i;
   int j;
   int add_one(int i, int j);
   };

class increment      // ERROR! SAME CLASS NAME
   {
   // public member list follows
   public:
   int k;
   int sub_one(int k);
   };

// var1 is an instance of class increment
// var2 is an instance of class increment
increment var1;
increment var2;

main(void)
{
   // x and y are local to main()
   int x, y;

   // initialize class members of object var1
   var1.i = 1;
   var1.j = 2;

   x = var1.add_one(var1.i, var1.j);

   // initialize class members of object var2
   var2.k = 5;

   y = var2.sub_one(var2.k);
   cout << "x is " << x << " \n"
             "y is " << y << " \n";
```

```
}

// add_one is qualified by class name
int increment::add_one(int i, int j)
{
   int l;
   l = i + j;
   return l;
}

// sub_one is qualified by class name
int increment::sub_one(int k)
{
   k -= 1;
   return k;
}
```

Compiling this program results in this error:

```
Error:  Multiple declaration for increment()
```

The problem can be fixed by changing one of the class names, as follows:

```
//    test7_2.cpp

#include <iostream.h>

class increment
   {
   // public member list follows
   public:
   int i;
   int j;
   int add_one(int i, int j);
   };

// ** Notice different class name
class decrement
   {
   // public member list follows
   public:
   int k;
   int sub_one(int k);
   };

increment var1;      // var1 is an instance of class increment
decrement var2;      // var2 is an instance of class decrement

main(void)
{
   // x and y are local to main()
   int x, y;
```

```
   // class members of object var1 are initialized
   var1.i = 1;
   var1.j = 2;

   x = var1.add_one(var1.i, var1.j);

   // class member of var2 are initialized
   var2.k = 5;

   y = var2.sub_one(var2.k);
   cout << "x is " << x << " \n"
         "y is " << y << " \n";
}

// add_one is qualified by class name
int increment::add_one(int i, int j)
{
   int l;
   l = i + j;
   return l;
}

// sub_one is qualified by class name
int decrement::sub_one(int k)
{
   k -= 1;
   return k;
}
```

Compiling and running this program result in the following output:

```
x is 3
y is 4
```

Now take a look at this program, in which two classes are assigned the same name:

```
//   test7_3.cpp

#include <iostream.h>

class increment
     {
    // public member list follows
     public:
     int i;
     int j;
     int add_one(int i, int j);
     };

// var1 is an instance of class increment
increment var1;
```

```
// function prototype follows
int sub_one(int y);

main(void)
{
   // x and y are local to main()
    int x, y;

   // class members of object var1 are initialized
    var1.i = 1;
    var1.j = 2;

    x = var1.add_one(var1.i, var1.j);

    y = sub_one(y);  .

    cout << "x is " << x << " \n"
       << "y is " << y << " \n";
}

// add_one is qualified by class name
int increment::add_one(int i, int j)
{
     int l;
     l = i + j;
     return l;
}

// sub_one is not qualified by class name
int sub_one(int k)
{
// ** Notice same class name
class increment
     {
     public:
     int k;
     };

// var2 is an object of type class increment
increment var2;

// member of class increment is initialized
var2.k = 5;
return var2.k;
}
```

This program produces the following output:

```
x is 3
y is 5
```

This version worked, even though two class names (increment) were assigned the same name. The reason for this is because the second declaration of the class increment() is out of scope of the first declaration. So what is the scope of a class name? It starts at the point of declaration and ends at the end of the enclosing block. Two classes of the same name will be correctly recognized by the compiler, as long as they are not within scope of each other. In the sample program, the second declaration of increment() is within the function sub_one, which is out of scope of the first declaration of increment().

7.4 Class Member Data Types

The class member list can comprise any valid C++ data type. It can contain the usual primary types:

```
class primary
   {
   int a;     // integer
   char b;    // character
   float c;   // float
   double d;  // double
   };

// class_1 is an object of type primary
primary class_1;
```

It can contain structures:

```
class structure_1
   {
   // member list contains structure of type family
   struct family;
   };

// Anderson is object of type structure_1
structure_1 Anderson
```

It can contain pointers to any valid type:

```
class pointer_1
   {
   // ptr is pointer to structure of type family
   struct family;
   struct family *ptr;
   };

// Anderson is an object of type pointer_1
pointer_1 Anderson;
```

It can even contain classes. However, the class inside a class must have been previously declared elsewhere.

Take a look at the following program:

```
//   test7_4.cpp

#include <iostream.h>

class class_2
   {
   public:
   int i;
   };

class class_1
   {
   public:
   int j;

   // variable_2 is a nested class
   class_2 variable_2;
   };

// variable_1 is an object of type class_1
class_1 variable_1;

main(void)
{
   variable_1.variable_2.i = 12;
   cout << "i is " << variable_1.variable_2.i << "\n";
}
```

This program gives the following output:

```
i is 12
```

This program worked because class_2 is defined, and then it is declared as a class member of class_1. Notice the syntax for accessing a member of a nested class:

```
variable_1.variable_2.i
```

The rule is to start with the object name of the outermost class, and then work your way to the class that is being accessed. Now look at what happens if the declaration of class_1 is moved below class_2:

```
//   test7_5.cpp

#include <iostream.h>

class class_1
     {
     public:
     int j;
```

```
     // variable_2 is a nested class
     class_2 variable_2;
     };

// variable_1 is an object of type class_1
class_1 variable_1;

// class_2 is declared after class_1 references it
class class_2
     {
     public:
     int i;
     };

main(void)
{
     variable_1.variable_2.i = 12;
     cout << "i is " << variable_1.variable_2.i << "\n";
}
```

Compiling this version results in the following message:

```
Error:   Type name expected
```

This is because the class class_2 is declared inside class_1, but class_2 has not been defined yet.

7.5 Class Member Storage Specifiers

The class member list declarations can be preceded with any storage class specifier except auto, extern, and register. A class declared this way:

```
class invalid_1
   {
   // invalid storage class specifiers follow:
   auto int a;
   extern char b;
   register int c;
   };

// variable is object of type invalid_1
invalid_1 variable;
```

will cause the compiler to generate the following messages:

```
Error:   Storage class 'auto' not allowed for a field
Error:   Storage class 'extern' not allowed for a field
Error:   Storage class 'register' not allowed for a field
```

7.5.1 Static Class Members

Take a look at this class declaration:

```
class add_1
   {
   int counter;
   int i;
   int add_number(int);
   };
```

The declaration above declares a class called add_1, which contains declarations for two integers and one function. When several variables of that class type are declared, for example,

```
add_1 variable_1, variable_2, variable_3;
```

copies of the data members of add_1 are assigned to each. That is, variable_1, variable_2, and variable_3 will each be a class of type add_1.

Now suppose that the value of counter is the same for all variables. (Perhaps counter counts the number of times a loop is entered). For the duration of the program, three copies of this value will exist, when, in fact, it would be more efficient to have just one. C++ allows us to get around situations such as these by allowing the keyword static to precede the declaration of that specific type.

Static implies that there will be only one copy of the type declared as such, and it will be shared by all data objects or instances of that type. Now look at the following declaration:

```
class add_1
   {
   private:

   // notice keyword static
   static int counter;

   public:
   int i;
   int add_number(int);
   };
```

The keyword static precedes the declaration of counter. Now when objects of this class are declared:

```
add_1 variable_1, variable_2, variable_3;
```

the location in memory for their static member counter will be the same.

This is more efficient, since there is only one copy of the member and its contents will not vary for each instance of that type.

The advantages offered by static members can now be summarized:

- They reduce the need for global variables.
- They make obvious which data can be logically shared within a class.

7.6 Class Member Access Specifiers

You should be able to read through this section rapidly, since it mainly reinforces concepts that you have already read about and seen extensively in previous programs.

Class members can be made public, private, or protected. Within a class declaration, each one of these keywords can be used to precede one or more class member declarations. The class members acquire special characteristics, based on their access specifier.

7.6.1 Public Access

In C++, all members of a structure are public by default. In the declaration below:

```
struct familiy
   {
   char *husband;
   char *wife;
   char *son;
   char *daughter;
   };

// Anderson is structure of type family
family Anderson;
```

the structure members husband, wife, son, and daughter can be accessed from anywhere within the program. Class members, on the other hand, are private by default. Hence, all public members must be specified explicitly.

```
class family
   {
   // public class members follow
   public:
   char *husband;
   char *wife;
   char *son;
```

```
   char *daughter;
   };

// Anderson is class of type family
family Anderson;
```

An access modifier remains effective for all declarations that follow it, until a different access modifier is encountered. The modifier can be reinserted more than once. The following declaration is valid:

```
class family
   {
   // public class members follow
   public:
   char *husband;
   char *wife;

   // private class members follow
   private:
   char *son;
   char *daughter;

   // class members that follow are public again
   public:
   char *neice;
   };
```

Here's a short program that illustrates the use of public class members:

```
//    test7_6.cpp

#include <iostream.h>

void function_1(int i);

class add_numbers
   {
   // public class members follow
   public:
   int i;
   int add_sum(int);
   };

// one is an object of type add_numbers
add_numbers one;

main(void)
{
   one.i = 1;
   function_1(one.i);
}
```

```
void function_1(int i)
{
   i += 5;
   cout << "i is " << i << "\n";
}
```

The output is:

```
i is 6
```

Notice that function_1() is not a member function of the class add_numbers. Yet the compiler allowed it to take i as an argument and change its value. This is because i was declared as public, and therefore there are no access restrictions on it.

7.6.2 Private Access

In C++, all member declarations are private by default. Thus, the following declaration:

```
class family
   {
   char *husband;
   char *wife;
   char *son;
   char *daughter;
   };
```

is equivalent to

```
class family
   {
   private:
   char *husband;
   char *wife;
   char *son;
   char *daughter;
   };
```

Private members can be accessed by their class member functions only (and by *friends* of a class, a topic that we will discuss later on in this chapter). Here's another version of test7_6.cpp, which specifies its class members as private instead of public:

```
//    test7_7.cpp

#include <iostream.h>

void function_1(int i);
```

```
class add_numbers
   {
   // class members are private by default
   int i;
   int add_sum(int);
   };

// one is an object of type add_numbers
add_numbers one;

main(void)
{
   one.i = 1;
   function_1(one.i);
}

void function_1(int i)
{
   i += 5;
   cout << "i is " << i << "\n";
}
```

Compiling this version gives an error:

```
Error:   add_numbers::i is not accessible
```

This error is caused by a call to function_1() inside main(), in which an argument of type integer is being sent. However, the integer that is being sent happens to be a private member of the class add_numbers, and function_1() does not have access privileges to it because it is not a member (or friend) function.

Let's modify test7_7.cpp to see what would happen if some other variable is sent to function_1(). We will send the variable k, which is initialized in main().

```
//    test7_8.cpp

#include <iostream.h>

void function_1(int i);

class add_numbers
   {
   // class members are private by default
   int i;
   int add_num(int);
   };

// one is an object of type add_numbers
add_numbers one;
main(void)
{
```

```
    // k is local to main()
    // k is sent as an argument to function_1()
    int k = 10;
    function_1(k);
}

void function_1(int k)
{
    k += 5;
    cout << "k is " << k << "\n";
}
```

This program compiles correctly, and results in the following output:

```
k is 15
```

The reason for this is simple. The variable k is declared within main(), it is not a class member, and therefore it has no access restrictions. Hence, it can be sent as an argument to function_1(), which is also not a class member.

Now let's try to send the class member i to its class member function add_num():

```
//    test7_9.cpp

#include <iostream.h>

void function_1(int i);

class add_numbers
   {
   // class members are private by default
   int i;
   void add_num(void);
   };

// one is an object of type add_numbers
add_numbers one;

main(void)
{
   // k is local to main()
   // k is sent as argument to function_1()
   int k = 10;
   function_1(k);

   // add_num() is called
   one.add_num();

}
void function_1(int k)
{
```

```
   k += 5;
   cout << "k is " << k << "\n";
}

void add_numbers::add_num(void)
{
   one.i = 5;
   cout << "i is " << one.i << "\n";
}
```

Compiling this program results in the following message:

```
Error:   add_numbers::add_num is not accessible
```

The reason for this message is obvious. `add_num` is a private member of its class, and therefore not accessible from `main()`. So how can `add_num()` be accessed? It is common (and logical) to declare data members of a class as `private` and member functions as `public`. The majority of class declarations in C++ programs are declared in this way. Doing so to `test7_9.cpp` will fix the problem:

```
class add_numbers
   {
   // class members are private by default
   // class method is public
   int i;
   public:
   void add_num(void);
   };
```

The output is as follows:

```
k is 15
i is 5
```

7.6.3 Protected Access

Protected access concerns member access by a derived class. But since derived classes have not been discussed yet, a discussion on this topic will be deferred until then.

7.7 Class Member Functions

All functions that are declared within a class are called *member functions* or *methods*. Member function scope and access rules are the same as regular class members.

7.8 Friend Functions

A class member function name can be prefixed with the keyword *friend*. This is a `friend` function. Take a look at the following declaration of a `friend` function:

```
class family
   {
   // private members follow
   private:
   char *husband;
   char *wife;
   char *son;
   char *daughter;
   family *ptr;

   // public members follow
   public:
   void initialize(void);

   // ** notice friend function
   friend void output(family *ptr);
   };
```

A class of type `family` is declared, with private members `husband`, `wife`, `son`, `daughter`, and `ptr` and public function member `initialize()`. The function `output()` is prefixed with the keyword `friend`, thus, this is a friend function. A friend function is not a member of that class. However, it has full access to the private and protected members of that class.

We now illustrate the use of a friend function inside a program. Take a look at a program that uses this class.

```
//    test7_11.cpp

#include <iostream.h>;

class family
   {
   private:
   char *husband;
   char *wife;
   char *son;
   char *daughter;
   family *ptr;
   public:
   void initialize(void);

   // notice friend function
   friend void output(family *ptr);
   };
```

```
// Anderson is object of type family
family Anderson;

// ** notice function prototype for output()
void output(family *ptr);

main(void)
{
  Anderson.initialize();
}

// notice class name and scope resolution operator
void family::initialize(void)
{
  Anderson.ptr = &Anderson;
  ptr->husband =  "John Anderson";
  ptr->wife    =  "Mary Anderson";
  ptr->son     =  "Joey Anderson";
  ptr->daughter = "Marla Anderson";
  output(ptr);
}

// notice no class name
void output(family *ptr)
{
  cout << "husband is " << ptr->husband  << "\n"
       << "wife is " << ptr->wife  << "\n"
       << "son is " << ptr->son << "\n"
       << "daughter is " << ptr->daughter << "\n";
}
```

In the declaration of the class called `family`, we find that `output()` is declared as a friend function. This means that it is not a member function of the class `family`. However, it can access its private members `husband`, `wife`, `son`, `daughter`, and `ptr` since it is a friend. The output for this program follows:

```
husband is John Anderson
wife is Mary Anderson
son is Joey Anderson
daughter is Marla Anderson
```

Friend functions are not affected by access specifiers. If the declaration of `output()` within class `family` is moved as follows:

```
class family
  {
  // private members follow
  private:
  char *husband[25];
  char *wife[25];
  char *son[25];
  char *daughter[25];
```

```
// friend function inside private list
friend void output(family *ptr);

family *ptr;

// public members follow
public:
void initialize(void);
};
```

it would not mean that the friend function is private. That's the whole point of friend functions. They are *outside* functions that can access private and protected members of the class that they are friends of. Also, their function prototype need not necessarily exist. We included it to illustrate that no error messages would be generated during compilation, as they would have if it were a class member.

All members of one class can become friends of another class via a single statement. Take a look at the following program that illustrates this concept.

```
//    test7_12.cpp

#include <iostream.h>

// ** notice incomplete class declaration
class neighbor;

class family
   {
   // all functions of class neighbor are friends of
   // class family.
   friend neighbor;
   char *husband;
   char *wife;
   family *ptr;

   // public members follow
   public:
   void initialize(void);
   };

// Anderson is object of type family
family Anderson;

class neighbor
   {
   public:
   void output(family *ptr);
   };

// Davis is object of type neighbor
neighbor Davis;
```

```
main (void)
{
   Anderson.initialize();
}

void family::initialize(void)
{
   Anderson.ptr = &Anderson;
   ptr->husband = "John Anderson";
   ptr->wife    = "Mary Anderson";

   // send ptr to freind function output()
   Davis.output(Anderson.ptr);
}

void neighbor::output(family *ptr)
{
   cout << "husband is " << ptr->husband << " \n"
        << "wife is " << ptr->wife    << " \n";
}
```

Compiling and running this program give the desired result:

```
husband is John Anderson
wife is Mary Anderson
```

Notice the incomplete declaration of class neighbor. It was necessary to do so, since reference is made to the class neighbor before it is declared. Remember, also, that objects of type neighbor cannot be declared unless the class declaration for neighbor is complete.

The function output() is declared as a member function of class neighbor. The class neighbor is declared a friend of the class family. Hence, all functions of the class neighbor become friends of the class family, even without this keyword having to prefix their individual declarations. This is why the friend function output() is able to access the private member ptr of family.

7.9 Inline Functions

There is one more subject to be discussed before this chapter is concluded, and that is the *inline* function. Inline functions provide a method for reducing function call overhead.

A member function can be defined within a class declaration, as is illustrated in the following example:

```
//    test7_13.cpp

#include <iostream.h>

class display
   {
   int i;
   public:

   // output() is an inline function
   void output(void)
      { cout << "i is " << i << "\n"; }

   };

// object_1 is an object of type display
display object_1;

main(void)
{
   object_1.output();
}
```

Compiling and executing this program give the following output:

```
i is 0
```

In the class declaration of display, the function output() is defined within the class itself. This is an example of an implicit inline definition.

Inline function declarations, as mentioned in previous chapters, reduce function call overhead. Because the code of an inline function will become a part of each instance of that class, small functions are best suited to be inline within class declarations.

Inline functions can also be declared explicitly. Following is an example of an explicit declaration:

```
//    test7_14.cpp

#include <iostream.h>

class display
   {
   int i;
   public:

   // output() is defined inline elsewhere
   void output(void);
   };

// object_1 is an object of type display
display object_1;
```

```
// display is defined inline explicitly
inline void display::output(void)
{
   cout << "i is " << i << " \n";
}

main(void)
{
   object_1.output();
}
```

Executing this program gives the following output:

```
i is 0
```

The explicit declaration of the inline function `output()` is outside the class declaration, and is preceded by the keyword `inline`. This results in inline expansion of the code for the function `output()` each time this function is called. Remember that inline functions must be defined before they can be referenced. Our program would not have compiled properly if the definition for `output()` existed below `main()`.

7.10 Review

In this chapter features specific to class member declarations and definitions were described.

- Class names must be unique within their scope.
- A class member list can comprise any valid C++ data type.
- Static class members allow multiple objects of a class type to share a location in memory. This reduces the need for global variables.
- Structure members are public by default.
- Class members are private by default.
- Class members can have public, private, and protected access.
- Class member functions follow the same scope and access rules as regular class members.

- Friend functions have access to the private and protected members of a class.

- Inline functions reduce function call overhead. Small functions are best declared inline within a class.

Chapter

8

Fundamental Concepts of Derived Classes

8.1 INTRODUCTION

When a child is born, he or she inherits certain characterisitics from the mother and some from the father. With the passage of time, this child develops traits which uniquely identify him or her. This child is a combination of characteristics inherited from the parents and those derived from the environment in which he or she lives.

As we grow older, our outlook on life changes. Our dreams, goals, and ambitions are derived from what we are taught and what we experience in the circle in which we grow and interact.

And then we pass on what we have learned and achieved to those who are near and dear to us, and give them the oppurtunity to build on what we built ourselves.

If you think of your life in a nutshell, you will realize just how much of it has been derived from what you inherited from your parents, what you learned in school, what you learned from the social structure, and what your own ambition drives you to achieve. If features inherited from your parents could be grouped together as one class, features learned in school as another, and features derived from your social structure as another, then you are analogous to a *derived* class, since you have inherited features from your *base* classes (your parents, education, and social strucuture), and you have added a few unique characteristics of your own (your ambitions, achievements, and more!). Derived classes, as they exist in C++, are analogous to the simple life story presented above. A derived class *inherits* characteristics from one or more base classes. Then, it adds a few unique features of its own. This class can then be used as a base class for some other derived class, and so on.

This is also how a *hierarchy* of classes is created. This is how one object is built from another. This is what makes C++ the powerful language that it is.

8.2 A Simple C Application

We will deviate from the main subject of this chapter for a moment. But we have a good reason for doing so, and this reason will become apparent as you read this section.

A simple C application will be developed that will add, find, modify, and delete records from a file. The code for the individual functions that will perform these tasks is not important. Therefore it will suffice to simply output a statement indicating which function is being executed at the time. We want you to understand how a C program handles a certain situation, and how C++ improves on it. Here's the code.

```
/* test8_1.c */

#include <stdio.h>

/* function prototypes follow */
void add(void);
void find(void);
void modify(void);
void delete(void);

main()
{
   char string[2], option = '\0';

   while (option != 'q')
   {
   printf ("Please enter option: \n");
   printf ("<a>dd, <f>ind, <m>odify, <d>elete or <q>uit:");
   gets(string);
   option = string[0];

   switch(option)
      {        /* start switch */
      case 'a':
         add();
         break;
      case 'f':
         find();
         break;
      case 'm':
         modify();
         break;
      case 'd':
         delete();
```

```
            break;
         case 'q':
            exit();
         default:
            printf ("Invalid input! Please re-enter. \n");
      } /* end switch */

   } /* end while() */

   return (0);
} /* end main() */

void add(void)
{
   printf ("Inside add() \n");
}

void find(void)
{
   printf ("Inside find() \n");
}

void modify(void)
{
   printf ("Inside modify() \n");
}

void delete(void)
{
   printf ("Inside delete() \n");
}
```

Compiling and running this program result in the following message being output on the screen:

```
Please enter option
<a>dd, <f>ind, <m>odify, <d>elete or <q>uit
```

On entry of a valid option, the corresponding function is executed. Otherwise, the message `Invalid option! Please re-enter` is displayed. Now we bring a small company into the picture. This company provides consulting services to its clients. Customer information is stored inside a master file.

Mr. Edward Heath is the owner of this company. He has four employees: Mary, Joseph, Ronald, and Sandra. Mr. Heath is interested in classifying the functions that can be performed by his employees. All of them should have the ability to find records from the master file. Only Mary and Joseph are allowed to add and modify records. Only he is allowed to delete them.

This logic can be incorporated inside the C program by assigning passwords to each employee. Access to various functions is allowed only on entry of a valid password. Mary and Joseph are assigned the passwords 10 and 20. Mr. Heath is assigned the password 99. Now take a look at the modified program.

```
/* test8_2.c */

#include <stdio.h>

/* stdlib.h is required for atoi() */
#include <stdlib.h>

/* function prototypes follow */
void add(void);
void find(void);
void modify(void);
void delete(void);

main()
{
   char string[2], option = '\0';
   int i, *intptr;
   char *password, *charptr;

   printf ("Please enter password: ");

   /* get input from user */
   charptr = gets(password);

   /* convert to integer */
   i = atoi(charptr);

   while (option != 'q')
   {
   printf ("Please enter option: \n");
   printf ("<a>dd, <f>ind, <m>odify, <d>elete or <q>uit:");

   /* get option from user */
   gets(string);
   option = string[0];

   /* switch on option entered */
   switch(option)
      {
      case 'a':
         /* add() can be accessed by select employees */
            if (i == 10 || i == 11 || i == 99)
            add();
         else
            printf ("Permission denied!\n");
         break;

        /* find() is accessible by all */
      case 'f':
         find();
```

```
         break;

        /* modify() is accessible by select employees */
      case 'm':
         if (i == 10  || i == 20 || i == 99)
            modify();
         else
            printf ("Permission denied! \n");
         break;

        /* delete is accessible by 1 person only */
      case 'd':
         if (i == 99)
            delete();
         else
            printf ("Permission denied! \n");
         break;

      case 'q':
         exit();

      default:
         printf ("Invalid input! Please re-enter. \n");

      }  /* end switch */

   }  /* end while() */

   return (0);
}  /* end main() */

void add(void)
{
   printf ("Inside add() \n");
}

void find(void)
{
   printf ("Inside find() \n");
}

void modify(void)
{
   printf ("Inside modify() \n");
}

void delete(void)
{
   printf ("Inside delete() \n");
}
```

Notice that the header file `<stdlib.h>` is included. This header file contains the definition of the function `atoi()`, which simply converts an ASCII string to an integer. In the example, input for the password has to be converted to an integer to perform the correct checking. Based on the password entered, code is added inside the switch-case construct to restrict access to various functions.

Now let's rewrite this program in C++. The functions that can be performed by various employees will be grouped together into classes. The program will be broken up into its logical fragments, and each fragment will be explained before proceeding to the next. First, take a look at the class declarations:

```
// test8_1.cpp
// iostream.h is necessary for I/O
// stdio.h is necessary for getch()
// stdlib.h is necessary for atoi()
#include <iostream.h>
#include <stdio.h>
#include <stdlib.h>

class group_1
     {
     public:
     void find(void);
     };

// everyone is object of type group_1
group_1 everyone;

class group_2
     {
     public:
     void add(void);
     void modify(void);
     };

// select_few is object of type group_2
group_2 select_few;

class group_3
     {
     public:
     void add(void);
     void modify(void);

    // notice function name remove()
    // delete is a reserved word in C++
     void remove(void);
     };

// heath is object of type group_3
group_3 heath;
```

Three classes are declared. These are group_1, group_2, and group_3. Notice that group_2 and group_3 have two sets of functions that are exactly the same in name. These functions are add() and modify(). It is necessary for us to do this since we are interested in grouping together the set of functions that can be performed by one group as a separate entity. C++ allows us to do this through the use of classes. The function called delete() in the C program is called remove() in the C++ program because delete is a reserved word in C++ (it is an operator that will be discussed in later chapters).

Here's the main processing loop:

```
main(void)
{
     char string[2], option = '\0';
     int i, *intptr;
     char *password, *charptr;

     cout << "Please enter password: ";

    // get input from user
    // convert to integer
     charptr = gets(password);
     i = atoi(charptr);

     while (option != 'q')
     {    /* begin while() */

     cout << "Please enter option \n"
          << "<a>dd, <f>ind, <m>odify, <d>elete or <q>uit: ";

     cin  >> option;

     switch(option)
          {    // switch on option entered

          // select employees can access add()
          case 'a':
          if (i == 10 || i == 20)
          {
          select_few.add();
          }
          else if (i == 99)
          {
          heath.add();
          }
          else
          cout << "Permission denied \n";
          break;

      // everyone can access find()
     case 'f':
          everyone.find();
          break;

      // select few can access modify()
```

```
    case 'm':
         if (i == 10 || i == 20)
         {
         select_few.modify();
         }
         else if (i == 99)
         {
         heath.modify();
         }
         else
         cout << "Permission denied!";
         break;

  // only heath can access remove()
    case 'd':
         if (i == 99)
         {
         heath.remove();
         }
         else
         cout << "Permission denied! \n";
         break;

    case 'q':
     break;

    default:
         cout << "Invalid option entered! \n";

    }    /* end switch */

    }    /* end while() */

}   /* end main() */
```

In `main()`, the inherent logic is the same as in `test8_2.c`. However, we invoke member functions of different classes, based on the password entered, instead of the same copy of the appropriate function as we did in the C program. Take a look at the function definitions next:

```
//   function definitions follow

void group_1::find(void)
{
     cout << "Inside group1 find() \n";
}

void group_2::add(void)
{
     cout << "Inside group2 add() \n";
}

void group_2::modify(void)
{
```

```
     cout << "Inside group3 modify() \n";
}

// function definition of add() in group_3 follows
void group_3::add(void)
{
     cout << "Inside group3 add() \n";
}

// function definition of modify() in group_3 follows
void group_3::modify(void)
{
     cout << "Inside group3 modify() \n";
}

void group_3::remove(void)
{
     cout << "Inside group3 remove() \n";
}
```

Notice that there are two versions of add() and modify(), which are member functions of classes group_2 and group_3, respectively. There is only one version of remove(), which is a member function of class group_3. The output statement has been modified, in order to qualify exactly which function is being executed at any time.

Now if you look at the code for each version of these functions, you will realize that it is exactly the same. So how can multiple versions of the same code be eliminated, without the loss of the reasons for having them grouped together in the same class? The answer is through the use of derived classes.

8.3 Derived Classes in C++

C++ allows you to derive a class from one or more base classes. *A derived class inherits all members of its base class.* Access privileges of inherited members can be changed by the derived class through access specifiers that prefix the declaration of the base class. Valid access specifiers are public and private.

Take a look at this fragment of code:

```
class group_1
   {
   public:
   void find(void);
   };

// everyone is an object of type group_1
group_1 everyone;
```

This is a declaration of a base class. There is nothing unusual here. Now let's derive the class group_2 from it:

```
// notice declaration of class group_2
class group_2:public group_1
   {
   // notice missing declaration of find()
   public:
   void add(void);
   void modify(void);
   };

// select_few is an object oftype group_2
group_2 select_few;
```

Now it's time to understand what happened.

The class group_2 is derived from the class group_1 via the statement:

```
class group_2:public group_1
```

The name of the first class in the list is that of the derived class. The name of the class following the colon (:) is that of the base class. The class group_2 inherits all members of its base class group_1. These members now belong to the member list of the class group_2. However, only the public and protected members of the base class can be used. (Protected members will be discussed in detail in the next chapter). The private members of the base class are not accessible to the derived class.

The access specifier public, which precedes the name of the base class, is used to specify access privileges of the inherited member list as they relate to the derived class:

```
class group_2:public group_1
```

This keyword indicates that the public members of the base class will also be public members inside the derived class. Along the same lines, protected members of the base class will be protected members inside the derived class. In other words, *the keyword public indicates that the access privileges of the inherited members in the derived class will be the same as they exist in the base class.*

Remember, however, that *the private members of the base class continue to remain private because they cannot be accessed by the derived class.* This makes sense. The very idea behind private members of a class is to limit their access privileges. The whole point would be lost if derived classes were to inherit access to these members. A derived class is often used as a building block for some other object. If a hierarchy of 10 derived classes were created and the private members of each class accessible to the next, then the advantages derived from the restriction of class members would be lost completely.

The following declaration of the derived class:

```
// ** notice keyword private
class group_2:private group_1
   {
   // notice missing declaration of find()
   public:
   void add(void);
   void modify(void);
   };

// select_few is an object of type group_2
group_2 select_few;
```

is synonymous to the following:

```
class group_2:group_1
   {
   public:
   void add(void);
   void modify(void);
   };
group_2 select_few;
```

This is because the default is `private` for a derived class. If this keyword prefixes the name of the base class, then both the public and protected members of the base class become private members of the derived class.

Now `test8_1.cpp` will be modified to use derived classes. The code will once again be presented in fragments, and each will be explained before proceeding to the next. First, the class declarations:

```
// test8_2.cpp

// iostream.h is necessary for I/O
// stdio.h is necessary for getch()
// stdlib.h is necessary for atoi()
#include <iostream.h>
#include <stdio.h>
#include <stdlib.h>

class group_1
     {
     public:
     void find(void);
     };

// everyone is an object of type group_1
group_1 everyone;
```

```
class group_2
     {
     public:
     void add(void);
     void modify(void);
     };

// select_few is an object of type group_2
group_2 select_few;

class group_3:public group_2
     {
     public:
     void remove(void);
     };

// heath is an object of type group_3
group_3 heath;
```

The class group_3 is derived from the class group_2. The base class group_2 is specified as public. This results in the functions add() and modify() also being public members for the class group_3. Now look at the code for main().

```
main(void)
{
     char string[2], option = '\0';
     int i, *intptr;
     char *password, *charptr;

     cout << "Please enter password: ";

     charptr = gets(password);
     i = atoi(charptr);

     while (option != 'q')
     {    /* begin while() */

     cout << "Please enter option \n"
          << "<a>dd, <f>ind, <m>odify, <d>elete or <q>uit: ";

     cin  >> option;

     switch(option)
          {    // start switch

          // select employees can access add()
          case 'a':
          if (i == 10 || i == 20)
          {
          select_few.add();
          }
          else if (i == 99)
```

```
        {
        heath.add();
        }
        else
        cout << "Permission denied \n";
        break;

    case 'f':
        everyone.find();
        break;

    // select few can access modify()
    case 'm':
        if (i == 10 || i == 20)
        {
        select_few.modify();
        }
        else if (i == 99)
        {
        heath.modify();
        }
        else
        cout << "Permission denied!";
        break;

    case 'd':
        if (i == 99)
        {
        heath.remove();
        }
        else
        cout << "Permission denied! \n";
        break;

    case 'q':
     break;

    default:
        cout << "Invalid option entered! \n";

    }    /* end switch */

    }    /* end while() */

}    /* end main() */
```

The code is the same as test8_1.cpp. Now look at the function definitions:

```
//   function definitions follow
void group_1::find(void)
{
    cout << "Inside group1 find() \n";
}
```

```
void group_2::add(void)
{
     cout << "Inside group2 add() \n";
}

void group_2::modify(void)
{
     cout << "Inside group3 modify() \n";
}

void group_3::remove(void)
{
     cout << "Inside group3 remove() \n";
}
```

Notice that only one version of each function is defined. Compiling and running this program result in the following message being displayed on the screen:

```
Please enter password
```

Let's pretend that we are the designated empolyee of the month who has the privilege of deleting records from the master file (and the burden of living with the knowledge that a valid record might have been deleted!).

We enter the password 99. Let's enter option `f` to find a record. The following message is displayed on the screen:

```
Inside group1 find()
Please enter option
<a>dd  <f>ind  <m>odify  <d>elete, or <q>uit
```

Entering option `a` results in the following message being displayed:

```
Inside group2 add
Please enter option
<a>dd  <f>ind  <m>odify  <d>elete, or <q>uit
```

Entering `d` results in this message:

```
Inside group3 remove()
Please enter option
<a>dd  <f>ind  <m>odify  <d>elete, or <q>uit
```

and entering `q` allows exit from the program.

Now look at this fragment of code again:

```
          case 'a':
               // select employees can access add()
          if (i == 10 || i == 20)
```

```
{
select_few.add();
}
else if (i == 99)
{
heath.add();
}
```

As you can see, heath.add() is supposed to execute if the password is 99. However, there is no definition for heath.add()! The compiler accepted this because heath is an instance of the class group_3, and group_3 is derived from the class group_2. Hence, it inherits all public members of its base class. If functions are inherited by one class, then there is no need to redefine them.

Refer to Figure 8.1 for a diagram of the logic implemented by the code.

Figure 8.1 Creation of Objects

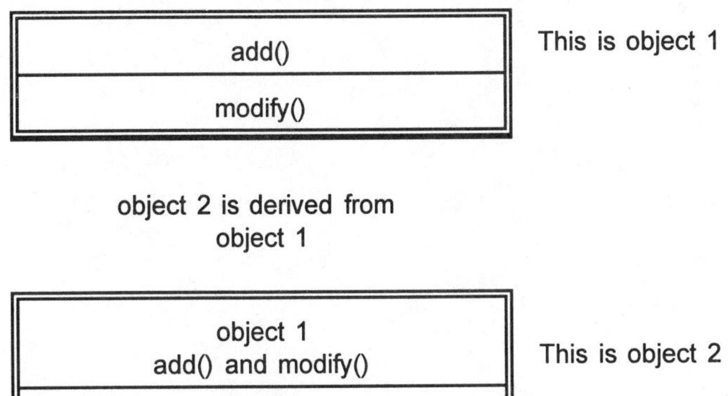

If the class group_2 can be considered an object, then the class group_3 contains that object, plus a unique function that differentiates it from group_2. group_3 cannot be group_3 without group_2. Thus, one object is used as a building block for another. The concept of derived classes should be clear to you now.

8.4 Review

In this chapter we learned the reasons for deriving a class from a base class, and how to do so. You should already understand the reason for using a class instead of a structure. Derived classes offer the advantages of classes in general, in addition to the ability to build a hierarchical structure of objects. The object at the top of the hierarchy is the most generalized object of the set. Each object derived from it contains features of the object from which it is derived, along with a few characteristics that make it unique.

You should now be thinking in terms of building objects, instead of writing procedural loops, as you were used to doing when you wrote code in C. The possiblities that can be gained from derived classes should now be emerging.

Chapter

9

Access Privileges of Members of Derived Classes

9.1 INTRODUCTION

In this chapter, access privileges of inherited members of classes derived from public and private base classes will be explained. But first, here's a discussion on protected members.

9.2 PROTECTED MEMBERS IN A CLASS

Consider the following class declaration:

```
class group_1
   {
   int a;  // a is private by default;
   protected:
   int b;  // b is protected
   public:
   void output1(void);
   }
group_1 everyone;
```

group_1 is a class in which a is a private member, b is a protected member, and the function output1() is public. Now look at the complete program.

```
//   test9_1.cpp

#include <iostream.h>

class group_1
     {
     // a is private by default
     int a;

     // b is protected
     protected:
     int b;

     // output() is public
     public:
     void output1(void);
     };
group_1 everyone;

// group_2 is derived from group_1
class group_2:public group_1
     {
     // c is private by default
     int c;

     public:
     void output2(void);
     };
group_2 a_few;

void main(void)
{
     everyone.output1();
}

void group_1::output1(void)
{
     a = 5;
     b = 10;
     cout << "a is " << a << " b is " << b << "\n";
     a_few.output2();
}
void group_2::output2(void)
{
     c = 15;
     b += 10;
     cout << "c is " << c << " b is " << b << "\n";
}
```

Compiling and running this program yield the following output:

```
a is 5 b is 10
c is 15 b is 20
```

Class members a and b are private and public members, respectively, of the class group_1. Hence, there are no suprises when the compiler allows access to these members from the function output1(), which is also a member function of that group. The protected member b is also accessed from this function and output2. output2 is a public member of the class group_2. This program illustrates that protected members of a base class are also accessible by members of the derived class.

Note here that group_2 is derived from group_1; that is, it inherits all members of group_1. Hence, the compiler does not issue any error messages when a class member of group_1 is accessed by a class member function of group_2 (if the class members of group_1 are either public or protected).

Let's modify the program and try to access the private member a from output2().

```
//   test9_2.cpp

#include <iostream.h>

class group_1
      {
      int a;
      protected:
      int b;
      public:
      void output1(void);
      };
group_1 everyone;

// group_2 is derived from group_1
class group_2:public group_1
      {
      int c;
      public:
      void output2(void);
      };
group_2 a_few;

void main(void)
{
      everyone.output1();
}

void group_1::output1(void)
{
      a = 5;
      b = 10;
      cout << "a is " << a << " b is " << b << "\n";
      a_few.output2();
}
```

```
void group_2::output2(void)
{
     c = 15;
     b += 10;

    // private member is accessed
     cout << "a is " << a << "\n";
     cout << "c is " << c << " b is " << b << "\n";
}
```

Compiling and running this program result in the following error message:

```
Error:   'group_1::a' is not accessible
```

This program illustrates that private members of a base class are not accessible to members of the derived class. (Recall that we stated that in the previous chapter.) Note that no error message is generated when a is accessed inside group_1::output1().

Now let's modify this program one more time and see if private and protected members of a base class are accessible to the public at large. You should already know the answer to this one, but we will present the code to reinforce what you may already know.

```
//   test9_3.cpp

#include <iostream.h>

class group_1
     {
     int a;
     protected:
     int b;
     public:
     void output1(void);
     };
group_1 everyone;

// group_2 is derived from group_1
class group_2:public group_1
     {
     int c;
     public:
     void output2(void);
     };
group_2 a_few;

void main(void)
{
     cout << "a is " << a " b is " << b << "\n";
     everyone.output1();
}
```

```
void group_1::output1(void)
{
      a = 5;
      b = 10;
      cout << "a is " << a << " b is " << b << "\n";
      a_few.output2();
}

void group_2::output2(void)
{
      c = 15;
      b += 10;
      cout << "c is " << c << " b is " << b << "\n";
}
```

Compiling this program results in the following error messages:

```
Error: Undefined symbol 'a'
       Undefined symbol 'b'
```

It would be safe to conclude that private and protected members of a base class can be accessed only by members of that class, and protected members of a base class can be accessed by members of classes derived from the same base class.

9.3 Access Privileges of Publicly Derived Classes

The following short program illustrates the access rules of members of base classes in derived classes.

```
//   test9_4.cpp

#include <iostream.h>

class group_1
      {
      int a;
      protected:
      int b;
      public:
      void output1(void);
      };
group_1 class1;

// group_2 is derived from group_1
class group_2:public group_1
      {
      public:
      void output2(void);
      };
group_2 class2;
```

```
// group_3 is derived from group_2
class group_3:public group_2
      {
      public:
      void output3(void);
      };
group_3 class3;

void main(void)
{
      class1.output1();
      class2.output2();
      class3.output3();
}

void group_1::output1(void)
{
      a = 5;
      b = 10;
      cout << "a is " << a << " b is " << b << "\n";
}

void group_2::output2(void)
{
      cout << "a is " << a << " b is " << b << "\n";
}

void group_3::output3(void)
{
      cout << "a is " << a << " b is " << b << "\n";
}
```

Compiling this program results in the following error messages:

```
Error: group_1::a is not accessible
       group_1::a is not accessible
```

Notice that no error messages were issued for accessing b, a protected member, from either one of the member functions of the derived classes group_2 or group_3. In conclusion, we can say that:

- Public members of a base class continue to remain public for the derived class, and therefore, accessible to the public at large. The functions output2() and output3() were declared as public members of the derived classes group_2 and group_3. Hence, they could be called from main().

- Protected members of a base class continue to remain protected for the derived classes. b is a protected member inside the base class group_1. Yet the compiler does not issue any error messages for this variable when it is accessed from member functions of the derived classes. The compiler would issue an error message if an attempt was made to access this variable from a nonmember function.

- Private members of a base class continue to remain private to the base class. They cannot be accessed by member functions of derived classes.

9.4 Access Privileges of Privately Derived Classes

`Test9_4.cpp` will now be modified to prefix the base class with the keyword `private` instead of `public`. Here's the code.

```
//   test9_5.cpp

#include <iostream.h>

class group_1
     {
     int a;
     protected:
     int b;
     public:
     void output1(void);
     };
group_1 class1;

// ** notice private declaration
class group_2:private group_1
     {
     public:
     void output2(void);
     };
group_2 class2;

// ** notice private declaration
class group_3:private group_2
      {
      public:
      void output3(void);
      };
group_3 class3;

void main(void)
{
      class1.output1();
      class2.output2();
      class3.output3();
}
```

```
void group_1::output1(void)
{
     a = 5;
     b = 10;
     cout << "a is " << a << " b is " << b << "\n";
}

void group_2::output2(void)
{
     cout << "a is " << a << " b is " << b << "\n";
}
void group_3::output3(void)
{
     cout << " b is " << b << "\n";
}
```

Compiling this program results in the following set of rather interesting error messages:

```
Error:   group_1::a is not accessible
         group_1::a is not accessible
         group_1::b is not accessible
         group_1::b is not accessible
```

Take a moment to analyze these error messages.

The first one states that group_1::a is not accessible in function group_2::output2(). This is understandable. a is a private member of the class group_1, and continues to remain private to its class. It cannot be accessed by members of derived classes.

The second message states that group_1::a is not accessible in the function group_3::output3(). This makes sense for the same reason as the first error message.

The third message states that group_1::b is not accessible in function group_3::output3(). This one should have gotten you thinking a bit. The reason this message was generated is because b is a protected member inside its base class. group_2 is privately derived from group_1. This private derivation results in protected members of the base class becoming private members inside the derived class. Hence, b is now a private member for the derived class group_2. Therefore, b is inaccessible from a member function of group_3, since it is private for its base class, which is group_2. So why didn't we get this message when b was accessed from group_2::output2()? The reason is because b is a protected member inside group_1, and therefore accessible by members of the derived class group_2. However, since group_2 is privately derived, b becomes a private member for group_2, and therefore inaccessible to any subsequent derived classes.

Now that you understand the rules for access of private base members inside privately derived classes, let's modify test9_5.cpp and see how access privileges of public base members are affected by private derivation.

```
//   test9_6.cpp
#include <iostream.h>

class group_1
     {
     int a;
     protected:
     int b;
     public:
     void output1(void);
     };
group_1 class1;

// group_2 is privately derived
class group_2:private group_1
     {
     public:
     void output2(void);
     };
group_2 class2;

// group_3 is privately derived
class group_3:private group_2
      {
      public:
      void output3(void);
      };
group_3 class3;

void main(void)
{
     class1.output1();
     class2.output2();
     class3.output3();

     // public member output1() is accessed
     class2.output1();
     class3.output1();
}

void group_1::output1(void)
{
     a = 5;
     b = 10;
     cout << "a is " << a << " b is " << b << "\n";
}
void group_2::output2(void)
{
     cout << "a is " << a << " b is " << b << "\n";
}
```

```
void group_3::output3(void)
{
     cout << "a is " << a << " b is " << b << "\n";
}
```

Compiling this program results in the set of three error messages that the compiler issued in the previous program, in addition to these two:

```
Error: group_1::output1() is not accessible
       group_1::output1() is not accessible
```

These messages are generated for the following statements:

```
     class2.output1();
     class3.output1();
```

The reason for these messages is that public members of privately derived classes become private for the derived class. output1() is a public member of the class group_1. group_2 is privately derived from group_1. Hence, output1() becomes a private member of group_2.

class2 is an instance of the class group_2. The statement class2.output1() is invoked from main(). But since output1() is now a private member of group_2, it can be accessed only by its class member list, and main() does not fall inside that category. This problem could be fixed by invoking class2.output1() inside the function group_2::output2() instead of main(), for example:

```
void group_2::output2(void)
{
   class2.output1();
   cout << "a is " << a << " b is " << b << "\n";
}
```

However, the following code would still present a problem:

```
void group_3::output3(void)
{
   class3.output1();
   cout << "a is " << a << " b is " << b << "\n";
}
```

The first invocation would be acceptable, since output1() is being accessed from output2(), which is a member function of the class group_2, and group_2 is derived from group_1. The second invocation would be unacceptable, since group_2 is privately derived from group_1; hence the public member output1() becomes private to group_1, and therefore inaccessible to group_3. Following is a complete program that would work. Code for the output of the variables a and b inside output2() and output3() have been taken out, as they are not applicable to what is being currently explained.

```
// test9_7.cpp

#include <iostream.h>

class group_1
     {
     int a;
     protected:
     int b;
     public:
     void output1(void);
     };
group_1 class1;

//* notice private specifier for group_1 and group_2
class group_2:private group_1
     {
     public:
     void output2(void);
     };
group_2 class2;

class group_3:private group_2
      {
      public:
      void output3(void);
      };
group_3 class3;

void main(void)
{
     class1.output1();
     class2.output2();
     class3.output3();
}

void group_1::output1(void)
{
     a = 5;
     b = 10;
     cout << "a is " << a << " b is " << b << "\n";
}

void group_2::output2(void)
{
     // * output1 is accessed from output2()
     cout << "Inside output2() \n";
     class2.output1();
}

void group_3::output3(void)
{
      cout << "Inside output3() \n";
}
```

Another solution would have been simply to derive group_2 and group_3 publicly instead of privately. Which alternative you choose depends on how you want the visibility of these variables and functions to be affected.

The important point to note here is that *data hiding*, such as can be achieved via access specifiers for class member lists and base classes, is the key to designing *modular* programs. Your program should be composed of stand-alone sections that are easily identifiable, and therefore that much more flexible and modifiable. You can achieve this if you understand the scope of each variable, based upon the use of access specifiers. What is required is that you take the time to plan a hierachy of classes, determine access privileges for members of base classes inside derived classes, and understand exactly why you did what you did!

9.5 Review

In this chapter, we described access privileges of base class members inside derived classes. Table 9.1 summarizes the major concepts with regard to access privileges.

Table 9.1 Access Privileges of Base and Derived Classes

Base class specifier	Access inside base class	Access inside derived class
public	Public Private Protected	Public Nonaccessible Protected
private	Public Private Protected	Private Nonaccessible Private

Chapter

10

Constructors and Destructors

10.1 INTRODUCTION

In this chapter, we will discuss how C++ offers a mechanism for initializing classes when they are created and a corresponding mechanism for destroying them when they are no longer in scope, that is, no longer needed. C++ allows automatic initialization of objects when they are created through *constructors*. *Destructors* are the opposite of constructors. They provide a way to deallocate memory that may have been allocated to objects through constructors.

Before we begin our discussion on constructors and destructors, we want you to understand that the functionality that is available for constructors and destructors is called automatically if it is not invoked explicitly. The reason for explicitly calling constructors or destructors is to allocate or deallocate memory in those instances when the compiler does not operate as expected. For example, if a class object is not created properly, it may be necessary to deallocate memory originally allocated to it, and then to recreate it in a different location in memory. The reasons should become clearer to you as you read the remainder of this chapter.

The discussion will begin with constructors.

10.2 AN INTRODUCTION TO CONSTRUCTORS

Consider the following sample program:

```
// test10_1.cpp

#include <iostream.h>

class sum
   {
   public:
   int sum_1;
   int sum_2;
   };
sum object_1, object_2;

void main(void)
{
   cout << "Inside main() \n";
   cout << "object_1.sum_1 is "<< object_1.sum_1 << "\n";
   cout << "object_1.sum_2 is "<< object_1.sum_2 << "\n";
   cout << "object_2.sum_1 is "<< object_2.sum_1 << "\n";
   cout << "object_2.sum_2 is "<< object_2.sum_2 << "\n";
}
```

Compiling and executing this simple program result in the following output:

```
Inside main()
object_1.sum_1 is 0
object_1.sum_2 is 0
object_2.sum_1 is 0
object_2.sum_2 is 0
```

sum_1 and sum_2 are automatically initialized to zeros, since they are declared outside of main(), and never set to any other value. But suppose these class members were to contain some other values. Let's try to initialize these members inside the class declaration:

```
// test10_2.cpp

#include <iostream.h>

class sum
   {
   // ** We try to initialize class members
   public:
   int sum_1 = 1;
   int sum_2 = 2;
   };
sum object_1, object_2;

void main(void)
{
   cout << "Inside main() \n";
   cout << "object_1.sum_1 is "<< object_1.sum_1 << "\n";
```

```
    cout << "object_1.sum_2 is "<< object_1.sum_2 << "\n";
    cout << "object_2.sum_1 is "<< object_2.sum_1 << "\n";
    cout << "object_2.sum_2 is "<< object_2.sum_2 << "\n";
}
```

Compiling this program results in the following error message:

```
Error:  Cannot initialize a class member here
```

Obviously, class members cannot be initialized at the time that they are declared. Instead, C++ allows objects to be initialized at the time that they are created through constructors.

10.3 DEFAULT CONSTRUCTORS

A constructor is a function that has the same name as the class that it initializes. It can be defined inline, or outside the class declaration. However, like ordinary function prototypes and definitions, it has no return value, and it is called automatically by the compiler if you fail to call it explicitly! Take a look at test10_3.cpp.

```
// test10_3.cpp

 #include <iostream.h>

// function sum() has same name as class sum()
class sum
   {
   public:
   int sum_1;
   int sum_2;
   sum();
   };
sum object_1, object_2;

void main(void)
{
   cout << "Inside main() \n";
   cout << "object_1.sum_1 is "<< object_1.sum_1 << "\n";
   cout << "object_1.sum_2 is "<< object_1.sum_2 << "\n";
   cout << "object_2.sum_1 is "<< object_2.sum_1 << "\n";
   cout << "object_2.sum_2 is "<< object_2.sum_2 << "\n";
}

// sum::sum() is the constructor function
sum::sum()
{
   cout << "Inside sum() \n";
}
```

Compiling and executing this program result in the following output:

```
Inside sum()
Inside sum()
Inside main()
object_1.sum_1 is 0
object_1.sum_2 is 0
object_2.sum_1 is 0
object_2.sum_2 is 0
```

As you look at the declaration of the class sum, you see that it has a class member also called sum(). This is a default constructor, and it is called as such because it has no arguments. (Constructors with arguments will be discussed later on in the chapter.) It is important to note that it has the same name as the class for which it is a member and it has no return type.

The output of this program demonstrates an interesting feature about constructors. You were perhaps suprised to see that the print statement Inside sum() output before Inside main(). The reason for this is that the sum() constructor is called at the time that objects of type sum are created. Saying it a little bit differently, constructors for objects are called at the time that objects of that type are declared. If you take a look at the test10_3.cpp, you will see that object_1 and object_2 are created outside of main(). Hence Inside sum() is output before Inside main(). Also, Inside sum() outputs twice, since two objects of type sum are created. sum() would have been called three times if three objects of that type had been created, and so on.

Another interesting feature is that a default constructor is called implicitly by the compiler each time an object is declared, if one is not specified inside the class declaration. Just think back to all the programs in the previous chapters. Default constructors were being generated each time an object was declared, and you never even knew it!

The value of sum_1 and sum_2 continues to be zero, because these class objects are declared outside main() and they are not set to anything else. Let's see what happens if object_1 and object_2 are declared inside main().

```
// test10_4.cpp

#include <iostream.h>

// function sum() has same name as class sum
class sum
   {
   public:
   int sum_1;
   int sum_2;
   sum();
```

```
   };

void main(void)
{
   // object_1 and object_2 are declared inside main()

   cout << "Inside main() \n";

   sum object_1, object_2;

   cout << "object_1.sum_1 is "<< object_1.sum_1 << "\n";
   cout << "object_1.sum_2 is "<< object_1.sum_2 << "\n";
   cout << "object_2.sum_1 is "<< object_2.sum_1 << "\n";
   cout << "object_2.sum_2 is "<< object_2.sum_2 << "\n";
}

// sum::sum() is the constructor function
sum::sum()
{
   cout << "Inside sum() \n";
}
```

Compiling and executing this program give us the following results:

```
Inside main()
Inside sum()
Inside sum()
object_1.sum_1 is 0
object_1.sum_2 is 8815
object_1.sum_1 is 1
object_1.sum_2 is 0
```

This time the class members display garbage values. This is because objects of type `sum` are being created inside `main()`, so they are not global in scope, and hence not initialized to zero. So how can class members be initialized to specific values? The answer is through the use of parameters, or default arguments. Parameters will be discussed next.

10.4 Constructors with Parameters

Take a look at `test10_5.cpp`:

```
// test10_5.cpp

#include <iostream.h>

class sum
   {
    // sum_1 and sum_2 are now private
   int sum_1;
   int sum_2;
```

```
   public:

    // sum() has no return type & arguments
   sum(int i, int j);
   };

void main(void)
{
   // ** object_1 & object_2 are created with parameters
   sum object_1(10,20), object_2(20,30);

   cout << "Inside main() \n";
}

sum::sum(int i, int j)
{
   // ** notice initialization to parameters
   sum_1 = i;
   sum_2 = j;

   cout << "sum_1 is " << sum_1 <<
      " sum_2 is " << sum_2 << "\n";
}
```

sum_1 and sum_2 are declared as private, since we are interested in utilizing the data hiding features that are offered by C++. Next, the constructor sum() is declared with arguments:

```
   sum(int i, int j);
```

Inside main(), object_1 and object_2 are declared with values substitued for the arguments:

```
   sum object_1(10,20), object_2(20,30)
```

Inside sum(), the two private class members sum_1 and sum_2 are initialized to the corresponding arguments i and j:

```
   sum_1 = i;
   sum_2 = j;
```

Compiling and executing this program give the following output:

```
sum_1 is 10 sum_2 is 20
sum_1 is 20 sum_2 is 30
Inside main()
```

A couple of warnings are also issued in this (and subsequent programs, stating that object_1 and object_2 are never used inside main(). But these warnings will be overlooked, since these programs are meant to demonstrate specific features that relate to constructors, and the code does just that.

Notice that the class members of each object are initialized in the same order in which they are declared. Class members sum_1 and sum_2 of object_1 are created first, then initialized to 10 and 20, respectively. Next, class members sum_1 and sum_2 of object_2 are created, then initialized to 20 and 30, respectively.

10.5 CONSTRUCTORS WITH DEFAULT ARGUMENTS

Class members can be initialized in a variety of ways. Default arguments can be specified in the constructor declaration. Class members will be initialized to these default values, if no others are specified, as is demonstrated by the following program:

```
// test10_6.cpp

#include <iostream.h>

class sum
   {
   // ** notice sum_1 and sum_2 are now private
   int sum_1;
   int  sum_2;

   public:
   // ** notice default arguments
   sum(int i, int j = 5);
   };

// ** object_1 is created with only 1 argument
sum object_1(10), object_2(20,30);

void main(void)
{
   cout << "Inside main() \n";
}
sum::sum(int i, int j)
{
   sum_1 = i;
   sum_2 = j;
   cout << "sum_1 is " << sum_1 <<
       " sum_2 is " << sum_2 << "\n";
}
```

The output for this program is as follows:

```
sum_1 is 10 sum_2 is 5
sum_1 is 20 sum_2 is 30
Inside main()
```

The declaration of the constructor sum is:

```
sum(int i, int j = 5);
```

The second parameter is initialized to a default value. Now notice the way object_1 and object_2 are created:

```
sum object_1(10), object_2(20,30);
```

Class member sum_1 for object_1 is initialized to 10 and sum_2 defaults to 5. The values for class members sum_1 and sum_2 for object_2 are self-explanatory.

10.6 Overloading Constructors

Constructors can be overloaded, that is, a constructor can have the same name, but different data types for arguments. The correct constructor will be invoked by the compiler, based on the data type of its argument. Take a look at test10_7.cpp:

```
// test10_7.cpp

#include <iostream.h>

class sum
   {
   int sum_1;
   double sum_2;
   public:

   // notice function name is overloaded
   sum(int i);
   sum(double k);
   };

void main(void)
{
   // ** sum(int) is called
   // ** sum(double) is called
   sum object_1(10);
   sum object_2(10.5);

   cout << "Inside main() \n";
}

sum::sum(int i)
{
   sum_1 = i;
   cout << "Inside sum(int) \n";
}
```

```
sum::sum(double k)
{
   sum_2 = k;
   cout << "Inside sum(double) \n";
}
```

Compiling and executing this program produce the following output:

```
Inside sum(int)
Inside sum(double)
Inside main()
```

When object_1 is declared, the constructor sum(int) is invoked, since the parameter 10 is of type int. When object_2 is declared, the constructor sum(double) is invoked.

10.7 ORDER OF CALLING CONSTRUCTORS

The following program demonstrates the order in which constructors are called when dealing with base and derived classes:

```
// test10_8.cpp

#include <iostream.h>

class one
   {
   public:
   one();
   };

// ** two is derived from one
class two : public one
   {
   int b;
   public:
   two(int j);
   };

main(void)
{
   one object_1();
   two object_2(20);
   cout << "Inside main() \n";
}

one::one()
{
   cout << "Inside one \n";
}
```

```
two::two(int j)
{
   b = j;
   cout << "Inside two  b is " << b << "\n";
}
```

The class two is derived from one. Inside main, an object of type one is declared and then an object of type two. The constructor one is a default constructor, since it takes no arguments. The constructor two is passed an argument. Compiling and executing this program result in the following output:

```
Inside one
Inside two  b is 20
Inside main()
```

The order in which the constructors are called is self-explanatory. But what would happen if an object of the type of the derived class only is created, and an object for the base class is not? Take a look at test10_9.cpp:

```
// test10_9.cpp

#include <iostream.h>

class one
   {
   public:
   one();
   };

// two is derived from one
class two : public one
   {
   int b;
   public:
   two(int j);
   };

main(void)
{
   // ** We do not create object of type base class first
   two object_2(20);
   cout << "Inside main() \n";
}

one::one()
{
   cout << "Inside one \n";
}
```

```
two::two(int j)
{
   b = j;
   cout << "Inside two  b is " << b << "\n";
}
```

Compiling and executing this program produce the following output:

```
Inside one
Inside two  b is 20
Inside main()
```

As you can see, the base class constructor is still called. This is necessary (and makes sense). Since two is derived from one, one must be constructed first. (How can you derive something from an object that does not exist? The base object must be created first.) The base class constructor is constructed first and then the derived class constructor.

Now take a look at the following program, which illustrates the order of calling constructors from multiple base classes.

```
// test10_10.cpp

#include <iostream.h>

class one
   {
   public:
   one();
   };

class three
   {
   public:
   three();
   };

// ** notice multiple base classes
class two : public one, public three
   {
   int b;
   public:
   two(int j);
   };

main(void)
{
   two object_2(20);
   cout << "Inside main() \n";
}

one::one()
{
```

```
   cout << "Inside one \n";
}

two::two(int j)
{
   b = j;
   cout << "Inside two  b is " << b << "\n";
}

three::three()
{
   cout << "Inside three \n";
}
```

Compiling and executing this program produce the following output:

```
Inside one
Inside three
Inside two  b is 20
Inside main()
```

As you can see, the base class constructors are called in the same order in which they are declared:

```
class two : public one, public three
```

10.8 Base Class Constructors with Parameters

So far, so good. But what happens if you wish to create an object of a derived class whose base class requires parameters? Look at the following code, and you will understand what we mean:

```
// test10_11.cpp

#include <iostream.h>

class one
   {
   int a;
   public:
   one(int i);
   };

// ** two is derived from one
class two : public one
   {
   int b;
   public:
   two(int j);
   };
```

```
main(void)
{
   two object_2(20);
   cout << "Inside main() \n";
}

one::one(int i)
{
   a = i;
   cout << "Inside one a is " << a << "\n";
}

two::two(int j) : one(j)
{
   b = j;
   cout << "Inside two  b is " << b << "\n";
}
```

As you can see, the constructor for the base class one requires a parameter:

```
   one(int i);
```

The object two is derived from one:

```
class two : public one
```

and an object of type two is created with the required parameter:

```
   two object_2(20);
```

Then, there is an interesting definition for the constructor for the derived class:

```
two::two(int j) : one(j)
{  .
   .
}
```

This is one of the ways in which parameters can be sent to the base class. The definition of the constructor of the derived class follows the usual syntax. However, it is appended with a colon (indicating derivation), the name of the base class, and the parameter list.

Compiling and executing this program result in the following output:

```
Inside one a is 20
Inside two  b is 20
Inside main()
```

The order of calling the constructors (base class, then derived class) remains the same.

Parameters can be passed to base classes in a variety of other ways as well. You can place a constant in the parameter list, as follows:

```
// test10_12.cpp

#include <iostream.h>

class one
   {
   int a;
   public:
   one(int i);
   };

// ** two is derived from one
class two : public one
   {
   int b;
   public:
   two(int j);
   };

main(void)
{
   two object_2(20);
   cout << "Inside main() \n";
}

one::one(int i)
{
   a = i;
   cout << "Inside one a is " << a << "\n";
}
// ** notice constant argument for one()
two::two(int j) : one(10)
{
   b = j;
   cout << "Inside two  b is " << b << "\n";
}
```

As you can see in the definition of the constructor for `two`:

```
two::two(int j) : one(10)
```

a constant is being sent as a parameter to `one`. Compiling and executing this program result in the following output:

```
Inside one a is 10
Inside two b is 20
Inside main()
```

The output should be self-explanatory.

Global parameters can also be passed to the base class constructor, as is illustrated by test10_13.cpp:

```
// test10_13.cpp
#include <iostream.h>

class one
   {
   int a;
   public:
   one(int i);
   };

class two : public one
   {
   int b;
   public:
   two(int j);
   };

// ** notice external variable declaration
int k;

main(void)
{
   // ** external variable is initialized
   k = 5;

   two object_2(20);
   cout << "Inside main() \n";
}

one::one(int i)
{
   a = i;
   cout << "Inside one a is " << a << "\n";
}

two::two(int j) : one(k)
{
   b = j;
   cout << "Inside two  b is " << b << "\n";
}
```

k is declared as a global variable, outside of main(), and initialized inside main() to 5. Then, it is passed as a parameter to the base class constructor:

```
two::two(int j) : one(k)
```

Compiling and executing this program result in the following output:

```
Inside one a is 5
Inside two b is 20
Inside main()
```

The output should be self-explanatory.

10.9 DESTRUCTORS

The complement of a constructor is a destructor. Destructors are used to deactivate the storage allocated to classes when they are created. Destructors have the same names as constructors, except that they are preceded by a tilde (~). Take a look at the following simple program, which illustrates the use of a constructor and destructor:

```
//    test10_14.cpp

#include <iostream.h>

class one
   {
   // ** one() is the constructor
   // ** ~one() is the destructor
   public:
   one();
   ~one();
   };

main(void)
{
   cout << "Inside main() \n";
   one object_1;
   cout << "Inside main() - after creating object_1 \n";
}

// ** this is the constructor function
one::one()
{
   cout << "Inside one \n";
}

// ** this is the destructor function
one::~one()
{
   cout << "Inside ~one \n";
}
```

There are two member functions for the class `one`: these are `one()` and `~one()`. `one()` is the default constructor, and `~one()` is the destructor.

Compiling and executing this program give the following output:

```
Inside main()
Inside one
Inside main() - after creating object_1
Inside ~one
```

As you can see, the destructor ~one is called automatically upon exit from main(). Like a constructor, it would have been called even if it had not explicitly defined.

Again, like a constructor, a destructor does not have a return type or value. But unlike constructors, it accepts no parameters. It is called implicitly when a variable goes out of scope (as it did in the sample program). For local variables, this occurs when they are no longer within block scope. For global variables, this occurs upon termination of the program.

10.10 ORDER OF CALLING DESTRUCTORS

Destructors are called in the exact opposite order as constructors. Take a look at the following program:

```
//    test10_15.cpp

#include <iostream.h>

class one
   {
   public:
   one();
   ~one();
   };

// ** two is derived from one
class two : public one
   {
   public:
   two();
   ~two();
   };

main(void)
{
   cout << "Inside main() \n";
   two object_1;
   cout << "Inside main() - after creating object_1 \n";
}

// ** this is the base class constructor
```

```
one::one()
{
  cout << "Inside one \n";
}

// ** this is the base class destructor
one::~one()
{
  cout << "Inside ~one \n";
}

// ** this is the derived class constructor
two::two()
{
  cout << "Inside two \n";
}

// ** this is the derived class constructor
two::~two()
{
  cout << "Inside ~two \n";
}
```

Here the class two is derived from one. Compiling and executing this program result in the following output:

```
Inside main()
Inside one
Inside two
Inside main() - after creating object_1
Inside ~two
Inside ~one
```

Inside main(), an object of type two is created. However, two is derived from one. Therefore, one is constructed first, and then two. Next, the program is exited. Here we see that first the destructor for the derived class is called (~two) and then the destructor for the base class (~one). Destruction follows the opposite order of construction, as it logically should.

10.11 Review

In this chapter we learned a lot of interesting things about constructors and destructors.

- Constructors are functions that have the same names as their classes. They initialize objects when they are created.

- They are called automatically by the compiler, if they are not explicity called within the program, at the time when objects of their class types are declared.
- Default arguments can be supplied to constructors.
- Constructors can be overloaded because the correct version will be automatically invoked by the compiler.
- They are called in the logical order that is followed by base and derived classes; i.e., base class constructors will precede derived class constructors.
- Destructors are the complement of constructors. They have the same names as constructors, except they are preceded by a tilde (~).
- Destructors deallocate memory allocated to objects created through constructors.
- They are called automatically upon exit from `main()`, if they are not explicitly called.
- They accept no parameters.
- Destructors are called in the opposite order as constructors; i.e., derived class destructors are called before base class destructors.

Chapter

11

Virtual Functions and Polymorphism

11.1 INTRODUCTION

You have come a long way since you first started reading Chapter 1 of this book (and it has been a fairly smooth journey, we hope). In Chapter 1, we introduced you to the concept of a virtual function. At the time, you probably did not understand the full power of this feature of C++. In this chapter, this concept will be reintroduced and illustrated in detail. You will be introduced to words such as *polymorphism*, and expressions such as *early binding* and *run-time binding*. By the time you conclude this chapter, you will feel comfortable with these little catch words, which C++ programmers and books freely use, and realize that these concepts are really not as difficult to understand as you may have originally thought.

11.2 BACK TO POINTERS

Before we begin our discussion of virtual functions, here is a short refresher on pointers. (Pointers will be discussed in detail in Chapter 12.) This discussion is necessary, since it is through pointers to base and derived classes that run-time polymorphism is achieved in C++.

A pointer, as you already know, contains the location in memory of a data type. The concept, syntax, and use of pointers is the same for C++ (save for a few enhancements) as it is in C. For example, if you declare an integer variable in your program:

```
int a;   // a is an integer data type
```

then, a pointer to this variable would be declared, as follows:

```
int *ptr;   // ptr is a pointer to an integer
```

Next, ptr would be set to the address or location in memory of a:

```
ptr = &a;   // ptr is set to the address of a
```

Once this is done, the contents of the variable a can be accessed indirectly through ptr. The following two statements result in the same output:

```
*ptr = 5;  // access contents of a through ptr, set a to 5
a = 5;     // access contents of a directly, set a to 5
```

The location in memory of a would be obtained by preceding ptr with the * operator. The following statement illustrates this:

```
cout << "At location " << ptr << "is stored " << *ptr
```

The statement above would result in the following output on your computer:

```
At location xxxxxx is stored 5
```

where xxxxxx is the address of a. The first invocation of ptr results in the address of a being output. The second invocation of ptr results in the output of the contents of a stored at that address.

11.3 Pointers to Classes

C++, like C, has pointers to characters, floats, doubles, arrays, and the like. There are pointers to structures, and, in C++, you also have pointers to classes. The syntax for accessing class members via pointers is the same as for accessing structure members in C. Take a look at the following program:

```
// test11_1.cpp

#include <iostream.h>

class one
   {
   public:
   void output(void)
      {
      cout << "Inside output \n";
```

```
        }
    };

main(void)
{
    // object_1 is object of type one
    // pointer is pointer to object of type one
    one object_1;
    one *pointer;

    // pointer is set to address of object_1
    // output() is executed
    pointer = &object_1;
    pointer->output();

    return(0);
}
```

Compiling and executing this program result in the following output:

```
Inside output
```

First, the class one is declared. The function output() is inline. Inside main(), object_1 as an object of type one. Then, pointer is declared as a pointer to objects of type one. pointer is set equal to the address of object_1. Next, the class member output() of the class one is executed via the statement:

```
pointer->output();
```

The -> operator is one way to access a class member through a pointer. The following statement would have given the same result:

```
pointer.output();
```

We will use the -> operator in our programs, since the arrow intuitively symbolizes that something is being pointed to, and that is exactly what is being implemented in the program.

11.4 Pointers to Derived Classes

In C++, you can have pointers to base classes and pointers to derived classes. You can access a member of a derived class via a pointer to the base class, as long as the member being accessed in the derived class has been inherited from the base class. This will become clear as you read the next program:

```
// test11_2.cpp

#include <iostream.h>

class one
   {
   public:
   void output(void)
      {
      cout << "Inside output \n";
      }
   };

// two is derived from one
class two : public one
   {
   public:
   void output2(void)
      {
      cout << "Inside output2 \n";
      }
   };

main(void)
{
   // object of type one is declared
   // object for derived class is declared
   // pointer to base class is declared
   one object_1;
   two object_2;
   one *pointer;

   // pointer is set to address of object_1
   // object_1::output() is executed
   pointer = &object_1;
   pointer->output();

   // pointer is now set to address of derived class
   // object_2::output() is executed
   pointer = &object_2;
   pointer->output();

   return(0);
}
```

Compiling and running this program result in the following output:

```
Inside output
Inside output
```

Here is the original definition of class one. Then class two is publicly derived from one. The class one has one class member: output(), and the class two has two class members: output(), which it inherits from class one, and output2(), which is unique to it.

Inside main(), a pointer is declared to the base class one. Next, it is set to the address of object_1, which is an object of type one. The function output() is executed as follows:

```
pointer->output();
```

Next, pointer is set to the address of an object of type two, which is the derived class:

```
pointer = &object_two;
```

and output() is executed again:

```
pointer->output();
```

The compiler did not generate any errors since the function output() for object_two is inherited from the base class one. If test11_2.cpp is modified to execute output2() via the pointer to the base class, then errors will be encountered, as this program illustrates:

```
// test11_3.cpp

#include <iostream.h>

class one
   {
   public:
   void output(void)
      {
      cout << "Inside output \n";
      }
   };

// two is derived from one
class two : public one
   {
   public:
   void output2(void)
      {
      cout << "Inside output2 \n";
      }
   };

main(void)
{
   // object of type one is declared
   // object for derived class is declared
   // pointer to base class is declared
   one object_1;
   two object_2;
```

```
    one *pointer;

    // pointer is set to address of object_1
    // object_1::output() is executed
    pointer = &object_1;
    pointer->output();

    // pointer is now set to address of derived class
    // object_2::output2() is executed
    pointer = &object_2;
    pointer->output2();

    return(0);
}
```

Compiling and executing this program result in the following message:

```
Error:  output2 is not a member of one
```

The compiler issued this complaint in response to the following statement:

```
pointer->output2();
```

This is because `pointer` is declared as a pointer to the base class `one`, and `output2()` is specific to the class `two`, not inherited from `one`.

Incidentally, you can typecast the base class pointer to a pointer to the derived class, and succeed in executing `output2` through pointer as follows:

```
((two *)pointer)->output2();
```

We don't want to get into too many messy details about statements that look like the one above (confusing, to say the least), and hence won't elaborate on it further in this chapter.

Elements of the derived class that are not inherited from the base class can be accessed conveniently through a pointer to the derived class. Take a look at this version of the program:

```
// test11_4.cpp

#include <iostream.h>

class one
  {
  public:
  void output(void)
    {
    cout << "Inside output \n";
```

```
        }
    };
// two is derived from one
class two : public one
    {
    public:
    void output2(void)
        {
        cout << "Inside output2 \n";
        }
    };

main(void)
{
    // object of type one is declared
    // object for derived class is declared
    // pointer to base class is declared
    // pointer to derived class is declared
    one object_1;
    two object_2;
    one *pointer;
    two *pointer2;

    // pointer is set to address of object_1
    // object_1::output() is executed
    pointer = &object_1;
    pointer->output();

    // pointer is now set to address of derived class
    // object_2::output2() is executed
    pointer2 = &object_2;
    pointer2->output2();

    return(0);
}
```

Compiling and running this program result in the following output:

```
Inside output
Inside output2
```

11.5 Virtual Functions Revisited

With this introduction to pointers to base and derived classes, we return to our discussion on virtual functions. It is necessary for you to understand how class members are accessed through pointers, since this is the fundamental mechanism by which virtual functions are executed.

So exactly what does the word *polymorphism* mean? We refer to our handy *Webster's Encyclopedic Unabridged Dictionary*, and narrow in on the following explanations:

"...existence of an animal or plant in several form or color varieties..."

"...state or condition of being polymorphous..."

Meanwhile, polymorphous means

"...having, assuming, or passing through many or various forms..."

Think about the first definition for a minute. Think of a rose. A rose is a rose, but some roses are red, and some are white, and some are pink, and maybe one day someone will somehow create a rose that is black or some other peculiar color.

Now think of a rose as an object. We know that a rose is a rose because it is of a certain shape, its petals are soft, it has a distinct bouquet, and it has thorns on its stems. Now we are not quite sure of how a rose came into existence, or who created it, but let's attribute its existence to nature. Nature created a flower of this specific shape, and gave it the remaining attributes that made it a rose. And when everything was ready, suppose it left the implementation of the color to a different entity. It would send a rose with no color, or a default color (say red), to the entity and allow it to determine the exact method in which a specific color would be assigned to that particular rose. This entity would determine the color of the rose in its own distinct way, and pass the color back to nature. Each time a new color had to be assigned to the rose, nature would send the default rose to the entity, and after the colo was assigned, the rose would be sent back to nature.

The interface or interconnection is the same each time a rose is sent: a rose with no or default color. The object returned from the entity is also always the same: a rose with a color. However, the way the color is determined, or the method in which it is assigned, is different for each color. If a green rose were to be created, then the colors yellow and blue would have to be mixed. If a purple rose were to be created, then the colors red and blue would have to be mixed, and so on. There is only one interface, but there are multiple implementations. Based on the definition from the dictionary, believe it or not, a rose is polymorphous because it can exist in several color varieties. Furthermore, believe it or not, this *one interface, multiple implementations concept is the key to understanding polymorphism in C++.*

We will now build on the one interface, multiple implementations concept, using a different example and sample programs, to help you further understand this powerful object-oriented mechanism.

We know of a little travel agency that specializes in Caribbean vacation packages. When this agency first started out, the owners decided to design a program in C++ that would list the salient attractions of the Caribbean resorts included in each package. The astute programmer who was assigned this task understood the advantages of using classes instead of structures, and so decided to build a class hierarchy where the base class would describe those features which are common to all Caribbean islands. Each island would then be derived from the base class and contain descriptions of the attractions that are specific to the island.

This program was designed to be as flexible as possible so that changes could be easily incorporated into it. What if a hurricane struck one island, or local tensions broke out in another? Obviously, these islands would have to be taken off the list of available packages. At the same time, new packages may be added as the company grows. What was needed was a program that could add and delete functions that were inherently the same (i.e., the listed attractions) but were implemented differently (a different set of attractions would be listed for each island). Based on these needs, it was apparent that virtual functions were the answer. Here's the result:

```
// test11_5.cpp

#include <iostream.h>

// caribbean_isles will be the main base class
class caribbean_isles
   {
   public:

   // ** notice keyword virtual
   virtual void other_attractions(void)
      {
      cout << "!!COME VISIT THE CARRIBBEAN ISLANDS!! \n";
      cout << "White sand beaches \n";
      cout << "Crystal clear water \n";
      cout << "No hassles - No worries - No cares \n\n";
      }
   };
```

The code is broken up into logical fragments, since it is longer than most of the other programs in this book. The program starts off by declaring a base class called `caribbean_isles`. This class contains one public function called `other_attractions()`. The definition of this function is preceded by the keyword *virtual*. It is inline (it does not have to be), and it outputs those features which are common to all Caribbean Islands in the list of available packages: white sand beaches; crystal clear water; and no hassles, worries, or cares. Let's continue with the code.

```
// bahamas, grand_cayman and st_thomas are derived from
// caribbean_isles.
```

```
class bahamas : public caribbean_isles
   {
   public:

   // ** notice same function name, no keyword virtual
   void other_attractions(void)
      {
      cout << "!!BAHAMAS!! \n";
      cout << "Fun-filled casinos \n";
      cout << "Action-packed water sports \n";
      cout << "Great rum punches \n\n";
      }
   };

class grand_cayman : public caribbean_isles
   {
   public:

   // ** notice same function name, no keyword virtual
   void other_attractions(void)
      {
      cout << "!!GRAND CAYMAN!! \n";
      cout << "Incredible scuba diving \n";
      cout << "Big time game fishing \n";
      cout << "Duty free shopping \n\n";
      }
   };

class st_thomas : public caribbean_isles
   {
   public:

   // ** notice same function name, no keyword virtual
   void other_attractions(void)
      {
      cout << "!!ST THOMAS!! \n";
      cout << "Excellent shopping \n\n";
      }
   };
```

Next, the bahamas, grand_cayman, and st_thomas are derived from the caribbean_isles. These islands inherit all features contained in the caribbean_isles, and then add a few features of their own. Notice here that each of these classes contains a member function whose name is common to the virtual function in the base class (other_attractions()). In addition to this, the return type is the same (void), and so are the parameters (void again). However, the implementation of each function is different (a different set of attractions is listed for each method). Now take a look at the code for main().

```
main(void)
{
   // ** object and ptr to caribbean_isles class is declared
   caribbean_isles islands, *ptr;

   // objects for derived classes are declared
   bahamas package_1;
   grand_cayman package_2;
   st_thomas package_3;

   // ptr is set to address of base class object
   ptr = &islands;

   // virtual function is executed
   // the compiler will know which version to execute!!
   ptr->other_attractions();

   // ptr is now set to address of derived class objects
   ptr = &package_1;
   ptr->other_attractions();
   ptr = &package_2;
   ptr->other_attractions();
   ptr = &package_3;
   ptr->other_attractions();

   return(0);
}
```

Inside `main()`, objects of the base and derived classes and a pointer to the base class are declared. Next, `ptr` is set to the address of the base class, and the function `other_attractions()` is implemented. But which version of the function will be implemented? Well, C++ determines the answer to this question at *run* time, as opposed to *compile* time, based on the type of object that is being pointed to. This is called *late binding*, and *run-time polymorphism*. These little catch words should be starting to make sense now.

Compiling and executing this program result in the following output:

```
!!COME VISIT THE CARRIBBEAN ISLANDS!!
White sand beaches
Crystal clear water
No hassles - No worries - No cares

!!BAHAMAS!!
Fun-filled casinos
Action-packed water sports
Great rum punches

!!GRAND CAYMAN!!
Incredible scuba diving
Big time game fishing
Duty free shopping
```

```
!!ST THOMAS!!
Excellent shopping
```

Now let's understand the output.

Initially, `ptr` is set to point to the object `islands`, which is an instance of the class object of type `caribbean_isles`. Hence, the statement:

```
ptr->other_attractions();
```

results in the execution of the version of `other_attractions()` that belongs to the base class.

Next, `ptr` is set to point to the object `package_1`, which is an instance of type `bahamas`. Hence, the statement:

```
ptr->other_attractions();
```

results in the execution of the version of `other_attractions()` that belongs to the derived class `bahamas`.

Step through the remainder of the program yourself, and you should be able to understand which version is being implemented, and why.

11.6 What Is a Virtual Function?

A *virtual function* is one that is declared as such in the base class. Then, it is redefined (although it does not have to be, as you will see shortly), in one or more classes derived from the base class. The correct implementation of the function is selected at run time, as opposed to compile time, based on the object that is being pointed to.

A virtual function is preceded by the keyword *virtual* inside the base class. Then, this function is redefined inside the derived classes. The name, return type, and parameters for the function must be exactly the same as those in the original prototype in the base class, otherwise the virtual nature of these functions is lost. For this reason, we do not use the term *overloaded* to describe these special functions. (Recall that overloaded functions have the same name, but different parameters.) Instead, the function is *overridden* inside the derived class.

Run-time polymorphism is achieved by accessing these functions through a pointer to the base class. The base class specifies the functions that will be common to all classes derived from it. It provides the uniform interface to these functions inside the derived classes. The actual method in which this function will be implemented is defined inside the derived class.

11.7 WHAT ARE EARLY BINDING AND LATE BINDING?

Early binding indicates the occurrence of the determination of events that are to take place at the time that a program is compiled. Examples of early binding are standard and overloaded function calls. Information required to implement standard and overloaded functions is known at the time that a program is compiled.

Late binding indicates the occurrence of the determination of events that are to take place at the time that a program is run. Examples of late binding include virtual functions. Information required to implement virtual functions is known at the time that a program is run, not when it is compiled. Let's explain this a little bit further.

Take a look at this very simple program:

```
// test11_6.cpp

main(void)
{
   int a = 5;  // 1st statement
   a += 2;     // 2nd statement
}
```

Compiling and executing this program generate no errors and produce no output; we have deliberately kept it this simple. However, this program illustrates two major points.

The first statement is executed at compile time. When `test11_6.cpp` is compiled, the compiler assigns storage for an integer to the variable `a`, and stores the value of 5 in it.

The second statement is executed at run time. When `test11_6.cpp` is run, 2 is added to whatever is stored in `a`.

So why are virtual functions a run-time phenomenon? Well, you already know that the function that is to execute is determined by the object being pointed to at the time. The value of `ptr` is modified at run time. Hence, the related version of the function that is to execute is also determined at run time.

11.8 REVIEW

In this chapter we learned the how and why of virtual functions. We learned:

- How pointers to base and derived classes are used to invoke function class members.

- That a pointer to a base class can be used to access a member of the derived class, as long as that class member has been inherited from the base.

- How virtual functions can be invoked using pointers to base classes to access objects of different types. Terms such as *late binding* and *run-time polymorphism* are used to describe this phenomenon.

Chapter

12

Virtual Functions and Abstract Classes

12.1 Introduction

In the previous chapter we reintroduced virtual functions and explained how they are invoked, and why. In this chapter we will build on this concept further, and introduce you to pure virtual functions and abstract classes.

12.2 Flexibility of Virtual Functions

In Chapter 11, a C++ program was designed that listed the main attractions of the vacation packages offered by our travel agency. This program was designed in such a way that it would be flexible enough to handle deletion and insertion of islands to the packages, without major redesign of the main code. This objective was achieved by utilizing virtual functions. It is presented in its entirety here for your convenience.

```
// test11_5.cpp

#include <iostream.h>

// caribbean_isles will be the main base class
class caribbean_isles
   {
   public:

   // ** notice keyword virtual
   virtual void other_attractions(void)
      {
```

```
     cout << "!!COME VISIT THE CARRIBBEAN ISLANDS!! \n";
     cout << "White sand beaches \n";
     cout << "Crystal clear water \n";
     cout << "No hassles - No worries - No cares \n\n";
     }
  };

// bahamas, grand_cayman and st_thomas are derived from
// caribbean_isles.

class bahamas : public caribbean_isles
  {
  public:

  // ** notice same function name, no keyword virtual
  void other_attractions(void)
     {
     cout << "!!BAHAMAS!! \n";
     cout << "Fun-filled casinos \n";
     cout << "Action-packed water sports \n";
     cout << "Great rum punches \n\n";
     }
  };

class grand_cayman : public caribbean_isles
  {
  public:

  // ** notice same function name, no keyword virtual
  void other_attractions(void)
     {
     cout << "!!GRAND CAYMAN!! \n";
     cout << "Incredible scuba diving \n";
     cout << "Big time game fishing \n";
     cout << "Duty free shopping \n\n";
     }
  };

class st_thomas : public caribbean_isles
  {
  public:

  // ** notice same function name, no keyword virtual
  void other_attractions(void)
     {
     cout << "!!ST THOMAS!! \n";
     cout << "Excellent shopping \n\n";
     }
  };


main(void)
{
```

```
   // ** object and ptr to caribbean_isles class is declared
   caribbean_isles islands, *ptr;

   // objects for derived classes are declared
   bahamas package_1;
   grand_cayman package_2;
   st_thomas package_3;

   // ptr is set to address of base class object
   ptr = &islands;

   // virtual function is executed
   // the compiler will know which version to execute!!
   ptr->other_attractions();

   // ptr is now set to address of derived class objects
   ptr = &package_1;
   ptr->other_attractions();
   ptr = &package_2;
   ptr->other_attractions();
   ptr = &package_3;
   ptr->other_attractions();

   return(0);
}
```

Now suppose a fourth hot-spot package comes into the picture. The code of the original program would be modified as follows:

```
// test12_1.cpp

#include <iostream.h>

// caribbean_isles will be the main base class
class caribbean_isles
   {
   public:

   // ** notice keyword virtual
   virtual void other_attractions(void)
      {
      cout << "!!COME VISIT THE CARRIBBEAN ISLANDS!! \n";
      cout << "White sand beaches \n";
      cout << "Crystal clear water \n";
      cout << "No hassles - No worries - No cares \n\n";
      }
   };

// bahamas, grand_cayman and st_thomas are derived from
// caribbean_isles.

class bahamas : public caribbean_isles
   {
   public:
```

```
   // ** notice same function name, no keyword virtual
   void other_attractions(void)
      {
      cout << "!!BAHAMAS!! \n";
      cout << "Fun-filled casinos \n";
      cout << "Action-packed water sports \n";
      cout << "Great rum punches \n\n";
      }
   };

class grand_cayman : public caribbean_isles
   {
   public:

   // ** notice same function name, no keyword virtual
   void other_attractions(void)
      {
      cout << "!!GRAND CAYMAN!! \n";
      cout << "Incredible scuba diving \n";
      cout << "Big time game fishing \n";
      cout << "Duty free shopping \n\n";
      }
   };

class st_thomas : public caribbean_isles
   {
   public:

   // ** notice same function name, no keyword virtual
   void other_attractions(void)
      {
      cout << "!!ST THOMAS!! \n";
      cout << "Excellent shopping \n\n";
      }
   };

class st_lucia : public caribbean_isles
   {
   public:

   // ** notice same function name, no keyword virtual
   void other_attractions(void)
      {
      cout << "!!ST. LUCIA!! \n";
      }
   };

main(void)
{
   // ** object and ptr to caribbean_isles class is declared
   caribbean_isles islands, *ptr;
   // objects for derived classes are declared
   bahamas package_1;
   grand_cayman package_2;
```

```
    st_thomas package_3;

    // ** st_lucia package is added here
    st_lucia package_4;

    // ptr is set to address of base class object
    ptr = &islands;

    // virtual function is executed
    // the compiler will know which version to execute!!
    ptr->other_attractions();

    // ptr is now set to address of derived class objects
    ptr = &package_1;
    ptr->other_attractions();
    ptr = &package_2;
    ptr->other_attractions();
    ptr = &package_3;
    ptr->other_attractions();

    // ** ptr to address of st_lucia is added here

    ptr = &package_4;
    ptr->other_attractions();

    return(0);
}
```

As you can see, a new class `st_lucia` has been added. This is the latest hot-spot package, which will contain its own implementation of `other_attractions()`. Now take a look at the code for `main()`.

The following lines of code are the only changes required inside `main()` to implement the function for the new derived class:

```
    st_lucia package_4;
    .
    ptr = &package_4;
    ptr->other_attractions();
```

The output for this program is the same as that of `test11_5.cpp`, in the previous chapter, with one additiona line of output: `!! ST. LUCIA!!`. This program illustrates the ease with which new functions can be integrated into the program. Removing the assignment of a pointer to a derived class would illustrate the corresponding ease with which virtual functions can be removed from the main logic.

12.3 Deviations from the Norm

There is a small island in the heart of the Caribbean. Not many know about it, but this quaint little haunt has majestic mountains, white sandy beaches, and breathtaking undersea cliffs. This island's name is Saba.

Suppose this island was to be included as one of the prime attractions, called the *mystery package*. However, at the moment, no one is quite sure how to classify its attractions. So, how would this situation be handled? Well, we forgot to tell you. If a virtual function is not defined inside the derived class, then the base virtual function is automatically executed instead. Or, to say it a different way, *if a derived class does not provide a function to override the base virtual function, then the base virtual function will execute when an object of the type of the new class is pointed to.* Take a look at this version of the original program:

```
// test12_2.cpp

#include <iostream.h>

// caribbean_isles is the main base class
class caribbean_isles
   {
   public:

   // ** we will output the header separately
   void header(void)
      { cout << "!!COME VISIT THE CARIBBEAN ISLANDS!! \n";}

   virtual void other_attractions(void)
      {
      cout << "White sand beaches \n";
      cout << "Crystal clear water \n";
      cout << "No hassles - No worries - No cares \n\n";
      }
   };
```

As you can see, this is a modified definition of the base class. It was modified by outputting the header line separately from the remainder of the original function. The new header function is not declared as virtual, since there is no need to do so. Let's continue with the program.

```
// bahamas, grand_cayman and st_thomas are derived from
// caribbean_isles.
// ** so is saba
class bahamas : public caribbean_isles
   {
   public:

   // ** notice same function name, no keyword virtual
   void other_attractions(void)
      {
      cout << "!!BAHAMAS!! \n";
      cout << "Fun-filled casinos \n";
      cout << "Action-packed water sports \n";
      cout << "Great rum punches \n\n";
```

```
      }
   };

class grand_cayman : public caribbean_isles
   {
   public:

   // ** notice same function name, no keyword virtual
   void other_attractions(void)
      {
      cout << "!!GRAND CAYMAN!! \n";
      cout << "Incredible scuba diving \n";
      cout << "Big time game fishing \n";
      cout << "Duty free shopping \n\n";
      }
   };

class st_thomas : public caribbean_isles
   {
   public:

   // ** notice same function name, no keyword virtual
   void other_attractions(void)
      {
      cout << "!!ST THOMAS!! \n";
      cout << "Excellent shopping \n\n";
      }
   };

class saba : public caribbean_isles
   {
   public:
   void name(void) { cout << "!!MYSTERY ISLAND SABA!! \n"; };

   // ** attributes of other_attractions() not defined yet

   };
```

The class saba is defined just as the rest. However, the attributes of its function other_attractions() have not been determined yet. These attributes are expected to be known some time in the future. For now, the mystery island simply inherits attributes from its base class. Let's continue with main().

```
main(void)
{
   // declare object and ptr to caribbean_isles class
   caribbean_isles islands, *ptr;

   // declare objects for derived classes
   bahamas package_1;
   grand_cayman package_2;
   st_thomas package_3;
```

```
   saba mystery_package;

   // output header
   islands.header();

   // set ptr to address of base class object
   ptr = &islands;

   // execute virtual function
   // the compiler will know which version to execute!!
   ptr->other_attractions();

   // now set ptr to address of derived class objects
   ptr = &package_1;
   ptr->other_attractions();
   ptr = &package_2;
   ptr->other_attractions();
   ptr = &package_3;
   ptr->other_attractions();

   // ** output name of mystery island
   // ** set ptr to address of package_4
   mystery_package.name();
   ptr = &mystery_package;

   // ** caribbean_isles::other_attractions executes
   ptr->other_attractions();

   return(0);
}
```

An object of type saba is given the name mystery_package. After the attractions of the other islands have been listed, the name of the mystery package island is output, ptr is set to point to an object of that type, and the function other_attractions() is executed. Here's the output of this program:

```
!!COME VISIT THE CARIBBEAN ISLANDS!!
White sand beaches
Crystal clear water
No hassles - No worries - No cares

!!BAHAMAS!!
Fun-filled casinos
Action-packed water sports
Great rum punches

!!GRAND CAYMAN!!
Incredible scuba diving
Big time game fishing
Duty free shopping

!!ST THOMAS!!
```

```
Excellent shopping

!!MYSTERY ISLAND SABA!!
White sand beaches
Crystal clear water
No hassles - No worries - No cares
```

As you can see, the base virtual function turns out to be the default function which executes in the absense of an overridding function in the derived class. At a future date, the `other_attractions()` function can be defined for the new derived class. Then, when the statement

```
ptr->other_attractions()
```

is executed

```
saba::other_attractions()
```

will be implemented instead of `caribbean_isles::other_attractions()`.

12.4 Pure Virtual Functions and Abstract Classes

Pure virtual functions exist for scenarios that are the flip side of the coin of the previous section. There are circumstances in which the attributes of the virtual function in the base class are undefined. A pure virtual function is created in these circumstances. This type of function is used simply as a *place holder* for functions that are *expected* to be derived from the base class in the future. Pure virtual functions have no definition in the base class; they are initialized to 0. For this reason, any class derived from them will be required to provide its own implementation of that function. The use of pure virtual functions is illustrated in `test12_3.cpp`.

```
// test12_3.cpp

#include <iostream.h>

// caribbean_isles is the base class
class caribbean_isles
   {
   public:

   // ** the header is output seperately
   void header(void)
      {cout << "!!COME VISIT THE CARRIBBEAN ISLANDS!! \n\n";}

   // attributes of other_attractions either do not exist,
   // or are simply a place holder.
```

```
// therefore, we define it as a pure virtual function
virtual void other_attractions(void) = 0;
};
```

As you can see, the virtual function `other_attractions()` in the base class is initialized to 0. This is a pure virtual function. *Declaring a pure virtual function results in each class that is derived from it being forced to provide its own implementation for that function.* Let's continue with the program.

```
// bahamas, grand_cayman and st_thomas are derived from
// caribbean_isles.
class bahamas : public caribbean_isles
   {
   public:

   // ** notice same function name, no keyword virtual
   void other_attractions(void)
      {
      cout << "!!BAHAMAS!! \n";
      cout << "Fun-filled casinos \n";
      cout << "Action-packed water sports \n";
      cout << "Great rum punches \n\n";
      }
   };

class grand_cayman : public caribbean_isles
   {
   public:

   // ** notice same function name, no keyword virtual
   void other_attractions(void)
      {
      cout << "!!GRAND CAYMAN!! \n";
      cout << "Incredible scuba diving \n";
      cout << "Big time game fishing \n";
      cout << "Duty free shopping \n\n";
      }
   };

class st_thomas : public caribbean_isles
   {
   public:

   // ** notice same function name, no keyword virtual
   void other_attractions(void)
      {
      cout << "!!ST THOMAS!! \n";
      cout << "Excellent shopping \n\n";
      }
   };
```

Now take a look at first few lines inside `main()`.

```
main(void)
{
   // ** declare ptr only to caribbean_isles class
   // ** we can not create an object of a class type that has
   // ** a pure virtual function.
   caribbean_isles *ptr;
```

As you can see, an object for the base class is not declared. This is because *a base class that has a pure virtual function is said to be abstract*. You cannot declare objects for abstract classes. However, also note that it is okay to declare pointers to this special type of class. This is necessary in order to implement run-time polymorphism. Here's the remainder of the code:

```
   // declare objects for derived classes
   bahamas package_1;
   grand_cayman package_2;
   st_thomas package_3;

   // ** we output header() function of the base class,
   // ** but as an element of the derived class.
   package_1.header();

   // ** set ptr to object of derived class
   ptr = &package_1;

   // execute virtual function
   // the compiler will know which version to execute!!
   ptr->other_attractions();
   ptr = &package_2;
   ptr->other_attractions();
   ptr = &package_3;
   ptr->other_attractions();

   return(0);
}
```

There are no further changes to the remainder of the code.

If we forgot to provide an implementation for the virtual function inside one of the derived classes, say, `st_thomas`, the compiler would issue the following error message:

```
Error:  Pure function 'caribbean_isles::other_attractions()'
        not overridden in 'st_thomas'
```

Therefore, pure virtual functions can be used as a safety mechanism inside programs where it is necessary for derived classes to provide their own version of the base virtual function.

12.5 REVIEW

In this chapter, we wrapped up our discussion on virtual functions. We learned:

- Just how easy it is to incorporate new virtual functions into a program or delete outdated ones, based upon current needs.

- That a base virtual function is invoked in those instances where a derived class fails to provide an implementation for it.

- That pure virtual functions force the programmer to provide an implementation of the virtual function inside the derived class.

- That classes which contain pure virtual functions are called abstract classes. Objects of this type cannot be declared, only pointers to them. The virtual function inside an abstract class is used as a place holder for classes that will be derived from it.

Chapter 13

Pointers and Pointer Arithmetic

13.1 INTRODUCTION

If you are a C programmer, then pointers should be no mystery to you. A brief introduction to pointers was presented in Chapter 11. In this chapter and the next, pointers will be discussed in detail. Section 11.2 is now redisplayed. It serves as a brief introduction to pointers and pointer syntax.

13.2 POINTER SYNTAX

A pointer contains the location in memory of a data type. The concept, syntax, and use of pointers is the same in C++ (save for a few enhancements) as it is in C. For example, if you declare an integer variable in your program:

```
int a;    // a is an integer data type
```

then, you would declare a pointer to this variable as follows:

```
int *ptr;   // ptr is a pointer to an integer
```

Next, you would set `ptr` to the address or location in memory of `a`:

```
ptr = &a;   // ptr is set to the address of a
```

Once this is done, you can access the contents of the variable a indirectly through ptr. The following two statements result in the same output:

```
*ptr = 5; // access contents of a through ptr, set a to 5
a = 5;    // access contents of a directly, set a to 5
```

If you were to output ptr without the * operator, you would get the location in memory where a is stored. The following statement illustrates what has just been said:

```
cout << "At location " << ptr << "is stored " << *ptr
```

The statement above would result in the following output on your computer:

```
At location 0xxxxxxxx is stored 5
```

where 0xxxxxxx is the address of a in hexadecimal. The first invocation of ptr results in the address of a being output. The second invocation of ptr results in the output of the contents of a, which are stored at that address.

To summarize, the & symbol is the address of operator, and gives us the location in memory of a data type. The indirection operator * allows us to access the contents of what is stored at that address. A pointer must be initialized to point to something, or it will contain garbage.

13.3 Pointers to Integer, Float, and Double Data Types

Based on this short discussion on pointers, here is a small program that illustrates the syntax and use of pointers to integer, float, and double data types.

```
// test13_1.cpp

#include <iostream.h>

main(void)
{
   // declare variables and ptr to data types
   int a, *ptr_int;
   float b, *ptr_float;
   double c, *ptr_double;

   // initialize and point to their addresses
   a = 5;
```

```
   ptr_int = &a;
   b = 10.3;
   ptr_float = &b;
   c = 50.5;
   ptr_double = &c;

   cout << "a is " << a
        << " ptr_int is " << ptr_int
        << " *ptr_int is " << *ptr_int << "\n";
   cout << "b is " << b
        << " ptr_float is " << ptr_float
        << " *ptr_float is " << *ptr_float << "\n";
   cout << "c is " << c
        << " ptr_double is " << ptr_double
        << " *ptr_double is " << *ptr_double << "\n";
}
```

Compiling and running this program give the following output:

```
a is 5 ptr_int is 0x8f51ffe6 *ptr_int is 5
b is 10.3 ptr_float is 0x8f51ffee *ptr_float is 10.3
c is 50.5 ptr_double is 0x8f51ffe6 *ptr_double is 50.5
```

The output statements first display the contents of what is stored in a, b, and c. Then, they display the contents of the pointers to these data types. As you can see, the pointers contain the locations in memory where the variables are stored. Next, the contents of what is stored at these memory locations are obtained.

Now take a look at this version of test13_1.cpp, in which the locations in memory of the pointers are displayed.

```
// test13_2.cpp

#include <iostream.h>

main(void)
{
   int a, *ptr_int;
   float b, *ptr_float;
   double c, *ptr_double;

   a = 5;
   ptr_int = &a;
   b = 10.3;
   ptr_float = &b;
   c = 50.5;
   ptr_double = &c;

   // ** output addresses of pointers in the 3rd column
   cout << " a is " << a
        << " ptr_int is " << ptr_int
        << " &ptr_int is " << &ptr_int << "\n";
```

```
   cout << " b is " << b
        << " ptr_float is " << ptr_float
        << " &ptr_float is " << &ptr_float << "\n";
   cout << " c is " << c
        << " ptr_double is " << ptr_double
        << " &ptr_double is " << &ptr_double << "\n";
}
```

The program output on our computer looks like this:

```
a is 5 ptr_int is 0x8f51fff4 &ptr_int is 0x8f51fff2
b is 10.3 ptr_float is  0x8f51ffee &ptr_float is  0x8f51ffec
c is 50.5 ptr_double is 0x8f51ffe4 &ptr_double is 0x8f51ffe2
```

As you can see, the third column outputs the locations in memory where the pointers are stored, which are the addresses of ptr_int, ptr_float, and ptr_double. Notice that the contents of the pointers are 2 bytes greater than the addresses of the pointers themselves.

Table 13.1 illustrates where each variable is stored, and what is stored in it:

Table 13.1 Addresses and Contents of Variables

Variable	Address	Contents
ptr_int	0x8f51fff2	0x8f51fff4
a	0x8f51fff4	5
ptr_float	0x8f51ffec	0x8f51ffee
b	0x8f51ffee	10.3
ptr_double	0x8f51ffe2	0x8f51ffe4
c	0x8f51ffe4	50.5

Now we are going to change the program to output the contents of what is stored at the addresses of the pointers. Take a look at this variation of test13_2.cpp:

```
// test13_3.cpp

#include <iostream.h>

main(void)
{
   int a, *ptr_int;
   float b, *ptr_float;
   double c, *ptr_double;
```

```
    a = 5;
    ptr_int = &a;
    b = 10.3;
    ptr_float = &b;
    c = 50.5;
    ptr_double = &c;

    // ** display contents of what is stored at addresses of
    // ** pointers.
    cout << "*&a: " << *&a
         << " ptr_int: " << ptr_int
         << " *(&ptr_int): " << *(&ptr_int) << "\n";
    cout << "*&b is " << *&b
         << " ptr_float: " << ptr_float
         << " *(&ptr_float): " << *(&ptr_float) << "\n";
    cout << "*&c: " << *&c
         << " ptr_double: " << ptr_double
         << " *(&ptr_double): " << *(&ptr_double) << "\n";
}
```

On our computer the output for this program is as follows:

```
*&a: 5 ptr_int: 0x8f51fff4 *(&ptr_int): 0x8f51fff2
*&b: 10.3 ptr_float: 0x8f51ffee *(&ptr_float): 0x8f51ffec
*&c: 50.5 ptr_double: 0x8f51ffe4 *(&ptr_double): 0x8f51ffe2
```

The output for the last two columns has already been explained. Notice the syntax for the output in the first column:

```
... *&a:  ...
```

Based on the rules of precedence, this expression is broken down as follows. First, the address of a is obtained:

```
....&a...
```

This indicates the location in memory where a is stored. Next, the indirection operator (*) is used to obtain the contents of what is stored at that address:

```
....*&a...
```

and that is why 5 is output.

13.4 Pointers to Arrays

Arrays can be accessed through indices, as follows:

```
int array[5];
```

```
int array[5];
array[3] = 5;
```

The above statements declare an array of five integers. The fourth element of the array is set to 5. The reason the fourth element is set to 5, and not the third, is because indexing starts at 0, not 1.

Arrays can also be accessed through pointers. Take a look at the following extension to the fragment of code above.

```
int array[5]; // declare array containing 5 elements
int *ptr;     // declare pointer to integer

ptr = array;  // set pointer to 1st element of array[]
ptr += 3;     // add 3 to ptr - ptr now points to 4rth element
*ptr = 5;     // set 4rth element of array to 5
```

An array of five elements and a pointer to integer data types are declared. Next, `ptr` is set to the address of the first element of the array via the statement:

```
ptr = array;
```

Notice that there is no index to the array, only its name. This form of syntax returns the first element of the array.

Next, 3 is added to `ptr`. Originally, the first element was being pointed to. Now the index in incremented by 3, which is equal to `array[3]`, which is the fourth element of the array. The statement

```
*ptr = 5;
```

sets the contents of what is being pointed to by `ptr` to 5. Hence, the fourth element of `array[]` is set to 5.

Here is a short program that summarizes most of what has been said:

```
// test13_4.cpp

#include <iostream.h>

main(void)
{
   char name[20] = "Jay Ranade";
   char *ptr;

   // set ptr to address of name[0];
   ptr = name;
   cout << "ptr is " << ptr << " name[0] is "
        << name[0] << "\n";
   ptr++;
```

```
   cout << "ptr is " << ptr << " name is " << name << "\n";

   // access contents of what is stored at name[0] + 1
   cout << "*(name + 1) is " << *(name + 1) << "\n";
}
```

The output for this program is as follows:

```
ptr is Jay Ranade name[0] is J
ptr is ay Ranade name is Jay Ranade
*(name + 1) is a
```

Here a 20- element character array is declared and initialized to Jay Ranade. ptr is declared as a pointer to character data types. ptr is initialized to the first element of name[].

The first time around, the complete string is output. The compiler knows the end of the string when it encounters the terminating (invisible to the human eye!) null at the end of the array. name[0], as expected, contains the letter J, which is duly output via the next cout. Next, ptr is incremented. It now points to the second element of the array, which is a, and hence ay Ranade is output. The name of the array without an index will always point to the first element of the array, and the complete array is output for name.

If name points to the first element of the array, then (name + 1) points to the second element. The contents of what is stored at that location are obtained via the expression:

```
*(name + 1)
```

and the second element of the array (a) is output.

13.5 Pointers to Structures

Pointers to structures are similar in syntax and function to pointers to any other data type. Take a look at the following program:

```
// test13_5.cpp

main(void)
{
struct family
   {
   char *husband;
   char *wife;
   char *son;
   };
```

```
    // anderson is a structure of type family
    // ptr is a pointer to family
    family anderson;
    family *ptr;

    // ptr now contains address of anderson
    ptr = &anderson;

    // point to structure members and initialize them
    ptr->husband = "John Anderson";
    ptr->wife = "Mary Anderson";
    ptr->son = "Joey Anderson";
}
```

A structure of type family is declared. This structure contains three elements, which are pointers to characters. anderson is declared as a structure of type family, and ptr is declared as a pointer to a structure of type family. Next, ptr is set to the address of anderson, and then structure members are accessed and initialized via the -> operator.

13.6 Pointer Arithmetic

Only three types of operations are permitted on pointers: addition, subtraction, and comparison. We will present a short program that illustrates each of these cases. Here's the program that illustrates how pointers are incremented:

```
// test13_6.cpp

#include <iostream.h>

main(void)
{
    int *ptr;

    // a[] is an array of integers
    int a[2] = {10, 20};

    // ptr contains address of 1st element of array
    ptr = a;

    cout << "ptr is " << ptr << " *ptr is " << *ptr << "\n";
    ptr += 1;
    cout << "ptr is " << ptr << " *ptr is " << *ptr << "\n";
}
```

The output for this program is as follows:

```
ptr is 0x8f93fff2 *ptr is 10
ptr is 0x8f94fff4 *ptr is 20
```

ptr is declared as a pointer to integer data types. Next, an integer array is declared and initialized. ptr is set to the first element of the array, and 10 is output. ptr is incremented by 1. It now points to the second element of the array, and 20 is output. Notice that ptr is incremented by 2 bytes, even though only 1 is added to it. This is because our computer stores an integer in 2 bytes, and a pointer is automatically incremented by the correct number of bytes in order to access subsequent elements. Your computer may take more or less bytes to store an integer, so refer to your system documentation for further details.

The following program illustrates how pointers are decremented:

```
// test13_7.cpp

#include <iostream.h>

main(void)
{
   int *ptr;

   // a[] is an array of integer
   int a[2] = {10, 20};

   // ptr contains address of 1st element of array
   ptr = a;

   cout << "ptr is " << ptr << " *ptr is " << *ptr << "\n";
   ptr += 1;
   cout << "ptr is " << ptr << " *ptr is " << *ptr << "\n";
   ptr--;
   cout << "ptr is " << ptr << " *ptr is " << *ptr << "\n";
}
```

The output for this program is as follows:

```
ptr is 0x8f97fff2 *ptr is 10
ptr is 0x8f97fff4 *ptr is 20
ptr is 0x8f97fff2 *ptr is 10
```

Notice that decrementing the pointer also results in a difference of 2 bytes in the address, not 1. This is once again because our computer stores an integer in 2 bytes. The correct offset is automatically calculated.

Pointers can also be compared. Here's a short program that does just that:

```
// test13_8.cpp

#include <iostream.h>
```

```
main(void)
{
   int *ptr1, *ptr2;

   // a[] is an array of integers
   int a[2] = {10, 10};

   // ptr contais address of 1st element of array
   ptr1 = a;
   cout << "ptr1 is " << ptr1 << " *ptr1 is " << *ptr1 << "\n";
   ptr2 = ptr1 + 1;
   cout << "ptr2 is " << ptr2 << " *ptr2 is " << *ptr2 << "\n";

   // compare 2 pointers
   if (ptr1 ==  ptr2)
      cout << "ptr1 is equal to ptr2 \n";
   else
      cout << "ptr1 is not equal to ptr2 \n";

   if (*ptr1 == *ptr2)
      cout << "*ptr1 equals *ptr2 \n";
   else
      cout << "*ptr1 does not equal *ptr2 \n";
}
```

Compiling and executing this program result in the following output:

```
ptr1 is 0x8f78fff2 *ptr1 is 10
ptr2 is 0x8f78fff4 *ptr2 is 10
ptr1 is not equal to ptr2
*ptr1 equals *ptr2
```

The output should be self-explanatory.

And now here's a program that illustrates what you cannot do with pointers:

```
// test13_9.cpp

main(void)
{
   int a = 5, b = 10, *ptr, *ptr2;

   ptr = &a;
   ptr2 = &b;

   // lines 10 thru 14 follow
   ptr *= 4;      // multiply pointer by constant
   ptr /= 2;      // divide pointer by constant
   ptr %= 3;      // obtain remainder by dividing pointer
   ptr *= ptr2;   // multiply 2 pointers
   ptr /= ptr2;   // divide 1 pointer into another
```

```
    // lines 18 and 19 follow
    ptr += ptr2;    // add 2 pointers
    ptr -= ptr2;    // subtract 1 pointer from another
}
```

Compiling this program results in the following error message being output for lines 10 through 14:

```
Error:  Illegal use of pointer
```

and the following messages are output for lines 18 and 19:

```
Error:  Invalid pointer addition
Error:  Invalid pointer subtraction
```

The error messages are self-explanatory. You simply cannot perform any other function with pointers but add, subtract, and compare.

13.7 Review

In this chapter we discussed pointer syntax and use. This chapter should have served as a review for seasoned (and for that matter, nonseasoned) C programmers. We will present the operations that can and cannot be performed in Table 13.2. But before you look at the table, take a look at this fragment of code. The results in the table indicate the values that will be obtained by manipulating the variables defined below.

```
main()
{
      // pointers to integer values follow
      // a and b are integer data types
      int *ptr1, *ptr2;
      int a[2], b;

      // ptr1 contains address of a[0]
      // ptr2 contains address of a[1]
      ptr1 = &(a[0]);      // ptr1 contains address of a[0]
      ptr2 = &(a[1]);      // ptr2 contains address of a[1]

 // Assume a[0] is stored at memory location 8000
 // Therefore, a[1] is stored at address 8002
         .
         .
         .
 }
```

The Result column in Table 13.2 displays the value of the variable or expression after evaluating the condition. All results are based on the initial values of the pointers. Remember that the contents being pointed to are 8000 by ptr1 and 8002 by ptr2.

Table 13.2 Operations on Pointers

Operation	Permitted	Pointer Syntax	Result
Increment	Yes	++ptr1;ptr1++; ++ptr2;ptr2++;	ptr1=8002 ptr2=8004
Decrement	Yes	--ptr1;ptr1--; --ptr2;ptr2--;	ptr1=7998 ptr2=8000
Compare	Yes	if (ptr1 < ptr2) while (ptr2 < ptr1)	TRUE FALSE
Subtract a pointer from a constant	No	z=8-ptr1; z=14-ptr2;	Error
Add 2 pointers	No	z=ptr1 + ptr2;	Error
Multiply pointer by a value	No	z=ptr1 * 9; z=ptr2 * 6;	Error
Divide pointer by a value	No	z = ptr1 / 8; z = ptr2 / 60;	Error
Multiply 2 pointers	No	z = ptr1 * ptr2	Error
Divide 1 pointer by another	No	z = ptr2 / ptr1	Error

Chapter

14

Fundamental Concepts of Operator Overloading

14.1 INTRODUCTION

In this chapter we will describe an unusual and interesting feature of C++ called *operator overloading*. This feature allows you to change the meaning of operators such as +, -, *, /, and others. If you take the time to think through the reasons to overload operators, then you will see how this can be a very powerful tool. On the other hand, indiscriminate use of overloaded operators can result in a debugging nightmare. Keep this in mind as you proceed with the remainder of the chapter.

14.2 OPERATOR OVERLOADING IS NOTHING UNUSUAL

Take a look at the following six line program.

```
//    test14_1.cpp

#include <iostream.h>

main(void)
{
   cout << "Notice the use of the << operator!! \n";
}
```

Compiling and running this program result in the following output:

```
   Notice the use of the << operator!!
```

There are no mysteries here. Now take a look at test14_2.cpp, in which the << operator is used in the context of a left shift operator:

```
//    test14_2.cpp

#include <iostream.h>

main(void)
{
   int a = 2;
   cout << "a is " << a << "\n";

   // shift a left by 12 bits
   a = a << 12 ;
   cout << "a is " << a << "\n";
}
```

Compiling and running this program result in the following output:

```
a is 2
a is 8192
```

What is interesting in this program is the use of the << operator. In the first instance, it is used as a *put to* operator. In the second program, the following statement

```
a = a << 12;
```

implies its use as the left shift operator. a is shifted left 12 bits, and so the value stored in a is output as 8192, instead of 2.

What you just encountered is an example of operator overloading. Operator overloading is a feature provided by C++ that allows you to change the meaning of operators. In the first example, the operator << is used as a *put to* operator. In the second example, it is used as a left shift operator, as well as a *put to* operator.

Operator overloading is an interesting concept, but you will be suprised to realize that it has existed all along, perhaps without your knowing about it. For example, you can add two integers using the + operator:

```
a = 5 + 2;
```

and you can add two floats using the same operator:

```
a = 5.5 + 2.8;
```

You are using the same operator to perform the same function on two different data types. The + operator is overloaded to perform addition on two integer types in the first instance and addition of two float types in the second.

Here's another example. The * operator is used to multiply two data types:

```
a = a * b;
```

However, the * operator can also be used to specifiy a pointer type when it is declared:

```
int *ptr;
```

The above statement declares `ptr` as a pointer to an integer type. The * operator can also be used to dereference a pointer variable, in order to manipulate the contents of what is stored at the location in memory that `ptr` is pointing to:

```
*ptr = 5;
```

The above statement sets the contents of the location in memory stored in `ptr` to 5. This is another instance of operator overloading.

14.3 SYNTAX OF OPERATOR OVERLOADING

Take a look at the following short program:

```
//    test14_3.cpp

#include <iostream.h>

class assign
   {
   public:
   int a;
   };

assign object_1, object_2;

main(void)
{
   object_1.a = 5;
   object_2 = object_1;

   cout << "object_2.a is " << object_2.a << "\n";
}
```

Compiling and running this program result in the following output:

```
object2.a is 5
```

This program demonstrates nothing but the simple assignment of an integer value to a class member, and then cout is used to display this value to your screen. Now take a look at the following program, which illustrates operator overloading.

```
//   test14_4.cpp

#include <iostream.h>

class assign
   {
   public:
   int a;

   // ** notice overloaded function syntax:
   void operator=(assign var1);
   };

// overloaded operator function returns no value (type void)
// it takes an object of type assign as an argument
// it follows the usual function definition rules
void assign::operator=(assign var1)
{
   a = 2 + var1.a;
}

// object_1 and object_2 are objects of type assign
assign object_1, object_2;

main(void)
{
   // class member a of object_1 is assigned the value of 5
   object_1.a = 5;

   // object_2 is set equal to object_1
   object_2 = object_1;
   cout << "object_2.a is " << object_2.a << "\n";
}
```

Compiling and running this program result in the following output:

```
object_2.a is 7
```

Interesting output, wouldn't you say? Under normal circumstances, object_2.a should have been 5, not 7, since object_2 is set equal to object_1, and object_1.a was previously set to 5. Well, the reason for this unusual output is that the operator = was *overloaded* to set the operand on the left equal to the operand on the right plus 2. That is why object_2.a was set equal to 7, instead of 5. Let's step through this program and understand what happened. Take a look at the declaration of the class assign:

```
class assign
   {
   public:
   int a;

   // ** notice overloaded function syntax:
   void operator=(assign var1);
   };
```

Notice the syntax for the member function assign():

```
   void operator=(assign var1);
```

This statement declares the existence of an overloaded operator function, and it is a member function of the class assign. The operator that will be overloaded is the assignment operator =. This function will return no value, and it takes an object of type assign as an argument. This function could just as well have been declared as follows:

```
   assign operator=(void);
```

This would imply that it returns an object of type assign, and takes no arguments. Or, it could have been declared as:

```
   int operator=(char);
```

or with any other valid return or argument type. In our example, it is declared as:

```
   void operator=(assign var1);
```

The definition of the class member function operator=() follows:

```
void assign::operator=(assign var1)
{
   a = 2 + var1.a;
}
```

The object on the left of the operator is assigned to the object on the right. The a class member inside the functions belongs to object_2. The definition of this function agrees with the function prototype in the class declaration. The function returns no value, it is a member of the class assign (shown by the scope resolution operator ::, which precedes the function name assign::operator=), it overloads the operator =, and it takes an object of type assign as an argument.

The function itself is only one line. It receives class object1 as a parameter and adds 2 to its object_2.a member. It assigns the resulting value to the class member a, and then returns back to main().

Inside main(), object_2 is assigned to object_1. This is a valid assignment, since both objects are of the same class type. Finally, the contents of object_2.a are output.

The reason for the unusual result is that the operator = has been overloaded for all objects that belong to the class of which the overloaded function is a member. Let's go over this concept in greater detail.

object_1 and object_2 are objects of type assign. The operator function = is a class member of assign. Each time the operator = is encountered or called to perform an operation on class objects that belong to the class type for which an overloaded function definition exists, the overloaded function definition will be substituted instead of the usual operation. (Friend function definitions can also be substituted, and these will be discussed later on in the chapter.)

Now take another look at the code for main().

```
assign object_1, object_2;

main(void)
{
   // class member a of object_1 is assigned the value of 5
   object_1.a = 5;

   // object_2 is set equal to object_1
   object_2 = object_1;
   cout << "object_2.a is " << object_2.a << "\n";
}
```

object_1 and object_2 are declared as objects of type assign. Inside main(), class member a of assign is set to 5. Next, object_2 is assigned to object_1. However, the operator = was previously declared as a member function of the class assign. Since object_1 and object_2 are objects of the same type, the compiler implements the code for that particular overloaded function.

Before trying to understand what happens inside the function itself, you should note that in the first assignment statement

```
   object_1.a = 5;
```

5 was, in fact, assigned to object_1, and 2 was not added to it. The reason for this is that both operands on the left and the right of the overloaded operator must belong to the same class that the overloaded operator (or friend function) belongs to. The operand on the right is a constant, not a member of the class object assign, hence the regular assignment operation is implemented. What this implies is that operators

preserve their existing functionality in the absence of the above mentioned conditions. (In the case of unary operators, i.e., those that operate on one operand only, e.g., ++ and --, the overloaded operator will always be called, given that the operand belongs to the same class. These will be discussed later on in the chapter.)

Now take another look at the code for the overloaded operator function:

```
void assign::operator=(assign var1)
{
   a = 2 + var1.a;
}
```

As you can see, an argument called var1 is accepted by assign. This is the template for an object of type assign. 2 is added to the a member of this object, and the result is assigned to the a member of the second object. You should be wondering by now exactly which object is being added to, and which object is being assigned to. The answer is that the operand on the right of the operator is passed as the explicit argument to the function. Hence, in the statement

```
   object_2 = object_1;
```

the argument that is passed to the overloaded operator as the explicit argument var1 is object_1. The object on the left of the operator is assigned to. The a class member inside the function itself belongs to object_2. (This particular mechanism will be discussed in greater detail shortly.) That is why the contents of object_2.a are changed from 5 to 7.

Meanwhile, the contents of object_1.a remain unchanged. We will modify test14_4.cpp to demonstrate just that.

```
//    test14_5.cpp

#include <iostream.h>

class assign
   {
   public:
   int a;

   // ** notice overloaded function syntax:
   void operator=(assign var1);
   };

// overloaded operator function returns no value
// it takes an object of type assign as an argument
// it follows the usual function definition rules
```

```
void assign::operator=(assign var1)
{
   a = 2 + var1.a;
}

// object_1 and object_2 are objects of type assign
assign object_1, object_2;

main(void)
{
   // class member a of object_1 is assigned the value of 5
   object_1.a = 5;

   // object_2 is set equal to object_1
   object_2 = object_1;
   cout << "object_2.a is " << object_2.a << "\n";
   cout << "object_1.a is " << object_1.a << "\n";
}
```

Compiling and running this program result in the following output:

```
object_2.a is 7
object_1.a is 5
```

The output should make sense. The operand on the right remains unchanged through the whole process.

14.4 Getting Carried Away with Operator Overloading

`Test14_5.cpp` will now be modified to demonstrate an instance where we get a little bit carried away with the concept just explained, and want to play tricks with your mind. Take a look at the following code.

```
//    test14_6.cpp

#include <iostream.h>

class assign
   {
   public:
   int a;

   // ** notice operator changed from = to +:
   void operator+(assign var1);
   };

// overloaded operator function returns object of type assign
// it takes an object of type assign as an argument
// it follows the usual function definition rules
```

```
void assign::operator+(assign var1)
{
   a = 2 + var1.a;
}

// object_1 and object_2 are objects of type assign
assign object_1, object_2;

main(void)
{
   // class member a of object_1 is assigned the value of 5
   object_1.a = 5;

   // ** the '+' actually performs an '='!!!!
   object_2 + object_1;
   cout << "object_2.a is " << object_2.a << "\n";
}
```

Two lines of code that you should pay special attention to are:

```
void operator+(assign var1);
object_2 + object_1;
```

In the first statement, the operator + is overloaded. In the second statement, `object_2` is added to `object_1`, and is not assigned to anything. Compiling and running this program result in the following output:

```
object_2.a is 5
```

If the operator + was not overloaded, the statement

```
object_2 + object_1;
```

would have resulted in an unfriendly compiler error message. However, no errors are generated because

```
object_2 + object_1;
```

results in exactly the same sequence of operations that occurred when the code looked like this:

```
object_2 = object_1;
```

For those of us of who inherit the code of programmers who inadvertently changed the meaning of operators, statements such as

```
object_2 + object_1;
```

can result in acute cases of confusion, headache, frustration, and insomnia. Hence, a word of advise from us. Please don't overload operators to mean something that goes against the grain of their original meaning. Don't overload a + operator to mean a -, a * to mean a /, and so on. Do what you have to do, but think things through before you proceed. Don't play tricks with other people's minds; you may end up playing a trick on yourself!

14.5 Overloaded Operators Are Simply Function Calls

An overloaded operator function syntax is simply an alternate form of a function call. Take a look at the following code. The function name `operator()` has been abbreviated to `op()`.

```
//    test14_7.cpp

#include <iostream.h>

class assign
   {
   public:
   int a;

   // ** notice that op is now a regular function
   // ** and it returns an object of type assign
   assign op(assign var1);
   };

assign object_1, object_2;

// op() is a regular function
// it returns an object of type assign
// it takes an object of type assign as a parameter
assign assign::op(assign var1)
{
   a = 2 + var1.a;
   object_2 = object_1;

   cout << "object_2.a in op() function is "
        << object_2.a << "\n";

   return var1;
}

main(void)
{
   // class member a of object_1 is assigned the value of 5
   object_1.a = 5;
```

```
   // object_1.op() is executed
   // the return value is assigned to object_2
   object_2 = object_1.op(object_1);

   cout << "object_2.a is " << object_2.a << "\n";
}
```

Compiling and running this program result in the following output:

```
object_2.a in op() function is 7
object_2.a is 5
```

The function `op()` is now a regular member function of the class `assign()`. `object_1` and `object_2` are declared as objects of type `assign`. Inside `main()`, the following statement

```
object_2 = object_1.op(object_1);
```

results in the function `object_1.op()` being called, `object_1` is passed as a parameter to it. Inside the function, 2 is added to a class member of `object_1`, and assigned to `object_2` in the statement

object_2 = object_1;

Hence, `object_2.a` in `op()` gets set to 7. However, `object_1.a` remains unchanged, and this is the value sent back to `main()`. `object_2` is assigned this value, and `object_2.a` is now once again set to 5.

As you are aware, the contents of variables inside functions can be manipulated or changed only through pointers (unless you are passing an array to the function or global variables). This is because copies of parameters are passed to functions, not the actual values. Here's a short program that illustrates this point:

```
//   test14_8.cpp

#include <iostream.h>

class assign
   {
   public:
   int a;

   // ** notice that op is now a regular function
   assign op(assign *object_1);
   };

assign object_1, object_2, *ptr;

// op() is a regular function
// it returns an object of type assign
```

```
// it takes a pointer to an object of type assign as a parameter
assign assign::op(assign *ptr)
{
   // modify contents of what ptr is pointing to
   // ptr is pointing to object_1.a
   ptr->a = 2 + ptr->a;

   // return object_1
   return object_1;
}

main(void)
{
   // class member a of object_1 is assigned the value of 5
   object_1.a = 5;

   // set ptr to location in memory of object_1
   ptr = &object_1;

   // object_2 is set equal to return value of op()
   // this return value is an object of type assign
   object_2 = object_1.op(ptr);

   cout << "object_2.a is " << object_2.a << "\n";
}
```

Compiling and running this program result in the following output:

```
object_2.a is 7
```

This time a pointer to `object_1` is sent to the function `op()`:

```
assign op(assign *object_1);
```

`ptr` is set to the location in memory of `object_1`, and then a call to `op()` is initiated.

Inside `op()`, the actual contents of `object_1` are modified, via `ptr`:

```
ptr->a = 2 + ptr->a;
```

A member of `object_1` is accessed via the -> operator. The dot (.) operator could also have been used as follows:

```
ptr.a = 2 + ptr.a;
```

The modified contents of `object_1` are sent back to `main()`, and `object_2` is assigned to this return value. Hence, `object_2.a` outputs as 7.

Now here's the trick question. Which version do you think looks cleaner and more natural? The one that uses pointers:

```
//    test14_8.cpp

#include <iostream.h>

class assign
   {
   public:
   int a;

   // ** notice that op is now a regular function
   assign op(assign *object_1);
   };

assign object_1, object_2, *ptr;

// op() is a regular function
// it returns an object of type assign
// it takes a pointer to an object of type assign as a parameter
assign assign::op(assign *ptr)
{
   // modify contents of what ptr is pointing to
   // ptr is pointing to object_1.a
   ptr->a = 2 + ptr->a;

   // return object_1
   return object_1;
}

main(void)
{
   // class member a of object_1 is assigned the value of 5
   object_1.a = 5;

   // set ptr to location in memory of object_1
   ptr = &object_1;

   // object_2 is set equal to return value of op()
   // this return value is an object of type assign
   object_2 = object_1.op(ptr);

   cout << "object_2.a is " << object_2.a << "\n";
}
```

or the one that uses operator overloading:

```
//    test14_4.cpp
#include <iostream.h>

class assign
   {
   public:
   int a;
   // ** notice overloaded function syntax:
   void operator=(assign var1);
```

```
};

// overloaded operator function returns no value
// it takes an object of type assign as an argument
// it follows the usual function definition rules
void assign::operator=(assign var1)
{
   a = 2 + var1.a;
}

// object_1 and object_2 are objects of type assign
assign object_1, object_2;

main(void)
{
   // class member a of object_1 is assigned the value of 5
   object_1.a = 5;

   // object_2 is set equal to object_1
   object_2 = object_1;
   cout << "object_2.a is " << object_2.a << "\n";
}
```

If you prefer the first version, then you probably don't feel comfortable with the syntax of overloaded operator calls. We recommend that you refrain from using overloaded operators until you feel more comfortable with the concept and syntax.

If you prefer the second version, then you are well on your way to adopting yet another powerful feature of C++.

14.6 ADVANTAGES OF OPERATOR OVERLOADING

One of the major advantages of operator overloading is that it allows you to use the same operators on user-defined data types as are used on built-in data types. You are used to expressions such as

```
a = a + b;
a = a * b;
```

but without operator overloading, the statements

```
object_1 = object_1 + object_2;
object_1 = object_1 * object_2;
```

would be invalid, given that `object_1` and `object_2` are user-defined data types. Operator overloading affords a more natural way for the expression of such statements. As another example, a concatenation of two strings would be expressed intuitively as follows:

```
"This is a " + "concatenation of 2 strings.";
```

The above statement would not compile properly without operator overloading.

14.7 Disadvantages of Operator Overloading

The major disadvantage of operator overloading is the possibility that the meaning of operators can become hidden inside obscure code, and the programmer does not understand why an operator such as + is not performing the function that he/she expects it to. The programmer is bound to experience feelings of inadequacy (since he/she does not understand the code), frustration, insomnia, and emotional distress.

14.8 Review

In this chapter we explained how operator overloading works, and why it can be a powerful or destructive tool. In particular, we learned that:

- We have been inadvertently overloading operators such as << and * all along; it is nothing new.

- This mechanism can be used to change the meaning of most operators provided by C++.

- Overloaded operator functions must be class members or friend functions.

- Overloaded operator functions are nothing more than an alternate form of a function call.

- The syntax for an overloaded function is as follows:

  ```
  type operator#(argument_list);
  ```

  where *type* is the return type of the function. This can be type `void` or any other valid data type; # is the operator that is being overloaded; *argument_list* is the list of arguments, if any, which are sent to the overloaded function.

- Overloaded operators allow a more natural way to express the relationship between two user-defined data types.

- Overloaded operators can be a programmer's nightmare, if their use results in obscure and impenetrable code.

Chapter

15

Operator Overloading, *this* and *friend*

15.1 Introduction

In this chapter, we will introduce a pointer called `this` (yes, it really is called `this`!). This pointer (no pun intended) is an integral part of the mechanism that allows operator overloading. Use of friend functions will also be illustrated. Friends can be used instead of class members to overload operators.

15.2 Binary and Unary Overloaded Operators

A binary operator is one that works on two objects. For example, + is a binary operator, because you have to add something to something in order for it to work. A unary operator is one that works on one object only. For example, ++ is a unary operator; `something++` results in `something` being incremented by 1.

Tables 15.1 and 15.2 list operators that cannot and can be overloaded, respectively.

Table 15.1 Operators That Cannot Be Overloaded

Operator	Function
,	comma
.	member
->	class or structure pointer
?:	ternary
sizeof	obtain size in bytes

Table 15.2 Operators That Can Be Overloaded

Operator	Function
++	increment
--	decrement
!	not
~	complement
+	add
-	minus
*	multiply
/	divide
%	modulus
()	function call
[]	array subscript
new	free store allocator
delete	free store deallocator
=	assign
+=	add and assign
-=	subtract and assign
*=	multiply and assign
/=	divide and assign
&	bitwise and
|	bitwise or
^	bitwise exclusive-or
||	logical or
&&	logical and
<	less than
<=	less than or equal to
>	greater than
>=	greater than or equal to
<<	left shift
>>	right shift
|=	or and assign
^=	exclusive-or and assign
&=	and and assign
<<=	left shift and assign
>>=	right shift and assign
==	logical equal
!=	not equal

15.3 Restrictions on Overloaded Operators

- You cannot make up your own operator. You can overload existing operators only.
- Operator overloading works when applied to class objects only.
- You cannot change the precedence or associativity of the original operators.
- You cannot change a binary operator to work with a single object.
- You cannot change a unary operator to work with two objects.
- Prefix and postfix application of the operators ++ and -- cannot be distinguished.
- You cannot overload an operator that works exclusively with pointers.

15.4 Expression Syntax of Overloaded Operators

We would like to bring your attention to the fourth and fifth restrictions from the previous section. These restrictions state that you must respect the general form of syntax that is associated with a particular operator; that is, you cannot change its basic template. Take a look at the following program.

```
//    test15_1.cpp

#include <iostream.h>

class assign
   {
   public:
   int a;

   // ** notice overloaded function syntax:
   void operator/(assign var1);
   };

// overloaded operator function returns type void (i.e. nothing)
// it takes an object of type assign as an argument
// it follows the usual function definition rules
void assign::operator/(assign var1)
{
   a = var1.a / 5;
}
```

```
// object_1 and object_2 are objects of type assign
assign object_1, object_2;

main(void)
{
   // class member a of object_1 is assigned the value of 5
   object_1.a = 15;
   object_2.a = 10;

   // The divide operator is treated as a unary operator
   object_2 / ;

   cout << "object_1.a is " << object_1.a << "\n";
   cout << "object_2.a is " << object_2.a << "\n";
}
```

Notice the statement:

```
object_2 / ;
```

As you can see, an attempt is made to use the division operator, which is binary, on a single object. Compiling this program results in the following error message:

```
Error:  Expression syntax
```

Now take a look at this program, which also overloads the divide operator but uses two objects instead of one.

```
//   test15_2.cpp

#include <iostream.h>

class assign
   {
   public:
   int a;

   // ** notice overloaded function syntax:
   void operator/(assign var1);
   };

// overloaded operator function returns type void
// it takes an object of type assign as an argument
// it follows the usual function definition rules
void assign::operator/(assign var1)
{
   a = var1.a / 5;
}
// object_1 and object_2 are objects of type assign
assign object_1, object_2;
```

```
main(void)
{
   object_1.a = 15;
   object_2.a = 10;

   cout << "object_2.a is " << object_2.a << "\n";

   // object_2 is divided by object_1
   object_2 / object_1;

   cout << "object_1.a is " << object_1.a << "\n";
   cout << "object_2.a is " << object_2.a << "\n";
}
```

Compiling and running this program result in the following output:

```
object_2.a is 10
object_1.a is 15
object_2.a is 3
```

object_1.a and object_2.a are initially set to 15 and 10, respectively. The division (/) operator is overloaded. object_2 is divided by object_1. The statement

```
a = var1.a / 5;
```

can be decoded as follows:

```
object_2.a = object_1.a / 5;
```

which is equal to

```
object_2.a = 15 / 5;
```

and so object_2.a is equal to 3. The output statements should now make sense. The contents of object_1.a remain unchanged. The contents of object_2.a are set to 3.

In the previous chapter, we had mentioned that the operator on the right of the operand is sent as an explicit argument to the calling overloaded operator function. The operand on the left is implicitly sent to the calling function. In this chapter, this concept will be elaborated on, so that you can understand how this mechanism works. Take another look at the function definition:

```
void assign::operator/(assign var1)
{
   a = var1.a / 5;
}
```

Based on what has just been said, var1 will contain the value assigned to object_1, since object_1 is to the right of the overloaded operator. This is the explicit argument sent to the calling function.

A pointer to the left operand is implicitly passed to operator/(). Hence, the variable a in the statement

```
a = var1.a / 5;
```

belongs to object_2. A pointer to object_2 is implicitly passed to the overloaded function. But exactly how does this occur? The answer is through a pointer that Mr. Stroustrup chose to call the this pointer.

15.5 THIS POINTER

Each time a member function is invoked, it is passed a pointer to the object that invoked it. The name of this pointer is this. This pointer is invisible to us because it is passed automatically or implicitly. The syntax of this pointer is similar to other pointer syntax. The only difference is that it is never declared, since its existence is automatic. And now, just to prove that a pointer to the operand on the left side of the overloaded operator is implicitly passed to the calling function through this pointer, here's a modified version of test15_2.cpp.

```
//    test15_3.cpp

#include <iostream.h>

class assign
   {
   public:
   int a;

   // ** notice overloaded function syntax:
   void operator/(assign var1);
   };

// overloaded operator function returns no value
// it takes an object of type assign as an argument
// it follows the usual function definition rules
void assign::operator/(assign var1)
{
   cout << "this->a is " << this->a << "\n";
   a = var1.a / 5;
}

// object_1 and object_2 are objects of type assign
assign object_1, object_2;
```

```
main(void)
{
   object_1.a = 15;
   object_2.a = 10;

   // ** object_2 is divided by object_1
   object_2 / object_1;

   cout << "object_1.a is " << object_1.a << "\n";
   cout << "object_2.a is " << object_2.a << "\n";
}
```

Compiling and running this program give the following output:

```
this->a is 10
object_1.a is 15
object_2.a is 3
```

As you can see, `this->a` contains the value 10, which was assigned to `object_2.a` in `main()`. The statement

```
a = var1.a / 5;
```

can be decoded as follows:

```
object_2.a = object_1.a / 5;
```

which is equal to

```
object_2.a = 15 / 5;
```

and so `object_2.a` is set equal to 3. The output statements should now be clear.

Let's switch the values of `object_1` and `object_2` inside `main()`, and see how the value of the `this` pointer is affected. Here's the code:

```
//    test15_4.cpp

#include <iostream.h>

class assign
   {
   public:
   int a;

   // ** notice overloaded function syntax:
   void operator/(assign var1);
   };
```

```
// overloaded operator function returns object of type assign
// it takes an object of type assign as an argument
// it follows the usual function definition rules
void assign::operator/(assign var1)
{
   cout << "this->a is " << this->a << "\n";
   a = var1.a / 5;
}

// object_1 and object_2 are objects of type assign
assign object_1, object_2;

main(void)
{
   object_1.a = 15;
   object_2.a = 10;

   cout << "object_2.a is " << object_2.a << "\n";

   // object_1 is divided by object_2
   object_1 / object_2;

   cout << "object_1.a is " << object_1.a << "\n";
   cout << "object_2.a is " << object_2.a << "\n";
}
```

Compiling and running this program result in the following output:

```
object_2.a is 10
this->a is 15
object_1.a is 2
object_2.a is 10
```

The statement

```
a = var1.a / 5;
```

can be decoded as follows:

```
object_1.a = object_2.a / 5;
```

which is equal to

```
object_1.a = 10 / 5;
```

and so `object_1.a` is set equal to 2, and `object_2.a` remains unchanged. The output should now be self-explanatory.

And now, to reinforce what you have just learned, here's another program that illustrates how operator overloading works. This time the * operator will be overloaded.

```
//    test15_5.cpp
#include <iostream.h>

class assign
   {
   public:
   int a;

   // ** notice return value of overloaded function
   int operator*(assign var1);
   };

// overloaded operator function returns integer
// it takes an object of type assign as an argument
// it follows the usual function definition rules
int assign::operator*(assign var1)
{
   cout << "this->a is " << this->a << "\n";
   a = this->a * var1.a;
   return a;
}

// object_1, object_2 and object_3 are objects of type assign
assign object_1, object_2, object_3;

main(void)
{
   object_1.a = 15;
   object_2.a = 10;

   // object_3.a receives the return value
   object_3.a = object_2 * object_1;

   cout << "object_1.a is " << object_1.a << "\n";
   cout << "object_2.a is " << object_2.a << "\n";
   cout << "object_3.a is " << object_3.a << "\n";
}
```

Notice that this time the overloaded function returns an `int`, instead of an object of type `assign`. Inside the function, `a` is returned, which is a class member of `object_2`. Since an `int` type is being returned, `main()` is modified to have an `int` type accept this value.

Compiling and running this program result in the following output:

```
this->a is 10
object_1.a is 15
object_2.a is 150
object_3.a is 150
```

The statement

```
object_3.a = object_2 * object_1;
```

results in object_2 being multiplied by object_1. The * operator is overloaded. Inside the overloaded function:

```
int assign::operator*(assign var1)
{
   cout << "this->a is " << this->a << "\n";
   a = this->a * var1.a;
   return a;
}
```

object_1 is sent explicitly, and a pointer to object_2 is sent implicitly. The variables a and this->a belong to object_2 (they are to the left of the overloaded operator). Thus, the statement

```
a = this->a * var1.a;
```

can be decoded as follows:

```
object_2.a = 10 * 15;
```

Thus, the value of object_1.a remains unchanged, and object_2.a is returned via the statement:

```
return a;
```

and assigned to object_3.a:

```
object_3.a = object_2 * object_1;
```

The output should now be absolutely clear to you.

15.6 Friend Functions

So far, member functions only have been used to illustrate how operator overloading works. Friend functions to the class that contains the overloaded operator function definition can also be used.

As you have seen, member functions that overload binary operators are passed only one argument, and a pointer to the argument is passed implicitly through the this pointer. Overloaded unary operator function definitions require no arguments.

In friend functions, overloaded unary operators take one argument, and binary operators take two arguments. Both arguments are passed explicitly. The this pointer cannot be used, since it returns the location in memory of a class member for member functions only, and a friend function does not fall into this category. Take a look at test15_6.cpp, which illustrates the use of a friend function that overloads an operator.

```
//   test15_6.cpp

#include <iostream.h>

class assign
   {
   public:
   int a;

   // ** notice friend function
   friend int operator*(assign var1, assign var2);
   };

// overloaded operator function returns integer
// it takes two objects of type assign as arguments
// it follows the usual function definition rules
// operator* is a friend function, therefore there is no
// scope resolution operator for it.
int operator*(assign var_1, assign var_2)
{
   var_2.a = var_1.a * var_2.a;
   return var_2.a;
}

// object_1, object_2 and object_3 are objects of type assign
assign object_1, object_2, object_3;

main(void)
{
   object_1.a = 15;
   object_2.a = 10;

   // object_3.a receives the return value
   object_3.a = object_2 * object_1;

   cout << "object_1.a is " << object_1.a << "\n";
   cout << "object_2.a is " << object_2.a << "\n";
   cout << "object_3.a is " << object_3.a << "\n";
}
```

Take another look at the function definition:

```
int operator*(assign var_1, assign var_2)
{
   var_2.a = var_1.a * var_2.a;
```

```
   return var_2.a;
}
```

Notice that the name of the function is not preceded by a scope resolution operator. This makes sense because there is no scope to resolve, since this is a friend function. Also notice that both arguments are passed explicitly.

Compiling and running this program result in the following output:

```
object_1.a is 15
object_2.a is 10
object_3.a is 150
```

Now take another look at the statement that calls the overloaded operator function:

```
object_3.a = object_2 * object_1;
```

The object on the left of the overloaded operator *, i.e., object_2, is assigned to var1. The object on the right, i.e., object_1, is assigned to var2. Inside the function, the values of the objects themselves do not change, since copies of these objects are manipulated. The return value is assigned to object_3.a, and therefore 50 is output for this data type.

If the contents of object_1 or object_2 are to be modifed, these objects can be sent as references. Here's a program that illustrates how parameters can be sent by reference, instead of value:

```
//   test15_7.cpp

#include <iostream.h>

class assign
   {
   public:
   int a;

   // ** notice friend function
   friend int operator*(assign object_1, assign &object_2);
   };

// overloaded operator function returns integer
// it takes two objects of type assign as arguments
// it follows the usual function definition rules
// operator* is a friend function, therefore there is no
// scope resolution operator for it.
// var_2 is passed as a reference.
int operator*(assign var_1, assign &var_2)
{
   var_2.a = var_1.a * 5;
   var_2.a = var_1.a * var_2.a;
```

```
    return var_2.a;
}

// object_1, object_2 and object_3 are objects of type assign
assign object_1, object_2, object_3;

main(void)
{
    object_1.a = 15;
    object_2.a = 10;

    // object_3.a receives the return value
    object_3.a = object_2 * object_1;

    cout << "object_1.a is " << object_1.a << "\n";
    cout << "object_2.a is " << object_2.a << "\n";
    cout << "object_3.a is " << object_3.a << "\n";
}
```

Notice the function prototype for the overloaded friend function:

```
friend int operator*(assign var1, assign &var2);
```

As you can see, the first parameter is sent by value; that is, a copy of this variable is sent to the calling function. The second parameter is sent by reference (the & sign precedes the variable name).

Compiling and running this program result in the following output:

```
object_1.a is 500
object_2.a is 10
object_3.a is 500
```

The statement

```
object_3.a = object_2 * object_1;
```

results in the overloaded operator function being called. Inside the function, `var_1` is assigned the value of `object_2` (10), since it is to the left of the overloaded operator, and `var_2` is assigned the value of `object_1` (15). The statement

```
var_2.a = var_1.a * 5;
```

is decoded as follows:

```
object_1.a = object_2.a * 5;
```

`object_1.a` is set to 10 * 5, which is equal to 50.

Since `object_1` is passed as a reference, its actual value is also changed to 50. The statement

```
var_2.a = var_1.a * var_2.a;
```

is decoded as follows:

```
object_1.a = object_2.a * object_1.a;
```

which is equal to

```
object_1.a = 10 * 50;
```

and `object_1.a` is set equal to 500. The output should now make sense.

Friend functions make the code for overloaded operators easier to read, since all arguments sent are visible to the human eye. There are no implicit or hidden arguments involved. Whether you use class members or friend functions to overload operators is your prerogative. Regardless of your choice, remember that one day someone will probably inherit your code. Make sure your overloaded function code is not impossible to penetrate, comment liberally, and don't play tricks with people's minds.

15.7 Review

In this chapter we described some additional features of overloaded operators.

- The majority of existing operators can be overloaded.
- There are some restrictions with reference to the extent to which operators can be overloaded.
- A pointer to the object on the left of a binary overloaded operator is implicitly passed to the calling function via the `this` pointer.
- The object to the right of the overloaded operator is passed explicitly as a parameter to the calling function.
- Binary overloaded operators are passed one argument.
- Unary overloaded operators are passed no arguments.
- Friend functions can be used to overload operators as well. Friends require that all parameters be sent to the calling function explicitly.

Chapter

16

Turbo C++ Preprocessor Directives

16.1 INTRODUCTION

In this chapter C++ preprocessor directives will be described. These directives allow the inclusion of files, implement simple string replacement, expand macros, and perform conditional compilation. Some directives help us in debugging the source code as well. But first, let's understand what a preprocessor is.

16.2 THE C++ PREPROCESSOR

If you are a C programmer, then you should be familiar with preprocessor control lines. Undoubtedly you have been including the header file `stdio.h` in your programs, so that you can utilize the pre-written I/O functions, such as `printf()`.

C++ also comes with a standard library of functions, which are normally included with the standard C++ compiler package. The rules for C++ preprocessor directives are the same as C. This chapter should serve as a review for most of you.

The preprocessor is a program that processes the source code of a program before it passes the source code on to the compiler. Preprocessor directives are preceded by the # symbol, and are called preprocessor control lines. Based on the control lines, the preprocessor performs one or more of the following functions:

- Includes files.
  Files are included when the following directive is encountered:

```
#include
```

- Replaces strings, and expands and/or undefines macros.
  The above two functions are implemented when the following directives are encountered:

```
#define
#undef
```

- Performs conditional compilation.
  Conditional compilation is implemented through the following sets of control lines:

```
#if
#else
#endif

#if
#elif
#endif

#ifdef
#endif

#ifndef
#endif
```

- Aids in debugging.
  The following control line helps debugging:

```
#pragma
```

  The following sections describe each of the directives.

16.3 Include Files

We have been including the file `<iostream.h>` in all our programs. Let's take a look at what happens if this file is not included.

```
//    test16_1.cpp
main(void)
{
   cout << "Hi there! \n";
   printf ("Hi there again! \n");
}
```

Compiling this program results in the following error messages:

```
Error:  Undefined symbol 'cout'
Error:  Function 'printf()' should have a prototype
```

Obviously, iostream.h has been included for good reason. Let's include the necessary files and recompile:

```
//    test16_2.cpp

// iostream.h is required for I/O
// stdio.h is required for printf()
#include <iostream.h>
#include <stdio.h>

main(void)
{
   cout << "Hi there! \n";
   printf ("Hi there again! \n");
}
```

Compiling and running this program result in the following output:

```
Hi there!
Hi there again!
```

The #include directive causes the entire contents of the name of the file that follows the directive to be included in the compilation. The header file iostream.h contains the definition for cout, and stdio.h contains the definition for printf().

The #include directive can take three forms.

- #include <filename>

  You should be familiar with this form. The name of the file inside angular brackets instructs the compiler to search for the file from the list of prearranged directories that are outside the current working directory.

- #include "filename"

  This form instructs the compiler to search for the file inside the current working directory.

- #include "C:\DIRNAME\FILENAME"

  This form instructs the compiler to search for the file inside the specified path. If it is not found in that directory, then the standard directories are searched.

Here's a short program that illustrates the form in which the path name is indicated.

```
//    test16_3.cpp

// iostream.h is required for I/O
// stdio.h is required for printf()
#include <iostream.h>
#include <stdio.h>

#include "C:\WP51\fileone"

main(void)
{
   cout << "Hi there! \n";
   printf ("Hi there again! \n");
   cout << "a from fileone is " << a << "\n";
}
```

We happen to have a directory called WP51 in our computer. (As a matter of fact, this is where our word processor resides.) This is what fileone looks like:

```
int a = 5;
```

That's right. fileone is only one line long. Normally, the file that is included is quite large. In fact, that's the whole point of include files. It helps break up a large source file into logical, manageable segments. Compiling and running this program result in the following output:

```
Hi there!
Hi there again!
a from fileone is 5
```

Although the preprocessor includes the file in the current source code, it is still the compiler's responsibility to check for syntax errors and the like. Unfriendly messages will be generated by the compiler if the file which is included does not compile properly. Suppose a file called filetwo is included, which looks like this:

```
int a = 5
```

Notice the missing semicolon. Now take a look at a program that includes filetwo:

```
//   test16_4.cpp

#include <iostream.h>
#include <stdio.h>
#include "C:\WP50\filetwo"

main(void)
{
   cout << "Hi there! \n";
   printf ("Hi there again! \n");
   cout << "a from filetwo is " << a << "\n";
}
```

Compiling this program results in five errors, the first one being:

```
Error:   Declaration syntax error
```

This is a slightly misleading error message, wouldn't you say? We will not list the remaining error messages, since they make no sense either. The lesson to be learned from this is to make sure that your `#include` files compile properly before you include them in your source code; otherwise you may have to face a debugging nightmare.

16.4 Simple String Replacement

Simple string replacement occurs with the `#define` directive. Take a look at this short program, which illustrates the use of this control line.

```
//   test16_5.cpp

#include <iostream.h>

#define HELLO "Hi there! \n"

main(void)
{
   cout << HELLO ;
}
```

Compiling and running this program result in the following output:

```
Hi there!
```

`HELLO` is replaced by the string `Hi there! \n` each time it is encountered in the source code. The statement

```
   cout << HELLO;
```

is replaced by

```
cout << "Hi there! \n";
```

and that is why you see the output

```
Hi there!
```

on your screen.

Most programmers use all capital letters when they use the #define control line. It is a good convention to follow, since it clearly identifies the variables which are defined in your program.

16.5 Macros without Arguments

Macro expansion is a form of string replacement. Arguments can be also be specified and these will be discussed in the next section. Take a look at the following program, which illustrates the expansion of a simple macro.

```
//    test16_6.cpp

#include <iostream.h>

#define SQUARE_TWO 2*2

main(void)
{
   int a;
   a = SQUARE_TWO;
   cout << "a is " << a << "\n";
}
```

In the line

```
#define SQUARE_TWO 2*2
```

#define is the control line, SQUARE_TWO is the macro template, and 2*2 is the macro expansion. This is a macro definition. Compiling this program results in the following output:

```
a is 4
```

This output is achieved because the statement

```
a = SQUARE_TWO;
```

is expanded to

```
a = 2 * 2;
```

which, of course, is equal to 4.

Macro expansions are valuable in that they define string replacement inside a program in one location only. Suppose you have a 500 line program in which 2 is squared 60 times, the code for each instance being scattered throughout the program. Now suppose you need to change the application to have 2 multiplied by 8, instead of 2. All you would have to do is change one line of code, the macro definition, as follows:

```
#define SQUARE_TWO  2*8
```

and all subsequent references to SQUARE_TWO will be changed accordingly.

16.6 Macros with Arguments

Here's a short program that expands a macro with an argument:

```
//    test16_7.cpp

#include <iostream.h>

#define ADD(X) (X + X)

main(void)
{
   int b;
   b = ADD(4);
   cout << "b is " << b << "\n";
}
```

The control line

```
#define ADD(X) (X + X)
```

is referenced in the following statement

```
b = ADD(4);
```

which expands to

```
b = 4 + 4;
```

Compiling and running this program result in the following output:

```
b is 8
```

Take another look at the control line:

```
#define ADD(X) (X + X)
```

Notice that there is no space between the macro template and its parameter X. If there was a space in between, then the token that follows it would become part of the macro expansion. Take a look at test16_8.cpp, which illustrates this form of expansion.

```
//    test16_8.cpp

#include <iostream.h>

// notice space between macro name and parameter
#define ADD (X) (X + X)

main(void)
{
   int b;
   b = ADD(4);
   cout << "b is " << b << "\n";
}
```

Compiling this program gives the following error message:

```
Error:   Undefined symbol 'X'
```

The compiler does not understand that the 4 inside the parentheses is the parameter that is to be substituted when the string is expanded. The space acts as a delimiter of the macro template.

Now suppose we forgot to place the parentheses in the control line, as follows:

```
#define ADD(X) X + X
```

This ommission can be potentially dangerous, as is illustrated by the following program:

```
//    test16_9.cpp

#include <iostream.h>

// notice space between macro name and parameter
#define ADD(X) X + X

main(void)
{
   int b;
```

```
   // we multiply the result of the macro expansion by 5
   b = ADD(4) * 5;

   cout << "b is " << b << "\n";
}
```

Compiling and running this program give the following output:

```
b is 24
```

The statement

```
b = ADD(4) * 5;
```

was expanded as follows:

```
b = 4 + 4 * 5;
```

and since multiplication takes precedence over addition, b was calculated as follows:

```
b = 4 + (4 * 5);
```

However, what we wanted was this:

```
b = (4 + 4) * 5
```

The expression was not evaluated as expected since the parentheses are missing. Make sure you don't forget them.

16.7 Undefining Macros

Macros that have been previously defined can be undefined with the following control line:

```
#undef
```

This control line will result in no string replacement. Take a look at test16_10.cpp, which illustrates its use.

```
//    test16_10.cpp

#include <iostream.h>

#define FOUR 4
```

```
main(void)
{
   int a = FOUR;
   cout << "a is " << a << "\n";

   #undef FOUR
   int b = FOUR;
   cout << "b is " << b << "\n";
}
```

Compiling this program results in the following error message:

```
Error:   Undefined symbol FOUR
```

This message is output for the following statement:

```
int b = FOUR;
```

This is because FOUR was undefined just before this statement. The compiler no longer substitutes 4 for FOUR.

The reason for undefining a macro would be so that macro names can be localized for those sections of code in which they are needed.

16.8 Conditional Compilation

Conditional compilation takes place when the following keywords are encountered in the source code:

```
#if - #else - #endif
#if - #elif - #endif
#ifdef - #endif
#ifndef - #endif
```

We will discuss each in the following subsections.

16.8.1 #if and #endif

The #if keyword is followed by a constant expression, a block of code, and then the #endif keyword. The block of code between these two control lines is included in compilation only if the constant expression between the braces evaluates to TRUE, or a nonzero value. Take a look at test16_11.cpp, which illustrates its use.

```
//    test16_11.cpp

#include <iostream.h>
```

```
main(void)
{
   const int a = 5;
   const int b = 0;

   #if (a)
      cout << "a is TRUE, i.e. non-zero \n";
   #else
      cout << "a is FALSE i.e. zero \n";
   #endif

   #if (b)
      cout << "b is TRUE, i.e. non-zero \n";
   #else
      cout << "b is FALSE, i.e. zero \n";
   #endif

   cout << "This code is outside the blocks \n";
}
```

Compiling and running this program give the following output:

```
a is TRUE, i.e. non-zero
b is FALSE i.e. zero
This code is outside the blocks
```

The output is self-explanatory. Note that it is necessary for a constant expression to be inside the test condition. An error message will be generated if it isn't, as is illustrated by `test16_12.cpp`:

```
//   test16_12.cpp

#include <iostream.h>

main(void)
{
   // a and b are declared as variables
   int a = 5;
   int b = 0;

   #if (a)
      cout << "a is TRUE, i.e. non-zero \n";
   #else
      cout << "a is FALSE i.e. zero \n";
   #endif

   #if (b)
      cout << "b is TRUE, i.e. non-zero \n";
   #else
      cout << "b is FALSE, i.e. zero \n";
   #endif
```

```
   cout << "This code is outside the blocks \n";
}
```

Compiling this program results in the following error message:

```
Error:   Constant expression required
```

The difference between the #if, #else, and #endif and the regular if, else, and endif control structures is that in the former case evaluation takes place before the program is compiled and run. You cannot have variables inside the test condition, since their value can change at run time.

16.8.2 #if, #elif, and #endif

These control lines are equivalent to the #if, #else, and #endif control lines just discussed, so they will not be elaborated on any further.

16.8.3 #ifdef and #endif

The block of code between these two control lines is compiled only if the macro name that follows the directive has been previously defined. Take a look at test16_13.cpp:

```
//    test16_13.cpp

#include <iostream.h>

#define  COMPILE

main(void)
{
   #ifdef COMPILE
      cout << "This code will be compiled \n";
   #endif
}
```

Compiling and running this program result in the following output:

```
This code will be compiled
```

As you can see, the macro COMPILE is defined; hence, the code within these two control lines is compiled. If the #define statement in the previous program is commented out, the code within the control lines will not be compiled. test16_4.cpp illustrates this.

```
//    test16_14.cpp

#include <iostream.h>

// we comment out the macro definition of COMPILE
// #define COMPILE

main(void)
{
   #ifdef COMPILE
      cout << "This code will be compiled \n";
   #endif
}
```

Compiling this program results in no output, since the macro called COMPILE is not defined.

This preprocessor feature can be used as a debugging aid. Debug statements can be inserted for a macro name, and then this name can be commented and uncommented, in order to exclude or include the debugging statements in the source code.

16.8.4 #ifndef and #endif

These control lines are the flip side of #ifdef and #endif statements. The block of code between these control lines is included in the compilation only if the macro name is not defined. Here's a program that illustrates just that.

```
//    test16_15.cpp

#include <iostream.h>

#define  COMPILE

main(void)
{
   // the following code is compiled only if macro
   // is not defined
   #ifndef COMPILE
      cout << "This code will be compiled \n";
   #endif
}
```

Compiling and running this program result in no output. This is because COMPILE is defined. There would have been output if the macro control line was commented out or deleted.

16.9 #PRAGMA

This control line allows various instructions to be given to the compiler. The instructions are specific to implementations. Please refer to your compiler's documentation for the #pragma directives that exist for your compiler.

16.10 REVIEW

In this chapter we discussed the preprocessor and its directives. We learned how to:

- Include files:

  ```
  #include <fileone>
  #include "fileone"
  #include "c:\dir\fileone"
  ```

- Perform simple string replacement, by defining macros:

  ```
  #define HELLO "hello"
  ```

  The above statement will result in HELLO being replaced by hello every time it is encountered in the source code file.

- Undefine macros, so that string replacement does not take place:

  ```
  #undef HELLO
  ```

- Define macros with arguments:

  ```
  #define square(x) (x*x)
  ```

  The above control line takes one argument, and expands it as indicated.

- Compile conditionally, through the following control lines:

  #if, #else, and #endif

  The code between the block is compiled only if the constant expression in the test condition evaluates to TRUE or a nonzero value.

These directives are equivalent to #if, #else, and #endif directives:

#if, #elif, and #endif

The code between the block is compiled only if the macro name that follows the directive has been previously defined:

#ifdef and #endif

The code between the control lines is compiled only if the macro name is not defined:

#ifndef and #endif

- How to use the #pragma directive, which issures instructions to the compiler. This directive is implementation dependent.

Part

3

Object-Oriented Approach Applied to C++

Chapter

17

Object-Oriented Analysis

17.1 INTRODUCTION

It is now time to put all of the pieces from Parts 1 and 2 of this book together and forge ahead armed with the tools that C++ provides. In this chapter, we will describe object-oriented analysis of a problem. In the next chapter, our analysis will be synthesized into object-oriented program design. The methodology described will be translated into a sample C++ application. Then, the ease with which the code can be revised, enhanced, and expanded will be illustrated. The true power of an object-oriented environment will be apparent to you as you conclude this section of the book.

17.2 WHAT IS OBJECT-ORIENTED ANALYSIS?

Take your eyes off this book just for a moment and look directly up at any object before you. Did you notice how your eyes focused on that object and everything else faded, almost out of view? Out of all possible objects, your eyes focused on a specific one because that was the object that held relevance for you at the time.

Undoubtedly, there must have been occasions at work when you were required to perform a set number of tasks before the start of the next business day. However, due to limitations of time and prior commitments, you realized that it would be impossible to perform all the assigned tasks. Assuming that you are of stable and sane mind, you probably proceeded as follows:

- Prioritized the tasks.
- Analyzed how the top priority tasks were to be performed.
- Implemented these tasks.
- Disregarded (at least for the time being) those tasks that had no crucial relevance at the time.

This was your way of handling the complexity at hand and your method of simplifying it in order to resolve the current problem. Well, what you did (perhaps without even realizing it) was to *apply the principle of abstraction to resolve a problem.* Rather than trying to comprehend and resolve the complete complexity of the problem right away, you chose to concentrate only on the part of it that was considered more relevant at the time.

If you take a moment to think about what you have just read, you will realize that abstraction is a method that we use constantly and consistently as we live our day-to-day lives. Life is too complex. In order to understand it, it has to be broken up into simpler components that are comprehensible and relevant at any particular time.

Abstraction lies at the very core of object-oriented analysis. With this introduction, we proceed to describe how this methodology can be applied to formulate an efficient, manageable, and powerful system.

17.2.1 Understand the Problem

The first step in the design of a system is to understand what the system is required to do. The best place to start is with the user or the client.

Users are almost always vague in their description of what they want (they are almost never vague about how soon they want it; tomorrow, or next week, at the latest!). It is unlikely that they understand the relationship between what they want and how it can be implemented.

Suppose you are required to implement a system that maintains a file of customer records. Users are to be given the ability to browse, add, change, and delete records from this file.

Talk to the user. Find out how he/she currently stores the data and manipulates it. Try to get a feeling for what the user really requires from this system. How should a customer search be done. Will it be through customer name and address, or through a preassigned customer number? What information is to be retrieved? Is there a system currently in use? What are its shortcomings? How can it be improved? Immerse yourself in the world of the user.

17.2.2 Identify Objects

An object is simply a package of information and knowledge of how that information can be manipulated. Based on the requirements stated in the previous section, the following objects can be identified:

1. An object that retrieves information for current customers.

2. An object that displays information for customers on the screen.

3. An object that adds customers to the file.

4. An object that deletes customers from the file.

We will assume that a unique identifying number is assigned to each customer, and all searches and manipulation of data are based on this key. Figure 17.1 illustrates these objects.

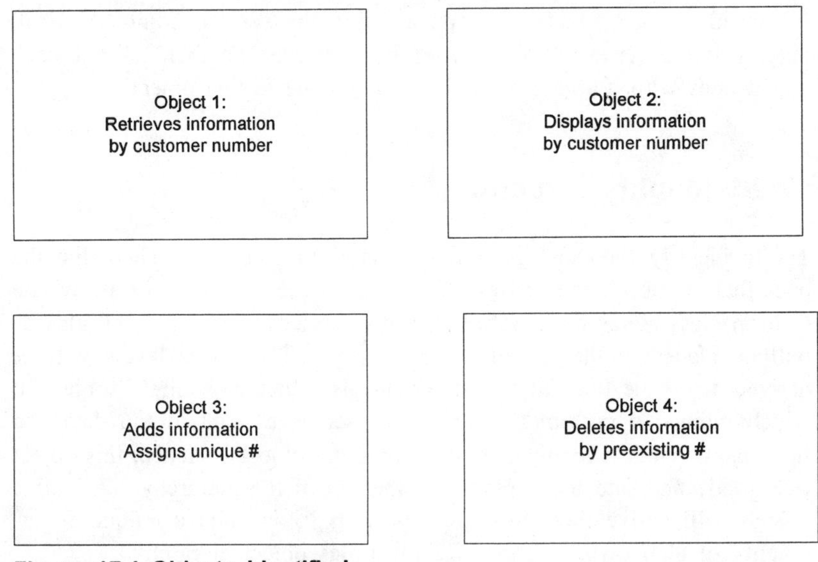

Figure 17.1 Objects Identified

Customers may come and go and the information required to be stored for each customer may vary over time. However, the functionality of each object will more or less remain the same. Objects are relatively stable. Of course, new requirements may emerge, for example, the storage and retrieval of customer responses to a survey. But this would mean the creation of a new self-contained object, which will have a functionality all its own. It should be no problem fitting this new object into the current schema, since it will be self-contained and hence will not interfere with the working of other objects. This is the beauty of object-oriented analysis. It results in a framework that can be easily expanded and modified.

Let's continue with the analysis.

17.2.3 Identify Common Attributes

Try to identify those attributes that apply to every single occurrence of the objects that you have created. In our example, we can safely state that the customer number is common to all objects.

17.2.4 Identify Common Services

In our example, the functionality of each object can be differentiated, as listed in Table 17.1.

Based on this analysis, it appears that the service common to all objects is the retrieval of a record by customer number. What each object does with it after it is retrieved is unique to that object.

17.2.5 Identify Structure

Try to identify the most general objects from your list. Then, list the ones that are specialized cases. This step of the analysis will allow you to form class hierarchies. Attributes and services common to all classes will be placed at the top of the hierarchy. The lower levels will be derived from the ones at the higher levels. In our example, object 1, which maintains customer information, seems to contain the data and functionality that is required by the remaining objects. Hence, this object is a good candidate to be placed at the top of the hierarchy. All other objects will derive their functionality from it, and add a unique functionality of their own. Figure 17.2 illustrates object hierarchy.

Table 17.1 Functionality of Objects

Object	Function
1	Retrieves information for customers. Searches for the existence of a customer number before it allows object 2 to display it. Searches for the existence of a duplicate customer number before it allows object 3 to add a new record. Searches for the existence of a customer number before it allows object 4 to delete it.
2	Displays information for customers. Searches the customer file for a customer number. If it finds the number, it displays relevant information for the number. Otherwise, it displays a message stating customer not found.
3	Adds customers. Searches the customer file for a customer number. If it finds the number, it disallows the transaction, since the customer already exists. It allows the transaction if it does not find the customer number.
4	Deletes customers. Searches the customer file for a customer number. If it does not find the number, it disallows the transaction, since the customer does not exist. It allows the transaction if the customer number is found.

17.2.6 Identify Object Dependency

Identify those objects that are dependent on others, i.e., need to access others, in order to perform the functions assigned to them. In our example, objects 2, 3, and 4 depend on object 1.

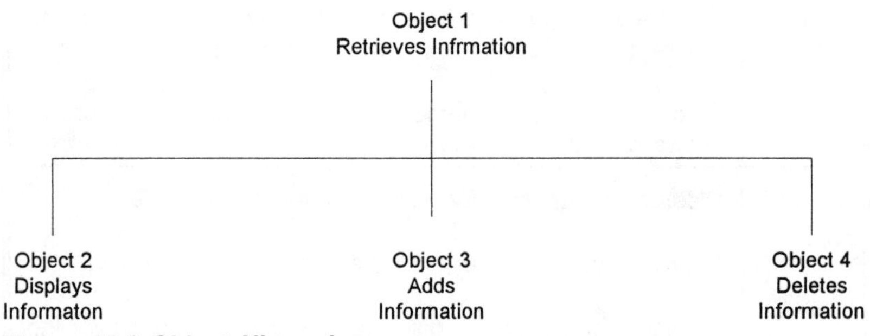

Figure 17.2 Object Hierarchy

17.2.7 Identify Message Flow of Objects

Identify the communication pattern between each object. The message pattern can be classified as inbound or outbound. Figures 17.3, 17.4, and 17.5 illustrate the message flow between the objects identified.

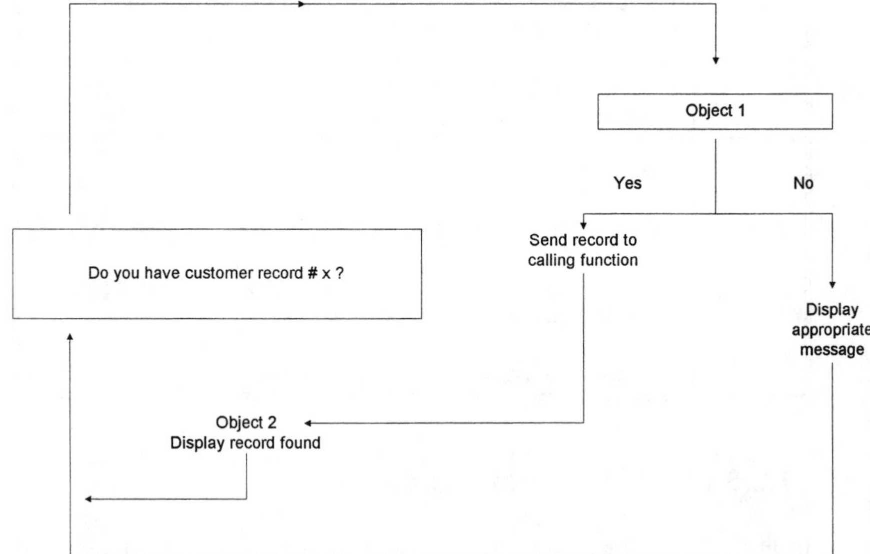

Figure 17.3 Message Flow between Objects 1 and 2

Object 1

Yes

No

Do you have customer record # x ?

Send record to calling function

Display appropriate message

Object 3
Disallow add - display message

Object 3
Add record

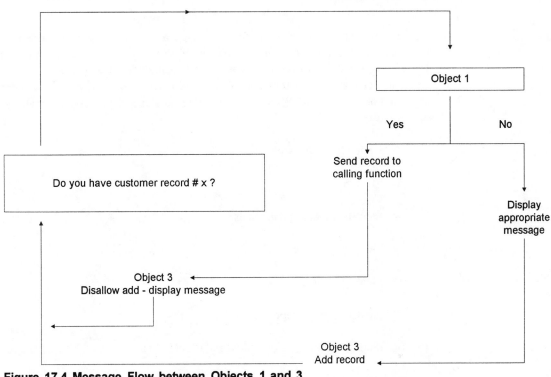

Figure 17.4 Message Flow between Objects 1 and 3

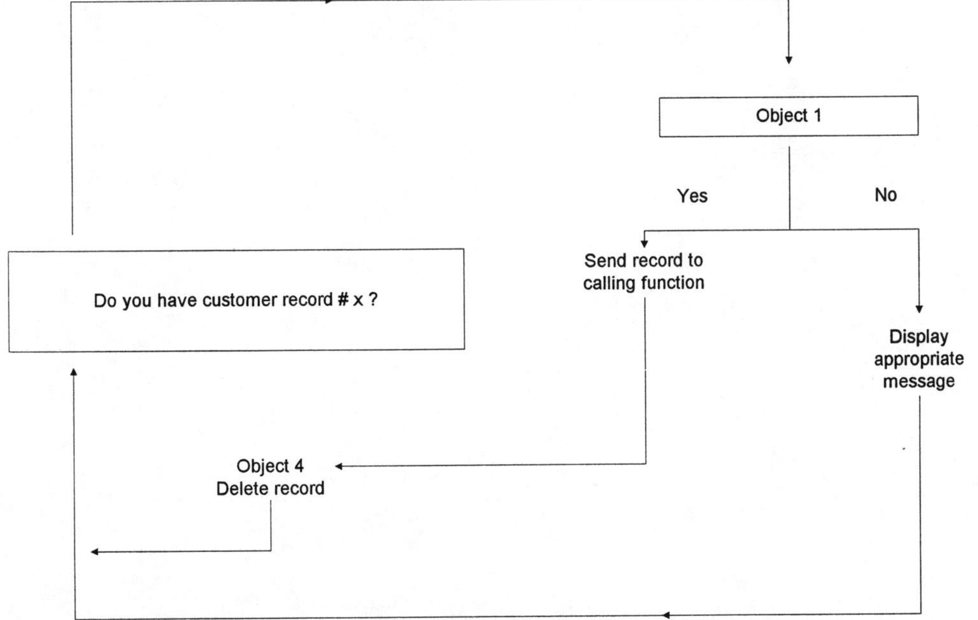

Figure 17.5 Message Flow between Objects 1 and 4

17.3 Review

In this chapter we learned how to design a system using object-oriented analysis techniques. We realized that abstraction lies at the very core of object-oriented analysis. Abstraction is a method in which aspects of a subject that are not relevant to the current purpose are ignored, in order to concentrate on those that are. Our analysis was broken down as follows:

- Understand the problem.
- Identify objects.
- Identify common attributes.
- Identify common services.
- Identify structure.
- Identify object dependency.
- Identify message flow between objects.

Chapter

18

Object-Oriented Program Design

18.1 INTRODUCTION

In the previous chapter, an object-oriented approach was used to analyze the requirements for a system that maintains and updates customer information. In this chapter, object-oriented program design will be described, and some parts of the resulting code will also be developed. As you proceed through the remaining chapters in this book, you will notice that code developed in previous chapters will be redisplayed as new code is added to it. This is done to reinforce concepts that you may have missed at the time the code was originally developed. It will also help you see the complete program all in one place, saving you the trouble of having to flip through the pages. New code will always be indicated via comments.

18.2 WHAT IS OBJECT-ORIENTED PROGRAM DESIGN?

Object-oriented programs have the remarkable ability to be continually modified, expanded, and refined with minimal changes to the basic structure of the program. The best way for you to understand the power that can be derived from object-oriented programs is by implementing the design itself. Let's begin.

18.3 A Brief Review

In the following subsections, a brief review is presented of the problem and the results of the analysis that were presented in the previous chapter.

18.3.1 Requirements

We were required to design a system that would maintain information for customers and display and update this information on an as-needed basis.

18.3.2 Objects Identified

Four objects were identified:

Object 1: Retrieves customer information
Object 2: Displays information
Object 3: Adds information
Object 4: Deletes information

18.3.3 Attributes Identified

The following attribute was found to be common to all objects:

- Customer number

18.3.4 Services Identified

The following service was found to be common between objects:

- To retrieve customer information via customer record number

18.4 Program Design

The data at hand will be analyzed and synthesized to design an object-oriented application. We will proceed as follows:

- Formulate classes

- Identify structure

- Identify object dependency
- Identify message flow between objects formulated
- Incorporate polymorphism/virtual functions into the program design

18.4.1 Formulate Classes

Upon review, we find that there is enough information to design the structure of each object. In Part 2 of the book, you learned how to declare and define classes. Recall that a class contains both data and code. The next step would be to translate the objects that have been identified into classes. Each class will be given a meaningful name. The name `del` instead of `delete` will be given to the class that will delete information, since delete is a reserved keyword.

For the sake of simplicity, assume that customer information comprises only customer number. We are more interested in the design of the program, rather than those details that do not affect the design in any way. The following elements are common to all classes:

- Customer number
- Retrieval of customer information via customer number

For now, assume that the class member functions take no parameters and return no value. Here's the first draft of each class:

```
class retrieve
   {
   int customer_numbers;

   void search(void);
   };

class display
   {
   int customer_numbers;

   void search(void);
   };

class add
   {
   int customer_numbers;

   void search(void);
   };
```

```
class del
   {
   int customer_numbers;

   void search(void);
   };
```

On further analysis, you may realize that modification of records has not been incorporated in any of the classes. It appears that the best option would be to allow modification of current records by the class `retrieve` only. In this way, the possibility of data being erroneously modified by some other unsuspecting class will be minimized. The classes `display`, `add`, and `del` are distinguished from each other by these very functions. Take a look at the new declarations of the classes:

```
class retrieve
   {
   int customer_numbers;

   void search(void);
   void modify(void);
   };

class display
   {
   int customer_numbers;

   void search(void);
   void display_info(void);
   };

class add
   {
   int customer_numbers;

   void search(void);
   void add_info(void);
   };

class del
   {
   int customer_numbers;

   void search(void);
   void delete_info(void);
   };
```

Now take a closer look at the data types of the parameters that will be passed to and returned from the member functions.

The function `search()` is required to search based on customer number, which will be unique and will be the key field. This function will be called by the remaining classes, and then sent a customer number for which to search. This customer number may or may not exist. If it exists, the function can return the customer number to the calling function. If it does not exist, the function can return a 0. The function `modify()` will take the customer number as a parameter and continue to return `void`, since it has nothing else to do. The prototypes for these functions will change inside each class as follows:

```
class retrieve
   {
   int customer_numbers;

   int search(int);
   void modify(int);
   };

class display
   {
   int customer_numbers;

   int search(int);
   void display_info(void);
   };

class add
   {
   int customer_numbers;

   int search(int);
   void add_info(void);
   };

class del
   {
   int customer_numbers;

   int search(int);
   void delete_info(void);
   };
```

An analysis of the remaining functions follows:

- `display_info()`

This function will assess the value sent back from the `search()` member function of the class `retrieve`. If it is 0, then no corresponding record was found. This function will do nothing, and the message stating as such will be displayed by the class `retrieve`. If a valid number is returned by `retrieve`, then the customer record will be displayed on the screen. Therefore, this function will take the customer number returned from search() as a parameter. It will still return void, since it has nothing else to do but display or not display the record. The prototype for display_info() will change as follows:

```
void display_info( int );
```

- add_info()

This function will also access the value returned by search(). If it is 0, then a corresponding record was not found. Hence, the current record may be added. If a nonzero value is returned, then the customer record already exists, and an attempt is being made to add a duplicate. The transaction will not be allowed. If a duplicate exists, then a message should be output stating as such. If the transaction is to be allowed, then all that has to be done is to insert the value in the next available slot of customer numbers. This function will take the customer number to be added as a parameter. It will return no value. The prototype for add_info() is as follows:

```
void add_info( int );
```

- delete_info()

This function, like add_info(), will check the value sent back from search(). If it is 0, then no corresponding record was found. This function will do nothing, since the message which indicates as such will be output within the class retrieve itself. If a nonzero value is returned, then the customer record can be deleted, and this function will display a message indicating as such. Hence, the function will take the customer number as a parameter. It will return no value. The prototype is as follows:

```
void delete_info( int );
```

Our class objects are now starting to take shape. Here's how they look:

```
class retrieve
   {
   int customer_numbers;

   int search(int);
   void modify(int);
   };

class display
   {
```

```
  int customer_numbers;

  int search(int);
  void display_info(int);
  };

class add
  {
  int customer_numbers;

  int search(int);
  void add_info(int);
  };

class del
  {
  int customer_numbers;

  int search(int);
  void delete_info(int);
  };
```

Let's take a breather and review our progress. It seems that we have:

- Figured out the different types of objects required to implement the system.
- Figured out the data and member functions each object requires.
- Figured out the data types of the return values and the arguments of the member functions.

Now it's time to incorporate the member access specifiers as private, public, and, if necessary, protected, into the class definitions. This will allow us to *encapsulate* data or *hide information.* An analysis of each class follows:

- `retrieve`

  The following conclusions can be made about this class:

  a) Customer number will be accessed by all classes. Hence, it should be made public.

  b) The `modify()` function should be the only function that is permitted to modify existing records. No other class object should be allowed to access this function. Therefore, it should be private.

c) The search() function is accessed by all other classes, hence it should be public.

This class with the appropriate access specifiers now follows:

```
class retrieve
   {
   private:
   void modify(int);

   public:
   int customer_numbers;
   int search(int number);
   };
```

■ display

The function display_info() is a general purpose function which simply displays the appropriate customer record. There is no need to make this function private. Here is the declaration:

```
class display
   {
   public:
   int customer_numbers;
   int search(int);
   void display_info( int );
   };
```

■ add

The function add_info() adds data to the current file. It has a specialized function to perform. However, we plan to to implement all of our processing inside main(). Therefore, this function should be accessible from it. This function will be public.

```
class add
   {
   public:
   int customer_numbers;
   int search(int);
   void add_info(int);
   };
```

■ delete

The function delete_info() deletes data from the current file. This function will be declared as public for the same reasons as add_info(). Here's the subsequent class declaration:

```
class del
   {
   public:
   int cutomer_no;
   int search(int);
   void delete_info(int);
   };
```

18.4.2 Identify Structure

In Chapter 17, the object hierarchy was identified. Based on this hierarchy, we can say that retrieve is the base class, and display, add, and del are derived from it. The following data items are common to all classes:

```
int customer_numbers;
int search(int);
```

Hence, these will be the common elements in retrieve, which will be derived by the remaining classes. Take a look at the class declarations:

```
class retrieve
   {
   private:
   void modify(int);

   public:
   int customer_numbers;
   int search(int);
   };

class display : public retrieve
   {
   public:
   int customer_numbers;
   void display_info(int);
   };

class add : public retrieve
   {
   public:
   int customer_numbers;
   void add_info(int);
   };

class del : public retrieve
   {
   public:
   int customer_numbers;
```

```
void delete_info(int);
};
```

Notice that the classes are being publicly derived. This results in the public members of the base class retrieve becoming public members of each class derived from it. This is fine, since the body of the code will be placed inside main(), and functions such as search() will be accessed from here. Remember, however, that the private members of retrieve, i.e., the function modify(), will continue to remain private to it. Other class objects will not be allowed to access this member. This is exactly what we want. It would be much too dangerous to allow any function to inadvertently change the information for the customer records, except those designated to do so; only the private member function modify() is given that capability.

18.4.3 Identify Object Dependency

Through the course of the discussion, the classes display, add, and del were found to be dependent on retrieve.

18.4.4 Identify Message Flow between Objects

Through the course of the program design, the communication pattern between objects was identified. This communication pattern is based on the parameters sent to and returned from class member functions. Please refer to Figures 17.3, 17.4, and 17.5 if you need to review the communication pattern. We will have each function output a response. A simple print() function in each class will be used to display the response. These print functions will be declared as public, since there is no need to make them private. In addition to this, the classes display, add, and del are derived from retrieve. Hence, they inherit customer_numbers[] from it. For this reason, there is no need to declare customer_numbers[] individually in these classes. We take these declarations out, and the result is displayed in the code that follows:

```
class retrieve
   {
   private:
   void modify(int);
   public:
   int customer_numbers;
   int search(int);
   void print(void);
   };
```

```
class display : public retrieve
   {
   public:
   void display_info(int);
   void print(void);
   };

class add : public retrieve
   {
   public:
   void add_info(int);
   void print(void);
   };

class del : public retrieve
   {
   public:
   void delete_info(int);
   void print(void);
   };
```

18.4.5 Incorporate Polymorphism/Virtual Functions

It seems that each step of the analysis stage has been translated into code, except for `main()`. Let's take another look at the class declarations, and see if they can somehow be refined further. You will notice that each class has a function called `print()`, which outputs a simple response. The name, parameters, and return value of this function are the same for all classes. However, the output will vary, based on the class object that invokes it. `print()` is a perfect candidate for a virtual function. Here are the final templates for each class:

```
class retrieve
   {
   private:
   void modify(int);

   public:
   int cutomer_numbers;
   int search(int);
   virtual void print(void);
   };

class display : public retrieve
   {
   public:
   void display_info(int);
   void print(void);
   };

class add : public retrieve
```

```
   {
   public:
   void add_info(int);
   void print(void);
   };

class delete : public retrieve
   {
   public:
   void delete_info(int);
   void print(void);
   };
```

The function is declared as `virtual` inside the base class. The appropriate response for each class will be determined at run time, based on the class object being pointed to at the time. The class declarations are now complete.

18.5 Definitions of Member Functions

We are now ready to define each member function. In the next section, the code for `main()` will be implemented. The following class member functions have to be defined, listed by class name:

- The class `retrieve`:

```
void modify(int);
int search(int);
virtual void print(void);
```

- The class `display`:

```
void display_info(int);
void print(void);
```

- The class `add`:

```
void add_info(int);
void print(void);
```

- The class `delete`:

```
void delete_info(int);
void print(void);
```

For now, to keep things simple, only the class members `search()`, print(), and display_info() will be defined. In the next two chapters, the code for the remaining member functions will be presented. This will help you understand how easy it is to expand and modify object-oriented programs. However, in order for the program to compile properly, function definitions must exist. Therefore, for now, a statement identifying the class member will be output.

In order to simplify things further, the list of valid customer numbers will be placed inside an array called customer_numbers[]. In the real world, customer number and information would be kept inside a file, which would need to be opened, read, updated, and modified as required. But this would mean getting into file I/O functions, which would just make the code longer and add unnecessary details. For now, we are more interested in program design.

You may have noticed that each class member function accesses customer_numbers[], and contains a variable with the same class name. However, just as a file is globally available to any function in a program that tries to access it, the same location in memory that contains the relevant information must be accessible to each class. Therefore, the declaration of customer_numbers[] will be moved outside of the class declarations, thereby enabling it to be a globally accessible array. Here are the definitions. Comments and identifying statements have been added for your convenience:

```
// valid customer numbers are delimited by a 0
int customer_numbers[6] = {100, 200, 300, 400, 500, 0};

// modify takes the customer number to modify as a parameter.
// it returns no value.
void retrieve::modify(int)
{
   cout << "Inside modify \n";
}

// retrieve takes the customer number to search
// for as a paramter.
// it returns the customer number if found.
// it returns 0 if customer number is not found.
int retrieve::search(int number)
{
   int i = 0;
   cout << "Inside search \n";

   while (customer_numbers[i] != 0)
      {
      if (number != customer_numbers[i])
         {
         i++;
         }
      else
```

```
            {
            // print() is a virtual function.
            // Based on the object which is accessing
            // search(), the appropriate print()
            // function will be called.
             print();

             number = customer_numbers[i];
             return number;
             }
        }

    // if a corresponding record is not found, then the print()
    // statement for the base class will be called.
    retrieve::print();

    return 0;
}

void retrieve::print(void)
{
    cout << "Record not found!! \n";
}

// display_info takes the customer number returned from search()
// as a parameter.
// It has nothing to return.
void display::display_info(int temp)
{
    cout << "Inside display_info \n";
    cout << "Customer number is " << temp << " \n";
}

void display::print(void)
{
    cout << "Here's a copy of the record! \n";
}

void add::add_info(void)
{
    cout << "Inside add_info \n";
}

void add::print(void)
{
    cout << "Attempt to add duplicate record! \n" <<
          "Transaction disallowed!! \n";
}

void del::delete_info(int)
{
    cout << "Inside delete_info \n";
}

void del::print(void)
```

```
{
  cout << "Record ready to be deleted! \n";
}
```

18.6 MAIN()

It is now time to implement the code for `main()`. Remember that the display function will request `search()` to find a customer record. If found, `display_info()` will display it. If not, the appropriate message will be dislayed. The remaining functions will be developed in the next two chapters. Here's the code for `main()`:

```
main(void)
{
   int temp, number;
   retrieve retrieve_customer;
   display display_customer;
   add add_customer;
   del delete_customer;

   // search for customer number 100
     number = 100;

   temp = display_customer.search(number);

   if (temp > 0)
   {
     display_customer.display_info(temp);
   }
}
```

And, for your convenience, the complete program is displayed in one place, so that you can see the logical progression of object-oriented analysis into object-oriented program design.

```
// test18_1.cpp

#include <iostream.h>

int customer_numbers[6] = {100, 200, 300, 400, 500, 0};

// retrieve is the base class
class retrieve
   {
   private:
   void modify(int);

   public:
   int search(int number);
   virtual void print(void);
```

```
   };

// display is publicly derived from retrieve
class display : public retrieve
   {
   public:
   void display_info(int temp);
   void print(void);
   };

// add is publicly derived from retrieve
class add : public retrieve
   {
   public:
   void add_info(void);
   void print(void);
   };

// del is publicly derived from retrieve
class del : public retrieve
   {
   public:
   void delete_info(int);
   void print(void);
   };

// modify takes the customer number to modify as a parameter.
// it returns no value.
void retrieve::modify(int)
{
   cout << "Inside modify \n";
}

// search() takes the customer number to search for
// as a paramter.
// it returns the customer number if found.
// it returns 0 if customer number is not found.
int retrieve::search(int number)
{
   int i = 0;
   cout << "Inside search \n";

   while (customer_numbers[i] != 0)
      {
      if (number != customer_numbers[i])
         {
         i++;
         }
      else
         {
         // print() is a virtual function.
         // Based on the object which is accessing
         // search(), the appropriate print()
         // function will be called.
          print();
```

```
            number = customer_numbers[i];
            return number;
            }
        }

    // if a corresponding record is not found, then the print()
    // statement for the base class will be called.
    retrieve::print();

    return 0;
}

void retrieve::print(void)
{
    cout << "Record not found!! \n";
}

// display_info takes the customer number returned from search()
// as a parameter.
// It has nothing to return.
void display::display_info(int temp)
{
    cout << "Inside display_info \n";
    cout << "Customer number is " << temp << " \n";
}

void display::print(void)
{
    cout << "Here's a copy of the record! \n";
}

void add::add_info(void)
{
    cout << "Inside add_info \n";
}

void add::print(void)
{
    cout << "Attempt to add duplicate record! \n" <<
        "Transaction disallowed!! \n";
}

void del::delete_info(int)
{
    cout << "Inside delete_info \n";
}

void del::print(void)
{
    cout << "Record ready to be deleted! \n";
}


main(void)
{
```

```
   int temp, number;
   retrieve retrieve_customer;
   display display_customer;
   add add_customer;
   del delete_customer;

   // search for customer number 100
   // display it, if found
   number = 100;
   temp = display_customer.search(number);

   if (temp > 0)
   {
      display_customer.display_info(temp);
   }
}
```

Compiling and running this program give the following output:

```
Inside search
Here's a copy of the record!
Inside display_info
Customer number is 100
```

The output should be self-explanatory. Notice the invocation of the virtual `print()` function inside `search()`. Inside `main()`, the code:

```
      else
         {
         // print() is a virtual function.
         // Based on the object which is accessing
         // search(), the appropriate print()
         // function will be called.
          print();
```

resulted in the following statement being output:

```
Here's a copy of the record!
```

This is the `print()` function version of the class `display`.

In those instances where the `search()` function fails to find a record, the `print()` function for the base class `retrieve` will will called:

```
   // statement for the base class will be called.
   retrieve::print();
```

`Test18_1.cpp` will now be modified to illustrate the search for a non-existent customer number:

```
// test18_2.cpp
```

```
#include <iostream.h>

int customer_numbers[6] = {100, 200, 300, 400, 500, 0};

// retrieve is the base class
class retrieve
   {
   private:
   void modify(int);

   public:
   int search(int number);
   virtual void print(void);
   };

// display is publicly derived from retrieve
class display : public retrieve
   {
   public:
   void display_info(int temp);
   void print(void);
   };

// add is publicly derived from retrieve
class add : public retrieve
   {
   public:
   void add_info(void);
   void print(void);
   };

// del is publicly derived from retrieve
class del : public retrieve
   {
   public:
   void delete_info(int);
   void print(void);
   };

// modify takes the customer number to modify as a parameter.
// it returns no value.
void retrieve::modify(int)
{
   cout << "Inside modify \n";
}

// search() takes the customer number to search for
// as a paramter.
// it returns the customer number if found.
// it returns 0 if customer number is not found.
int retrieve::search(int number)
{
   int i = 0;
   cout << "Inside search \n";
```

```
    while (customer_numbers[i] != 0)
        {
        if (number != customer_numbers[i])
            {
            i++;
            }
        else
            {
            // print() is a virtual function.
            // Based on the object which is accessing
            // search(), the appropriate print()
            // function will be called.
             print();

             number = customer_numbers[i];
             return number;
             }
        }

    // if a corresponding record is not found, then the print()
    // statement for the base class will be called.
    retrieve::print();
    return 0;
}

void retrieve::print(void)
{
    cout << "Record not found!! \n";
}

// display_info takes the customer number returned from search()
// as a parameter.
// It has nothing to return.
void display::display_info(int temp)
{
    cout << "Inside display_info \n";
    cout << "Customer number is " << temp << " \n";
}

void display::print(void)
{
    cout << "Here's a copy of the record! \n";
}

void add::add_info(void)
{
    cout << "Inside add_info \n";
}

void add::print(void)
{
    cout << "Attempt to add duplicate record! \n" <<
        "Transaction disallowed!! \n";
}
```

```
void del::delete_info(int)
{
   cout << "Inside delete_info \n";
}

void del::print(void)
{
   cout << "Record ready to be deleted! \n";
}

main(void)
{
   int temp, number;
   retrieve retrieve_customer;
   display display_customer;
   add add_customer;
   del delete_customer;

   // search for non-existent customer number 10
   // display it, if found
   number = 10;
   temp = display_customer.search(number);

   if (temp > 0)
   {
      display_customer.display_info(temp);
   }
}
```

Compiling and executing this program result in the following output:

```
Inside search
Record not found!!
```

The output should be self-explanatory.

18.7 Review

In this chapter, the object-oriented analysis of a problem was synthesized into the object-oriented design of a sample C++ application. Each step of the analysis was translated into code, as illustrated in Table 18.1:

Table 18.1 Object-Oriented Program Design

Object-oriented analysis	Object-oriented program design
Identify objects	Formulate classes
Identify attributes	Formulate class data members
Identify services	Formulate class member functions Include access specifiers
Identify structure	Formulate base and derived classes
Identify message flow	Formulate the code for main()
Identify object dependency	Formulate the code for main() Introduce virtual functions, if possible

Chapter

19

Expansion of Object-Oriented Programs

19.1 Introduction

In this chapter, the prewritten code for the system that was analyzed and designed in Chapters 17 and 18 will be expanded. This chapter will develop the code for the modify() function. The next two chapters will develop the code for the add_info() and delete_info() functions.

19.2 The modify() Function

For your convenience, the retrieve class is redisplayed. The modify() function is a private member of this class.

```
class retrieve
   {
   private:
   int modify(int);

   public:
   int search(int number);
   virtual void print(void);
   };
```

We are interested in somehow encapsulating the modification of existing customer records to one function only. That is why this function was made private in the first place, i.e., to be inaccessible to any object other than that of type retrieve. After reviewing the class declaration, it is obvious that only search() can access this function, because this is the only other class member function in the class. But the functionality of search() is unique, so the idea is not to incorporate any further logic into it. search() is required to search for the existence or nonexistence of a customer record and return an appropriate value, and that's it. It seems that a new function will have to be created within the class retrieve. This function will have to be public, so that it is accessible from main(). Here's the revised template:

```
class retrieve
   {
   private:
   int modify(int);

   public:
   int search(int number);
   virtual void print(void);
   void modify_record(int);
   };
```

The function modify_record will do a search on the customer number that is to be modified. If the number is found, the private function modify() will be called, with the customer number to be modified as an argument. modify() will return the modified customer number to modify_record().

However, it seems that we neglected to take into account that retrieve is a base class for display, add, and del. All public members of retrieve will become public members of the derived classes. Therefore, a class object of any one of these classes will be able to access modify_record(), for example:

```
display_customer.modify_record(100);
```

or

```
add_customer.modify_record(200);
```

and thereby gain access to the function modify(). This is not at all desirable. So how will this problem be resolved? Well, recall those friendly friend functions? We can make modify_record a friend function of the class retrieve. A friend function has the ability to access the private members of a class. But, at the same time, it is not a part of the class that it is a friend of. Therefore, it cannot be a derived member for any classes derived from the base class of which it is a friend. This is exactly what we want. Here's the code. First, here are the class declarations:

```
// test19_1.cpp

#include <iostream.h>

int customer_numbers[6] = {100, 200, 300, 400, 500, 0};

// retrieve is the base class
class retrieve
   {
   private:
   int modify(int);

   public:
   int search(int number);
   friend void modify_record(int number);
   virtual void print(void);
   };

// display is publicly derived from retrieve
class display : public retrieve
   {
   public:
   void display_info(int temp);
   void print(void);
   };

// add is publicly derived from retrieve
class add : public retrieve
   {
   public:
   void add_info(void);
   void print(void);
   };

// del is publicly derived from retrieve
class del : public retrieve
   {
   public:
   void delete_info(int);
   void print(void);
   };
```

Next, we present the class definitions. We are obliged to move the declaration of an instance of a class of type `retrieve` before the definition of `modify()`, since `modify()` references it. Failure to do so would result in an error message from the compiler stating that the object `retrieve_customer` is undefined.

```
retrieve retrieve_customer;

// modify_record calls modify().
// it takes the customer number to be modified as a parameter.
// it returns no value.
```

```
// it is a friend function of the class retrieve.
// This enables this function and this function alone
// to modify the customer record.
void modify_record(int number)
{
   int i = 0;
   cout << "Inside modify_record \n";

   while (customer_numbers[i] != 0)
      {
      if (number != customer_numbers[i])
         {
         i++;
         }
      else
         {
         customer_numbers[i] =
             retrieve_customer.modify(customer_numbers[i]);
         return;
         }
      }

   cout << "Record not found! \n";
}

// modify takes the customer number to be modified
// as a parameter. it returns the modified value to the
// calling function.
int retrieve::modify(int number)
{
   cout << "Inside modify \n";
   number = number + 55;
   cout << "Record modified \n";
   return number;
}

// search() takes the customer number to search for
// as a parameter. it returns the customer number if found.
// it returns 0 if customer number is not found.
int retrieve::search(int number)
{
   int i = 0;

   cout << "Inside search \n";

   while (customer_numbers[i] != 0)
      {
      if (number != customer_numbers[i])
         {
         i++;
         }
      else
         {
         // print() is a virtual function.
         // Based on the object which is accessing
```

```
            // search(), the appropriate print()
            // function will be called.
             print();
             number = customer_numbers[i];
             return number;
             }
        }

    // if a corresponding record is not found, then the print()
    // statement for the base class will be called.
    retrieve::print();

    return 0;
}

void retrieve::print(void)
{
    cout << "Record not found!! \n";
}

// display_info takes the customer number returned from search()
// as a parameter.
// It has nothing to return.
void display::display_info(int temp)
{
    cout << "Customer number is " << temp << " \n";
}

void display::print(void)
{
    cout << "Here's the record! \n";
}

void add::add_info(void)
{
    cout << "Inside add_info \n";
}

void add::print(void)
{
    cout << "Attempt to add duplicate record! \n" <<
       "Transaction disallowed!! \n";
}

void del::delete_info(int)
{
    cout << "Inside delete_info \n";
}

void del::print(void)
{
    cout << "Record ready to be deleted! \n";
}
```

And finally, here is the code for `main()`. The customer array is output so that you can see how it was modified:

```
main(void)
{
   int temp, i, number;

   display display_customer;
   add add_customer;
   del delete_customer;

   // search for customer number 200
   number = 200;
   temp = display_customer.search(number);

   if (temp > 0)
   {
      display_customer.display_info(temp);
   }

   // modify customer number 200
   modify_record(number);

   for (i = 0; i < 6; i++)
      {
      cout << "Customer_numbers[" << i << "] is " <<
          customer_numbers[i] << "\n";
      }
}
```

Compiling and running this program result in the following outptut:

```
Inside search
Here's the record!
Customer number is 200
Inside modify_record
Inside modify
Record modified
Customer_numbers[0] is 100
Customer_numbers[1] is 255
Customer_numbers[2] is 300
Customer_numbers[3] is 400
Customer_numbers[4] is 500
Customer_numbers[5] is 0
```

Customer number 200 is searched for and displayed, via `display_info()`. Then, this record is modified by adding 55 to its current value. The output should be self-explanatory.

19.3 MODIFCATION OF A NONEXISTENT CUSTOMER RECORD

Let's try to modify a nonexistent customer record. As usual, the class declarations and definitions are shown first:

```
// test19_2.cpp

#include <iostream.h>

int customer_numbers[6] = {100, 200, 300, 400, 500, 0};

// retrieve is the base class
class retrieve
   {
   private:
   int modify(int);

   public:
   int search(int number);
   friend void modify_record(int number);
   virtual void print(void);
   };

// display is publicly derived from retrieve
class display : public retrieve
   {
   public:
   void display_info(int temp);
   void print(void);
   };

// add is publicly derived from retrieve
class add : public retrieve
   {
   public:
   void add_info(void);
   void print(void);
   };

// del is publicly derived from retrieve
class del : public retrieve
   {
   public:
   void delete_info(int temp);
   void print(void);
   };

retrieve retrieve_customer;

// modify_record calls modify().
// it takes the customer number to be modified as a parameter.
// it returns no value.
// it is a friend function of the class retrieve.
```

```
// This enables this function and this function alone
// to modify the customer record.
void modify_record(int number)
{
   int i = 0;
   cout << "Inside modify_record \n";

   while (customer_numbers[i] != 0)
      {
      if (number != customer_numbers[i])
         {
         i++;
         }
      else
         {
         customer_numbers[i] =
              retrieve_customer.modify(customer_numbers[i]);
         return;
         }
      }
   cout << "Record not found! \n";
}

// modify takes the customer number to be modified as
// a parameter. it returns the modified value to the
// calling function.
int retrieve::modify(int number)
{
   cout << "Inside modify \n";
   number = number + 55;
   cout << "Record modified \n";
   return number;
}

// search() takes the customer number to search for
// as a paramter. it returns the customer number if found.
// it returns 0 if customer number is not found.
int retrieve::search(int number)
{
   int i = 0;

   cout << "Inside search \n";

   while (customer_numbers[i] != 0)
      {
      if (number != customer_numbers[i])
         {
         i++;
         }
      else
         {
         // print() is a virtual function.
         // Based on the object which is accessing
         // search(), the appropriate print()
         // function will be called.
```

```
          print();

          number = customer_numbers[i];
          return number;
          }
      }

   // if a corresponding record is not found, then the print()
   // statement for the base class will be called.
   retrieve::print();

   return 0;
}

void retrieve::print(void)
{
   cout << "Record not found!! \n";
}

// display_info takes the customer number returned from search()
// as a parameter.
// It has nothing to return.
void display::display_info(int temp)
{
   cout << "Customer number is " << temp << " \n";
}

void display::print(void)
{
   cout << "Here's the record! \n";
}

void add::add_info(void)
{
   cout << "Inside add_info \n";
}

void add::print(void)
{
   cout << "Attempt to add duplicate record! \n" <<
      "Transaction disallowed!! \n";
}

void del::delete_info(int)
{
   cout << "Inside delete_info \n";
}

void del::print(void)
{
   cout << "Record ready to be deleted! \n";
}
```

And here's the code for `main()`**:**

```
main(void)
{
   int temp, i, number;

   display display_customer;
   add add_customer;
   del delete_customer;

   // search for non-existent customer number 250
   number = 250;
   temp = display_customer.search(number);

   if (temp > 0)
   {
      display_customer.display_info(temp);
   }

   // modify non-existent customer number 250
   modify_record(number);

   for (i = 0; i < 6; i++)
      {
      cout << "Customer_numbers[" << i << "] is " <<
          customer_numbers[i] << "\n";
      }
}
```

Compiling and running this program give the following output:

```
Inside search
Record not found!!
Inside modify_record
Record not found!
Customer_numbers[0] is 100
Customer_numbers[1] is 200
Customer_numbers[2] is 300
Customer_numbers[3] is 400
Customer_numbers[4] is 500
Customer_numbers[5] is 0
```

The output should be self-explanatory.

19.4 Accessing modify() via Nonmember Class Objects

And now, let's try to have some other class object access modify(). Here's the code:

```
// test19_3.cpp

#include <iostream.h>

int customer_numbers[6] = {100, 200, 300, 400, 500, 0};

// retrieve is the base class
class retrieve
   {
   private:
   int modify(int);

   public:
   int search(int number);
   friend void modify_record(int number);
   virtual void print(void);
   };

// display is publicly derived from retrieve
class display : public retrieve
   {
   public:
   void display_info(int temp);
   void print(void);
   };

// add is publicly derived from retrieve
class add : public retrieve
   {
   public:
   void add_info(void);
   void print(void);
   };

// del is publicly derived from retrieve
class del : public retrieve
   {
   public:
   void delete_info(int);
   void print(void);
   };

retrieve retrieve_customer;

// modify_record calls modify().
// it takes the customer number to be modified as a parameter.
// it returns no value.
// it is a friend function of the class retrieve.
// This enables this function and this function alone
// to modify the customer record.
void modify_record(int number)
{
   int i = 0;
   cout << "Inside modify_record \n";
```

```
   while (customer_numbers[i] != 0)
      {
      if (number != customer_numbers[i])
         {
         i++;
         }
      else
         {
         customer_numbers[i] =
             retrieve_customer.modify(customer_numbers[i]);
         return;
         }
      }
   cout << "Record not found! \n";
}

// modify takes the customer number to be modified
// as a parameter. it returns the modified value to the
// calling function.
int retrieve::modify(int number)
{
   cout << "Inside modify \n";
   number = number + 55;
   cout << "Record modified \n";
   return number;
}

// search() takes the customer number to search for
// as a paramter. it returns the customer number if found.
// it returns 0 if customer number is not found.
int retrieve::search(int number)
{
   int i = 0;

   cout << "Inside search \n";

   while (customer_numbers[i] != 0)
      {
      if (number != customer_numbers[i])
         {
         i++;
         }
      else
         {
         // print() is a virtual function.
         // Based on the object which is accessing
         // search(), the appropriate print()
         // function will be called.
          print();

          number = customer_numbers[i];
          return number;
          }
      }
```

```
  // if a corresponding record is not found, then the print()
  // statement for the base class will be called.
  retrieve::print();

  return 0;
}

void retrieve::print(void)
{
  cout << "Record not found!! \n";
}

// display_info takes the customer number returned from search()
// as a parameter.
// It has nothing to return.
void display::display_info(int temp)
{
  cout << "Customer number is " << temp << " \n";
}

void display::print(void)
{
  cout << "Here's the record! \n";
}

void add::add_info(void)
{
  cout << "Inside add_info \n";
}

void add::print(void)
{
  cout << "Attempt to add duplicate record! \n" <<
     "Transaction disallowed!! \n";
}

void del::delete_info(int)
{
  cout << "Inside delete_info \n";
}

void del::print(void)
{
  cout << "Record ready to be deleted! \n";
}

main(void)
{
  int temp, i, number;

  display display_customer;
  add add_customer;
  del delete_customer;

  // search for customer number 200
```

```
    number = 200;
    temp = display_customer.search(number);

    if (temp > 0)
    {
       display_customer.display_info(temp);
    }

    // modify customer number 200
    // try to invoke modify as an instance of display_customer
    display_customer.modify(number);

    for (i = 0; i < 6; i++)
       {
       cout << "Customer_numbers[" << i << "] is " <<
           customer_numbers[i] << "\n";
       }
}
```

Inside main(), modify() is accessed as follows:

```
    display_customer.modify(number);
```

But modify() is a private function, so not only can no other class access it, but the function itself cannot be invoked from main(). Compiling this version yields the following unfriendly message from the compiler:

```
Error: retrieve::modify() is not accessible
```

Perfect! Just what we wanted. We have successfully encapsulated the functionality of the modify() function.

By now you must have noticed a few choice features about the sample programs and output:

- None of the existing class definitions were required to be modified, save for the addition of code for the function that was devloped.
- Therefore, if the preexisting classes worked before the insertion of the new code, they must work now.
- Therefore, there is no need to retest their functionality.

19.5 Review

In this chapter, we expanded the code for an existing program, and in the process realized the power that can be derived from object-oriented programs. The basic structure (given that you took the time to design it as best as you could in the first place) remains unaltered. Preexisting code for existing classes does not have to be retested. Functionality of each object is encapsulated. Debugging becomes easy for this very reason.

Chapter

20

Adding to Object-Oriented Application

20.1 INTRODUCTION

In this chapter, the system designed in Chapter 17, and developed in Chapters 18 and 19, will be expanded. In this chapter, code for the delete_info function will be developed.

20.2 THE DELETE_INFO() FUNCTION

To start things off, search() will be invoked to search for the customer number that is to be deleted. If it is found, delete_info() will proceed to delete it. In our example, the appropriate slot will simply be set to 0. The remaining elements of the array will be moved up one slot, so that all existing customer record numbers are contiguous. If customer record is not found, the appropriate message will be displayed by search(). Here's the code:

```
// test20_1.cpp

#include <iostream.h>

int customer_numbers[6] = {100, 200, 300, 400, 500, 0};

// retrieve is the base class
class retrieve
   {
   private:
   int modify(int);
```

```
   public:
   int search(int number);
   friend void modify_record(int number);
   virtual void print(void);
   };

// display is publicly derived from retrieve
class display : public retrieve
   {
   public:
   void display_info(int temp);
   void print(void);
   };

// add is publicly derived from retrieve
class add : public retrieve
   {
   public:
   void add_info(void);
   void print(void);
   };

// del is publicly derived from retrieve
class del : public retrieve
   {
   public:
   void delete_info(int temp);
   void print(void);
   };

retrieve retrieve_customer;

// modify_record calls modify().
// it takes the customer number to be modified as a parameter.
// it returns no value.
// it is a friend function of the class retrieve.
// This enables this function and this function alone
// to modify the customer record.
void modify_record(int number)
{
   int i = 0;
   cout << "Inside modify_record \n";

   while (customer_numbers[i] != 0)
      {
      if (number != customer_numbers[i])
         {
         i++;
         }
      else
         {
         customer_numbers[i] =
             retrieve_customer.modify(customer_numbers[i]);
         return;
         }
```

```
    }
  cout << "Record not found! \n";
}

// modify takes the customer number to be modified
// as a parameter. it returns the modified value to the calling
function.
int retrieve::modify(int number)
{
   cout << "Inside modify \n";
   number = number + 55;
   cout << "Record modified \n";
   return number;
}

// search() takes the customer number to search for
// as a paramter. it returns a copy of the customer number
// if found.
// it returns 0 if customer number is not found.
int retrieve::search(int number)
{
   int i = 0;

   cout << "Inside search \n";
   while (customer_numbers[i] != 0)
      {
      if (number != customer_numbers[i])
         {
         i++;
         }
      else
         {
         // print() is a virtual function.
         // Based on the object which is accessing
         // search(), the appropriate print()
         // function will be called.
          print();

          number = customer_numbers[i];
          return number;
          }
      }

   // if a corresponding record is not found, then the print()
   // statement for the base class will be called.
   retrieve::print();

   return 0;
}

void retrieve::print(void)
{
   cout << "Record not found!! \n";
}
```

```
// display_info takes the customer number returned from search()
// as a parameter.
// It has nothing to return.
void display::display_info(int temp)
{
   cout << "Customer number is " << temp << " \n";
}

void display::print(void)
{
   cout << "Here's the record! \n";
}

void add::add_info(void)
{
   cout << "Inside add_info \n";
}

void add::print(void)
{
   cout << "Attempt to add duplicate record! \n" <<
      "Transaction disallowed!! \n";
}
```

So far, the code is the same. The code for `del::delete_info()` is developed next:

```
void del::delete_info(int temp)
{
   cout << "Inside delete_info \n";
   int i = 0;
   while (customer_numbers[i] != 0)
      {
      if (temp != customer_numbers[i])
         {
         i++;
         }
      else
         {

         // move remaining array in by 1
         while (customer_numbers[i+1] != 0)
            {
            customer_numbers[i] = customer_numbers[i+1];
            i++;
            }

         // zero out the previous last element
         customer_numbers[i] = 0;
         return;
         }
      }
   retrieve::print();
}
```

```
void del::print(void)
{
   cout << "Record ready to be deleted! \n";
}
```

And finally, here's the code for `main()`. The code developed previously is intact.

```
main(void)
{
   int temp, i, number;

   display display_customer;
   add add_customer;
   del delete_customer;

   // search for customer number 200
   number = 200;
   temp = display_customer.search(number);

   if (temp > 0)
   {
      display_customer.display_info(temp);
   }

   // modify customer number 200
   modify_record(number);

   // search for customer number 300
   // if found, delete it.
   temp = delete_customer.search(300);

   if (temp > 0)
   {
      delete_customer.delete_info(temp);
   }

   for (i = 0; i < 6; i++)
      {
      cout << "Customer_numbers[" << i << "] is " <<
          customer_numbers[i] << "\n";
      }
}
```

Compiling and running this program result in the following output:

```
Inside search
Here's the record!
Customer number is 200
Inside modify_record
Inside modify
Record modified
```

```
Inside search
Record ready to be deleted!
Inside delete_info
Customer_numbers[0] is 100
Customer_numbers[1] is 255
Customer_numbers[2] is 400
Customer_numbers[3] is 500
Customer_numbers[4] is 0
Customer_numbers[5] is 0
```

The output should be self-explanatory.

20.3 Deletion of a Nonexistent Customer Record

Let's try to delete a record that does not exist in customer_numbers[]. Here's the code:

```
// test20_2.cpp

#include <iostream.h>

int customer_numbers[6] = {100, 200, 300, 400, 500, 0};

// retrieve is the base class
class retrieve
   {
   private:
   int modify(int);

   public:
   int search(int number);
   friend void modify_record(int number);
   virtual void print(void);
   };

// display is publicly derived from retrieve
class display : public retrieve
   {
   public:
   void display_info(int temp);
   void print(void);
   };

// add is publicly derived from retrieve
class add : public retrieve
   {
   public:
   void add_info(void);
   void print(void);
   };
```

```
// del is publicly derived from retrieve
class del : public retrieve
   {
   public:
   void delete_info(int temp);
   void print(void);
   };

retrieve retrieve_customer;

// modify_record calls modify().
// it takes the customer number to be modified as a parameter.
// it returns no value.
// it is a friend function of the class retrieve.
// This enables this function and this function alone
// to modify the customer record.
void modify_record(int number)
{
   int i = 0;
   cout << "Inside modify_record \n";

   while (customer_numbers[i] != 0)
      {
      if (number != customer_numbers[i])
         {
         i++;
         }
      else
         {
         customer_numbers[i] =
              retrieve_customer.modify(customer_numbers[i]);
         return;
         }
      }
   cout << "Record not found! \n";
}

// modify takes the customer number to be modified
// as a parameter. it returns the modified value to the
// calling function.
int retrieve::modify(int number)
{
   cout << "Inside modify \n";
   number = number + 55;
   cout << "Record modified \n";
   return number;
}

// search() takes the customer number to search for
// as a parameter. it returns the customer number if found.
// it returns 0 if customer number is not found.
int retrieve::search(int number)
{
   int i = 0;
```

```
   cout << "Inside search \n";
   while (customer_numbers[i] != 0)
      {
      if (number != customer_numbers[i])
         {
         i++;
         }
      else
         {
         // print() is a virtual function.
         // Based on the object which is accessing
         // search(), the appropriate print()
         // function will be called.
          print();
          number = customer_numbers[i];
          return number;
          }
      }

   // if a corresponding record is not found, then the print()
   // statement for the base class will be called.
   retrieve::print();

   return 0;
}

void retrieve::print(void)
{
   cout << "Record not found!! \n";
}

// display_info takes the customer number returned from search()
// as a parameter.
// It has nothing to return.
void display::display_info(int temp)
{
   cout << "Customer number is " << temp << " \n";
}

void display::print(void)
{
   cout << "Here's the record! \n";
}

void add::add_info(void)
{
   cout << "Inside add_info \n";
}

void add::print(void)
{
   cout << "Attempt to add duplicate record! \n" <<
      "Transaction disallowed!! \n";
}
```

```
void del::delete_info(int temp)
{
   cout << "Inside delete_info \n";
   int i = 0;

   while (customer_numbers[i] != 0)
      {
      if (temp != customer_numbers[i])
         {
         i++;
         }
      else
         {
         // move remaining array in by 1
         while (customer_numbers[i+1] != 0)
            {
            customer_numbers[i] = customer_numbers[i+1];
            i++;
            }

         // zero out the previous last element
         customer_numbers[i] = 0;
         return;
         }
      }
   retrieve::print();
}

void del::print(void)
{
   cout << "Record ready to be deleted! \n";
}

main(void)
{
   int temp, i, number;

   display display_customer;
   add add_customer;
   del delete_customer;

   // search for customer number 200
   number = 200;
   temp = display_customer.search(number);

   if (temp > 0)
   {
      display_customer.display_info(temp);
   }

   // modify customer number 200
   modify_record(number);

   // search for non-existent customer number 350
   // if found, delete it.
```

```
   temp = delete_customer.search(350);

   if (temp > 0)
   {
      delete_customer.delete_info(temp);
   }

   for (i = 0; i < 6; i++)
      {
      cout << "Customer_numbers[" << i << "] is " <<
          customer_numbers[i] << "\n";
      }
}
```

Compiling and running this program give the following output:

```
Inside search
Here's the record!
Customer number is 200
Inside modify_record
Inside modify
Record modified
Inside search
Record not found!
Customer_numbers[0] is 100
Customer_numbers[1] is 255
Customer_numbers[2] is 300
Customer_numbers[3] is 400
Customer_numbers[4] is 500
Customer_numbers[5] is 0
```

As you can see, the array of customer numbers remains unchanged. The output is self-explanatory.

20.4 ACCESS OF DELETE_INFO() BY A NONCLASS MEMBER

Finally, a nonclass member attempts to delete a customer number. Here's the code:

```
// test20_3.cpp

#include <iostream.h>

int customer_numbers[6] = {100, 200, 300, 400, 500, 0};

// retrieve is the base class
class retrieve
   {
   private:
   int modify(int);
```

```
   public:
   int search(int number);
   friend void modify_record(int number);
   virtual void print(void);
   };

// display is publicly derived from retrieve
class display : public retrieve
   {
   public:
   void display_info(int temp);
   void print(void);
   };

// add is publicly derived from retrieve
class add : public retrieve
   {
   public:
   void add_info(void);
   void print(void);
   };

// del is publicly derived from retrieve
class del : public retrieve
   {
   public:
   void delete_info(int temp);
   void print(void);
   };

retrieve retrieve_customer;

// modify_record calls modify().
// it takes the customer number to be modified as a parameter.
// it returns no value.
// it is a friend function of the class retrieve.
// This enables this function and this function alone
// to modify the customer record.
void modify_record(int number)
{
   int i = 0;
   cout << "Inside modify_record \n";

   while (customer_numbers[i] != 0)
      {
      if (number != customer_numbers[i])
         {
         i++;
         }
      else
         {
         customer_numbers[i] =
              retrieve_customer.modify(customer_numbers[i]);
         return;
         }
```

```
      }
   cout << "Record not found! \n";
}

// modify takes the customer number to be modified
// as a parameter.
// it returns the modified value to the calling function.
int retrieve::modify(int number)
{
   cout << "Inside modify \n";
   number = number + 55;
   cout << "Record modified \n";
   return number;
}

// store takes the customer number to search for as a paramter.
// it returns the customer number if found.
// it returns 0 if customer number is not found.
int retrieve::search(int number)
{
   int i = 0;
   cout << "Inside search \n";

   while (customer_numbers[i] != 0)
      {
      if (number != customer_numbers[i])
         {
         i++;
         }
      else
         {
         // print() is a virtual function.
         // Based on the object which is accessing
         // search(), the appropriate print()
         // function will be called.
          print();

          number = customer_numbers[i];
          return number;
          }
      }

   // if a corresponding record is not found, then the print()
   // statement for the base class will be called.
   retrieve::print();

   return 0;
}

void retrieve::print(void)
{
   cout << "Record not found!! \n";
}
```

```
// display_info takes the customer number returned from search()
// as a parameter.
// It has nothing to return.
void display::display_info(int temp)
{
   cout << "Customer number is " << temp << " \n";
}

void display::print(void)
{
   cout << "Here's the record! \n";
}

void add::add_info(void)
{
   cout << "Inside add_info \n";
}

void add::print(void)
{
   cout << "Attempt to add duplicate record! \n" <<
      "Transaction disallowed!! \n";
}
void del::delete_info(int temp)
{
   cout << "Inside delete_info \n";
   int i = 0;

   while (customer_numbers[i] != 0)
      {
      if (temp != customer_numbers[i])
         {
         i++;
         }
      else
         {
         // move remaining array in by 1
         while (customer_numbers[i+1] != 0)
            {
            customer_numbers[i] = customer_numbers[i+1];
            i++;
            }

         // zero out the previous last element
         customer_numbers[i] = 0;

         return;
         }
      }
   retrieve::print();
}

void del::print(void)
{
   cout << "Record ready to be deleted! \n";
```

```
}
main(void)
{
   int temp, i, number;

   display display_customer;
   add add_customer;
   del delete_customer;

   // search for customer number 200
   number = 200;
   temp = display_customer.search(number);

   if (temp > 0)
   {
      display_customer.display_info(temp);
   }

   // modify customer number 200
   modify_record(number);

   // search for customer number 300
   // if found, delete it.
   temp = delete_customer.search(300);

   if (temp > 0)
   {
      // object display_customer attempts to access
      // delete_info().
      display_customer.delete_info(temp);
   }

   for (i = 0; i < 6; i++)
      {
      cout << "customer_numbers[" << i << "] is " <<
          customer_numbers[i] << "\n";
      }
}
```

Compiling this program results in the compiler issuing an error message:

```
Error:   'delete_info' is not a member of 'display'
```

Perfect! This is just what we wanted! We have successfully used derivation to encapsulate the delete function in objects of type `del` only.

20.5 REVIEW

This chapter incorporated the code for the `delete_info()` function in the program designed and developed in the previous three chapters. Once again, the ease with which object-oriented programs can be expanded was illustrated.

Chapter

21

Concluding Expansion of Object-Oriented Application

21.1 Introduction

Last but not least, the code for add_info() will be developed and incorporated into the application designed and implemented in the previous four chapters.

21.2 The add_info() Function

First, the customer record that is to be added will be searched. If the record is found, then an attempt is being made to add a duplicate record, and the transaction will not be allowed. The record will be added if search() outputs Record not found!. Here's the code:

```
// test21_1.cpp

#include <iostream.h>

int customer_numbers[6] = {100, 200, 300, 400, 500, 0};

// retrieve is the base class
class retrieve
   {
   private:
   int modify(int);

   public:
   int search(int number);
   friend void modify_record(int number);
```

```
   virtual void print(void);
   };

// display is publicly derived from retrieve
class display : public retrieve
   {
   public:
   void display_info(int temp);
   void print(void);
   };

// add is publicly derived from retrieve
class add : public retrieve
   {
   public:
   void add_info(int temp);
   void print(void);
   };

// del is publicly derived from retrieve
class del : public retrieve
   {
   public:
   void delete_info(int temp);
   void print(void);
   };

retrieve retrieve_customer;

// modify_record calls modify().
// it takes the customer number to be modified as a parameter.
// it returns no value.
// it is a friend function of the class retrieve.
// This enables this function and this function alone
// to modify the customer record.
void modify_record(int number)
{
   int i = 0;
   cout << "Inside modify_record \n";

   while (customer_numbers[i] != 0)
      {
      if (number != customer_numbers[i])
         {
         i++;
         }
      else
         {
         customer_numbers[i] =
              retrieve_customer.modify(customer_numbers[i]);
         return;
         }
      }
   cout << "Record not found! \n";
}
```

```
// modify takes the customer number to be modified
// as a parameter. it returns the modified value to the
// calling function.
int retrieve::modify(int number)
{
   cout << "Inside modify \n";

   number = number + 55;
   cout << "Record modified \n";
   return number;
}

// retrieve takes the customer number to search for
// as a paramter.
// it returns the customer number if found.
// it returns 0 if customer number is not found.
int retrieve::search(int number)
{
   int i = 0;
   cout << "Inside search \n";

   while (customer_numbers[i] != 0)
      {
      if (number != customer_numbers[i])
         {
         i++;
         }
      else
         {
         // print() is a virtual function.
         // Based on the object which is accessing
         // search(), the appropriate print()
         // function will be called.
          print();

          number = customer_numbers[i];
          return number;
          }
      }

   // if a corresponding record is not found, then the print()
   // statement for the base class will be called.
   retrieve::print();

   return 0;
}

void retrieve::print(void)
{
   cout << "Record not found!! \n";
}

// display_info takes the customer number returned from search()
// as a parameter.
// It has nothing to return.
```

```
void display::display_info(int temp)
{
   cout << "Customer number is " << temp << " \n";
}

void display::print(void)
{
   cout << "Here's the record! \n";
}
```

The code for add_info is short and simple:

```
void add::add_info(int temp)
{
   cout << "Inside add_info \n";
   int i = 0;

   // find the slot to add to
   while (customer_numbers[i] != 0)
      {
      i++;
      }

   customer_numbers[i] = temp;
}

void add::print(void)
{
   cout << "Attempt to add duplicate record! \n" <<
      "Transaction disallowed!! \n";
}

void del::delete_info(int temp)
{
   cout << "Inside delete_info \n";
   int i = 0;

   while (customer_numbers[i] != 0)
      {
      if (temp != customer_numbers[i])
         {
         i++;
         }
      else
         {
         // move remaining array in by 1
         while (customer_numbers[i+1] != 0)
            {
            customer_numbers[i] = customer_numbers[i+1];
            i++;
            }

         // zero out the previous last element
         customer_numbers[i] = 0;
```

```
         return;
         }
      }
   retrieve::print();
}

void del::print(void)
{
   cout << "Record ready to be deleted! \n";
}

main(void)
{
   int temp, i, number;

   display display_customer;
   add add_customer;
   del delete_customer;

   // search for customer number 200
   number = 200;
   temp = display_customer.search(number);

   if (temp > 0)
   {
      display_customer.display_info(temp);
   }

   // modify customer number 200
   modify_record(number);

   // search for customer number 300
   // if found, delete it.
   temp = delete_customer.search(300);

   if (temp > 0)
   {
      delete_customer.delete_info(temp);
   }

   // search for customer number 600
   // if not found, add it.
   temp = add_customer.search(600);

   if (temp == 0)
   {
      add_customer.add_info(600);
   }

   for (i = 0; i < 6; i++)
      {
      cout << "Customer_numbers[" << i << "] is " <<
          customer_numbers[i] << "\n";
      }
}
```

The output for this program follows:

```
Inside search
Here's the record!
Customer number is 200
Inside modify_record
Inside modify
Record modified
Inside search
Record ready to be deleted!
Inside delete_info
Inside search
Record not found!!
Inside add_info
Customer_numbers[0] is 100
Customer_numbers[1] is 255
Customer_numbers[2] is 400
Customer_numbers[3] is 500
Customer_numbers[4] is 600
Customer_numbers[5] is 0
```

Even though the output is self-explanatory, it won't hurt to overview it briefly anyway. (Feel free to skip over to the next section if you understand it thoroughly.)

First, a search for customer record number 200 is initiated. The record is found and displayed by `display_info`. Following is the output for this segment of code:

```
Inside search
Here's the record
Customer number is 200
```

Next, record number 200 is modified, by adding 55 to its current value. The corresponding output for this segment of code is:

```
Inside modify_record
Inside modify
Record modified
```

Ideally, a duplicate search should have been issued for the modified record, but we just wanted to keep things as simple as possible. Next, record number 300 is successfully deleted. The output follows:

```
Inside search
Record ready to be deleted!
Inside delete_info
```

And then, record number 600 is added:

```
Inside search
```

```
Record not found!
Inside add_info
```

And after all has been said and done, here's the resulting array of customer numbers:

```
Customer_numbers[0] is 100
Customer_numbers[1] is 255
Customer_numbers[2] is 400
Customer_numbers[3] is 500
Customer_numbers[4] is 600
Customer_numbers[5] is 0
```

21.3 Addition of a Duplicate Record

Let's try to add a record that already exists in the array:

```
// test21_2.cpp

#include <iostream.h>

int customer_numbers[6] = {100, 200, 300, 400, 500, 0};

// retrieve is the base class
class retrieve
   {
   private:
   int modify(int);

   public:
   int search(int number);
   friend void modify_record(int number);
   virtual void print(void);
   };

// display is publicly derived from retrieve
class display : public retrieve
   {
   public:
   void display_info(int temp);
   void print(void);
   };

// add is publicly derived from retrieve
class add : public retrieve
   {
   public:
   void add_info(int temp);
   void print(void);
   };
```

```
// del is publicly derived from retrieve
class del : public retrieve
   {
   public:
   void delete_info(int temp);
   void print(void);
   };

retrieve retrieve_customer;

// modify_record calls modify().
// it takes the customer number to be modified as a parameter.
// it returns no value.
// it is a friend function of the class retrieve.
// This enables this function and this function alone
// to modify the customer record.
void modify_record(int number)
{
   int i = 0;
   cout << "Inside modify_record \n";

   while (customer_numbers[i] != 0)
      {
      if (number != customer_numbers[i])
         {
         i++;
         }
      else
         {
         customer_numbers[i] =
              retrieve_customer.modify(customer_numbers[i]);
         return;
         }
      }
   cout << "Record not found! \n";
}

// modify takes the customer number to be modified
// as a parameter. it returns the modified value to the
// calling function.
int retrieve::modify(int number)
{
   cout << "Inside modify \n";

   number = number + 55;
   cout << "Record modified \n";
   return number;
}

// retrieve takes the customer number to search for
// as a paramter.
// it returns the customer number if found.
// it returns 0 if customer number is not found.
int retrieve::search(int number)
{
```

```
  int i = 0;
  cout << "Inside search \n";

  while (customer_numbers[i] != 0)
     {
     if (number != customer_numbers[i])
        {
        i++;
        }
     else
        {
        // print() is a virtual function.
        // Based on the object which is accessing
        // search(), the appropriate print()
        // function will be called.
         print();

         number = customer_numbers[i];
         return number;
         }
     }

  // if a corresponding record is not found, then the print()
  // statement for the base class will be called.
  retrieve::print();

  return 0;
}

void retrieve::print(void)
{
  cout << "Record not found!! \n";
}

// display_info takes the customer number ret[illegible] search()
// as a parameter.
// It has nothing to return.
void display::display_info(int te[illegible]
{
  cout << "Customer number [illegible] temp << " \n";
}

void display::pri[illegible]
{
  cout << "[illegible] record! \n";
}

void [illegible]dd_info(int temp)
{
  cout << "Inside add_info \n";
  int i = 0;
  // find the slot to add to
  while (customer_numbers[i] != 0)
     {
     i++;
```

```
      }

   customer_numbers[i] = temp;
}

void add::print(void)
{
   cout << "Attempt to add duplicate record! \n" <<
      "Transaction disallowed!! \n";
}

void del::delete_info(int temp)
{
   cout << "Inside delete_info \n";
   int i = 0;

   while (customer_numbers[i] != 0)
      {
      if (temp != customer_numbers[i])
         {
         i++;
         }
      else
         {
         // move remaining array in by 1
         while (customer_numbers[i+1] != 0)
            {
            customer_numbers[i] = customer_numbers[i+1];
            i++;
            }

         // zero out the previous last element
         customer_numbers[i] = 0;

         return;
         }
      }
   retrieve::print();
}

void del::print(void)
{
   cout << "Record ready to be deleted! \n";
}

main(void)
{
   int temp, i, number;

   display display_customer;
   add add_customer;
   del delete_customer;

   // search for customer number 200
   number = 200;
```

```
    temp = display_customer.search(number);

    if (temp > 0)
    {
       display_customer.display_info(temp);
    }

    // modify customer number 200
    modify_record(number);

    // search for customer number 300
    // if found, delete it.
    temp = delete_customer.search(300);

    if (temp > 0)
    {
       delete_customer.delete_info(temp);
    }

    // try to add duplicate customer record 500
    temp = add_customer.search(500);
    if (temp == 0)
    {
       add_customer.add_info(500);
    }

    for (i = 0; i < 6; i++)
       {
       cout << "Customer_numbers[" << i << "] is " <<
           customer_numbers[i] << "\n";
       }
}
```

The output for this program follows:

```
Inside search
Here's the record
Customer number is 200
Inside modify_record
Inside modify
Record modified
Inside search
Record ready to be deleted!
Inside delete_info
Inside search
Attempt to add duplicate record!
Transaction disallowed!!
Customer_numbers[0] is 100
Customer_numbers[1] is 255
Customer_numbers[2] is 400
Customer_numbers[3] is 500
Customer_numbers[4] is 0
Customer_numbers[5] is 0
```

The following is the response of the program when a duplicate record is added:

```
Inside search
Attempt to add duplicate record!
Transaction disallowed!!
```

21.4 ACCESS OF ADD_INFO() BY A NONCLASS MEMBER

And finally, a nonmember class object, such as retrieve_customer, will access add_info(). Here's the code:

```
// test21_3.cpp

#include <iostream.h>

int customer_numbers[6] = {100, 200, 300, 400, 500, 0};

// retrieve is the base class
class retrieve
   {
   private:
   int modify(int);

   public:
   int search(int number);
   friend void modify_record(int number);
   virtual void print(void);
   };

// display is publicly derived from retrieve
class display : public retrieve
   {
   public:
   void display_info(int temp);
   void print(void);
   };

// add is publicly derived from retrieve
class add : public retrieve
   {
   public:
   void add_info(int temp);
   void print(void);
   };

// del is publicly derived from retrieve
class del : public retrieve
   {
   public:
   void delete_info(int temp);
```

```
   void print(void);
   };

retrieve retrieve_customer;

// modify_record calls modify().
// it takes the customer number to be modified as a parameter.
// it returns no value.
// it is a friend function of the class retrieve.
// This enables this function and this function alone
// to modify the customer record.
void modify_record(int number)
{
   int i = 0;
   cout << "Inside modify_record \n";
   while (customer_numbers[i] != 0)
      {
      if (number != customer_numbers[i])
         {
         i++;
         }
      else
         {
         customer_numbers[i] =
             retrieve_customer.modify(customer_numbers[i]);
         return;
         }
      }
   cout << "Record not found! \n";
}

// modify takes the customer number to be modified
// as a parameter. it returns the modified value to the
// calling function.
int retrieve::modify(int number)
{
   cout << "Inside modify \n";
   number = number + 55;
   cout << "Record modified \n";
   return number;
}

// retrieve takes the customer number to search for
// as a paramter. it returns the customer number if found.
// it returns 0 if customer number is not found.
int retrieve::search(int number)
{
   int i = 0;
   cout << "Inside search \n";

   while (customer_numbers[i] != 0)
      {
      if (number != customer_numbers[i])
         {
         i++;
```

```
        }
      else
        {
        // print() is a virtual function.
        // Based on the object which is accessing
        // search(), the appropriate print()
        // function will be called.
         print();

         number = customer_numbers[i];
         return number;
         }
      }

   // if a corresponding record is not found, then the print()
   // statement for the base class will be called.
   retrieve::print();

   return 0;
}

void retrieve::print(void)
{
   cout << "Record not found!! \n";
}

// display_info takes the customer number returned from search()
// as a parameter.
// It has nothing to return.
void display::display_info(int temp)
{
   cout << "Customer number is " << temp << " \n";
}

void display::print(void)
{
   cout << "Here's the record! \n";
}

void add::add_info(int temp)
{
   cout << "Inside add_info \n";
   int i = 0;

   // find the slot to add to
   while (customer_numbers[i] != 0)
      {
      i++;
      }

   customer_numbers[i] = temp;
}

void add::print(void)
{
```

```
  cout << "Attempt to add duplicate record! \n" <<
     "Transaction disallowed!! \n";
}

void del::delete_info(int temp)
{
  cout << "Inside delete_info \n";
  int i = 0;

  while (customer_numbers[i] != 0)
     {
     if (temp != customer_numbers[i])
        {
        i++;
        }
     else
        {
        // move remaining array in by 1
        while (customer_numbers[i+1] != 0)
           {
           customer_numbers[i] = customer_numbers[i+1];
           i++;
           }

        // zero out the previous last element
        customer_numbers[i] = 0;

        return;
        }
     }
  retrieve::print();
}

void del::print(void)
{
  cout << "Record ready to be deleted! \n";
}

main(void)
{
  int temp, i, number;

  display display_customer;
  add add_customer;
  del delete_customer;

  // search for customer number 200
  number = 200;
  temp = display_customer.search(number);

  if (temp > 0)
  {
     display_customer.display_info(temp);
  }
```

```
    // modify customer number 200
    modify_record(number);

    // search for customer number 300
    // if found, delete it.
    temp = delete_customer.search(300);

    if (temp > 0)
    {
       delete_customer.delete_info(temp);
    }

    // search for customer number 500
    // if not found, add it.
    temp = add_customer.search(500);

    if (temp == 0)
    {
       retrieve_customer.add_info(500);
    }

    for (i = 0; i < 6; i++)
       {
       cout << "customer_numbers[" << i << "] is " <<
           customer_numbers[i] << "\n";
       }
}
```

You can probably already anticipate the result of compiling this version. That's right; the error message is as follows:

```
Error:   'add_info' is not a member of 'retrieve'
```

This is good. We have successfully encapsulated the add function as well.

21.5 Review

Object-oriented programs are powerful and efficient, at the cost of perhaps being a little more difficult to design. But if you follow the simple methodology outlined in Part 3 of this book, and utilize the tools that C++ makes available, you will be able to design your own set of classes that can be utilized to build other classes.

And so the power of object-oriented analysis and design should now be apparent to you, and you should feel comfortable and capable of implementing, modifying, and expanding your very own system.

Chapter

22

Thinking Object Oriented!

22.1 Introduction

The title of this book is *C++ Primer for C Programmers*. Starting from Chapter 1, and right through Chapter 21, we have explained how C++ works, and how it falls into place in an object-oriented framework. Now that you understand the language and its power, we conclude this book by emphasizing something that perhaps has lurked in your mind as you became more and more proficient in this language! The fact of the matter is, C++ is nothing more than another language to use to write programs in, *unless* the system has been *designed using object-oriented techniques*. You have to *think object oriented*, in order to bring C++ to life. You have to take the time to think, and think hard, about the design of the system, the base classes, the classes that will be derived from them, the virtual functions, the data-hiding facilities, the objects, and so on, before you write a single line of code. Unless you think object oriented and modular, and thereby formulate the proper hierarchy of classes, C++ is a powerful tool which is entirely useless since it is not being used correctly. This concluding and brief chapter is designed to help you *think*!

22.2 Abstraction

You were introduced to the concept of abstraction earlier in this book. The art of abstraction lies in being able to concentrate on those features of a system that will formulate the building blocks of everything else that will ensue. Although it is a suprisingly simple concept to understand, it would suprise you to know how infrequently this method is used when it comes to designing anything. In this chapter, we will present a very simplified design of a very complex system. Our objective is to illustrate how complex problems are best analyzed when they are broken down into their simplest components, and how easy it is to build and modify a system that has been carefully analyzed and then created in a modular fashion.

Please note that in the interest of simplicity, we will take into consideration only the most generalized features of this system.

22.3 DESIGNING A TELECOMMUNICATIONS SYSTEM

When you pick up the telephone and call someone, a connection is made between yourself and the calling party. In the simplest terms, this is a connection between two points. Your goal is to design a system that captures this connection.

Of course, life is never as simple as a direct connection between two points! The two points (say A and B) that are to be connected can be adjacent to each other. Or they can be linked to different points (say C, D, and E), which in turn can be linked to other points (such as F, G, and H). The connection between A and B would have to be formulated through these other connections.

All calls are routed through specific types of devices. Each of the points referenced in the previous paragraph could actually be visualized as different devices. The complexity of the system is enhanced by the fact that the connection between the two points can be formulated between different types of devices, which behave in different ways. Thus, the rules that exist for one device may not necessarily apply to another. As the route (or connection between the two points) is formulated, it will be necessary to identify the kind of device that is being traversed, and direct the call to the other end based on the rules that are specific to that device.

Finally, let's add one more level of complexity to the system. Assume that a connection has to be formulated between devices A and B, and that a direct line exists between them. However, this connection cannot be utilized, since it is being used by some other call. Thus, an alternate path has to be formulated to complete the connection, traversing unused connections.

22.3.1 Rethinking the System

If you take a moment to reread the previous paragraph, you will find the following issues that need to be addressed in your design of the system:

- How to capture a connection between two points, which may or may not be adjacent to each other
- How to capture the behavior of different devices, which are used to formulate the connection
- How to reroute the call to a different device, if the logical connection that would have been chosen under normal circumstances is not available

Once the main issues that have to be addressed have been listed, the next task is to concentrate on the essential characteristics of these issues that will allow us to distinguish the different types of objects that will be formulated to implement this system. We try to simplify the complexity of the issues just presented, and this is the result:

- The simplest connection between two points is the one in which they are adjacent to each other, thereby allowing a direct connection between them. An *object* has to be formulated that captures the essence of this connection.
- All devices are ultimately required to implement one main function: the forwarding of the call to the next point. Another *object* has to be formulated that captures the essence of this feature of a *basic* device.
- Before a call is routed from one device to another, the first device has to send a message to the next device asking whether it is available to transport a call to the next point. The subsequent device has to send a message back to the calling device with the appropriate answer. If the device is available, the calling device will forward the call to this device. If it is unavailable, the calling device will try to find an alternate path. This could be classified as the *mechanism* by which the objects formulated will communicate with each other.

The simplified generalizations just presented will form the backbone of the entire system. Once a system has been designed that satisifies the requirements listed, it will be robust enough to handle subsequent complexities, as the next section illustrates.

22.3.2 Building on the Initial Abstractions

We now summarize the results of our analysis. The two base classes that will form the building blocks of all other classes will contain the following features:

- A class that captures the rules required to route a call between two adjacent points. We will call this `ClassA`.

- A class that captures the functionality of the most basic device used to route a call. We will call this `ClassB`.

In addition to this, we identified the mechanism by which objects of these classes will communicate with each other, in order to complete the route of a call.

With these basic building blocks, we add to the complexity of the system, and see how well our base classes are designed to handle these situations. Here are the additional features we want our system to handle:

- A call can be routed between two points that are not adjacent to each other, but instead are linked via other connections.

We implement this feature of the system by deriving a class from `ClassA`. This derived class will inherit the rules required to formulate a basic one-to-one connection between two points. However, it will contain additional methods that will contain the rules required to formulate a more complex connection.

- Different types of devices can be added to the system, which handle the route of a call in different ways. However, the basic mechanism by which a call is routed will always remain the same.

We implement this feature by deriving classes from `ClassB`. These derived classes will inherit the functionality of the most basic device. However, unique attributes or methods that distinguish this device from others will be added for each derivation.

We have already identified in general terms the mechanism by which the classes will communicate with each other.

And believe it or not, that's about it. These should be the basic thought patterns you use to analyze and design a complex system. This system will be flexible enough to handle changes in rules required to complete a route or changes in the attributes of devices. These changes would be implemented simply by modifying the applicable code in the derived classes.

The method for each device will be encapsulated in its class. If a new device is added to the system which does not have clearly defined attributes, it can utilize virtual functions to pick up the functionality of the device defined in the base class. These virtual functions can be overridden once the attributes of the device are made available.

22.4 CONCLUSIONS

Although this is really a very simplified representation of a system that can be incredibly complex, that is the very point we are making. Keep it simple. Try to simplify the complexity of the problem as much as possible, and concentrate on the main features and requirements without getting bogged down in details that are of no significance to the initial design phase. Do not over-design, but get to the root of what is to be conveyed by the system. If you have the ability to analyze and access the required system in this way, you will be suprised at how easily you will be able to build on the strong foundation that you will create. The complexities of a system are a disguise for the underlying simplicity with which it can be created and implemented, given that you take the time to think, and think hard, of how to break up a complex problem into its simplest components. Once this has been achieved, you will be amazed at how easily everything else will fit into place.

If, on the other hand, there is some flaw in your design, you will also be amazed at how the system will tangle you as you attempt to build on it. A good system will enforce the correct rules; a badly designed system will ultimately become so tangled that it is almost impossible to detangle, usually resulting in a complete rewrite.

Index